Bringing Life to Aberdeen

A History of Maternity and Neonatal Services

Bringing Life to Aberdeen

A History of Maternity and Neonatal Services

Edited by
LESLEY DUNBAR, ALISON McCALL,
FIONA RENNIE and GEORGE YOUNGSON

Luath Press Limited
EDINBURGH
www.luath.co.uk

First published 2022

ISBN: 978-1-80425-027-3 (PBK)
ISBN: 978-1-80425-025-9 (HBK)

The paper used in this book is recyclable. It is made from low chlorine pulps
produced in a low energy, low emissions manner from renewable forests.

Printed and bound by
Severnprint Ltd., Gloucester

Typeset in 11 point Sabon LT Pro by
Main Point Books, Edinburgh

The editors acknowledge the support provided by Aberdeen City Council
towards the publication of this book.

All royalties generated from sales of this book will be donated to the new
neonatal unit in the Baird Family Hospital, Aberdeen.

This book is dedicated to the memory of Sandie Youngson,
our first reader

Contents

PART 4: STORIES, TALES AND MEMORIES

PART 5: THEN, NOW — AND A NEW FUTURE

Barney Crockett, Lord Provost of Aberdeen (2017–22)
(Courtesy of Aberdeen City Council)

Preface

'Bringing Life to Aberdeen' and beyond...

AS FORMER LORD PROVOST of Aberdeen, it is a great honour to welcome this valuable, and yes, exciting publication.

It is a profoundly moving story which these editors have put together for us, the story of huge improvements in the care of mothers, the care of babies and the consequent improved rights of women and the creation of a more civilised society.

The story of Aberdeen's particular contribution to this global story is painstakingly described, not excluding when individual early pioneers were discouraged, or progress was delayed. The early pioneers laid the basis for the dramatic advances which overtook Aberdeen from the 1930s onwards. It meant in Aberdeen far fewer deaths in childbirth for mothers or babies, smaller, better cared for families and healthier, better educated children. Statistics on all of these marked out Aberdeen from anywhere else in the UK or far beyond in the middle years of the 20th century.

The legacy of that work has spread across the world. The editors deserve the intense thanks of all Aberdonians. This book will also be appreciated by researchers everywhere and by all who are interested in the crucial issues covered so comprehensively and interestingly here.

Councillor Barney Crockett
September 2022

Artist's impression of the new Baird Family Hospital which will contain a neonatal unit, maternity hospital, and other health services for women.
(Image courtesy of NHS Grampian)

Introduction

THE OCCASION OF the opening of a new hospital in Aberdeen seems to be a good time to look back and recall how we got to this point. Whilst the histories of Aberdeen Royal Infirmary (ARI) and the Royal Aberdeen Children's Hospital (RACH) are well recorded in a variety of books and publications, the same is not true for the Aberdeen Maternity Hospital (AMH) and the associated Neonatal Unit (or Special Nursery as it was previously known). Nor is the history of midwifery and neonatal services presented in a single record.

It is timely, therefore, to put together an account of the past before some of that history is lost amidst the digital era. The opening of a new hospital – the Baird Family Hospital provides that opportunity. This institution commemorates the contributions of the Baird Family (Sir Dugald and Lady May Baird, and their offspring) to women's health in the North East of Scotland, but it will also be a family hospital, providing care for women, mothers and their babies, and their partners. So, a new start with a new model of healthcare for a new era; but that new model is borne out of the lessons learned from the past. This new hospital will respond to new needs, with new facilities providing age and gender specific health care in a manner not previously considered and in an environment with facilities that can respond to specific needs.

That bringing together of women's, maternal and neonatal services prompts recollection of how care of mothers and their babies came to take place in the

North East of Scotland and how midwifery grew to its current status.

This book comprises five parts:

- Places;
- People;
- Services;
- Stories – then, now and to come.

Whilst attempts have been made to avoid duplication throughout the book, some overlap will occur between sections. This has been done intentionally in order to assist when reading individual sections and help in understanding the timeline of some events as outlined below.

Timeline

1740   The foundation stone of Aberdeen Infirmary laid

1755   West Wing of the Infirmary opened for maternity care

1795   Alexander Gordon publishes a treatise on the Epidemic of Puerperal Fever of Aberdeen

1823   General Dispensary, Vaccination and Lying-in Clinics established in Broad Street

1860   Dr Robert Dyce appointed as first Professor of Midwifery, University of Aberdeen

1877   Opening of Royal Aberdeen Hospital for Sick Children

1900   Aberdeen Maternity Hospital founded at Castle Terrace

1912   Dr Robert McKerron appointed as Professor of Midwifery

1926   Appeal for Joint Hospital Scheme (Matthew Hay)

1936   Aberdeen Royal Infirmary moves from Woolmanhill to Foresterhill

1937   Sir Dugald Baird appointed Regius Professor of Midwifery

1960   Dr Betty Macgregor works with Sir Dugald Baird's team to set up a pioneering cervical screening programme in Aberdeen

1953   Textbook of Midwifery by Maggie Myles published

1965   Neonatal unit AMH; Ian McGillivray appointed as Regius Professor of Obstetrics and Gynaecology

1988   New 'Special Nursery' opens adjacent to AMH

2018   On Tuesday 18 December a turf-cutting ceremony held to mark the site of the new Baird Family Hospital

Before We Start

THIS RECORD STARTS with the description of the first major hospital in Aberdeen, but there is an appreciation that a variety of institutions existed prior to Woolmanhill and, of course, midwifery preceded all of these.

For hundreds of years, if not millennia, women have helped and supported each other during childbirth. However, relatively little is known about women's experience of childbirth in the Middle Ages, apart from a few queens and aristocrats, according to Katherine French, and French says that we know even less about women's attitudes towards childbirth. Very few women were educated then and those few elite women that were, were not encouraged to record their life experiences in writing. Childbirth was seen as a private affair, and medieval folk considered it a part of life not related to medicine. From artefacts that still exist today, we do know medieval women feared infertility, miscarriage, a long and painful labour and the possibility of death for themselves or their child.

A common fertility device was the paternoster, strings of semi-precious stone beads that doubled as rosaries. The most popular stone, according to wills, was coral. In addition to promoting fertility, coral was thought to speed up the beginning and end of any business, including labour, protect children from the 'evil eye' and ease teething pain. Jet and amber beads were also used. Jet quelled childbirth pains. Amber also helped with childbirth and warded off the evil eye and fairy abduction. Beads were a common betrothal gift and women frequently left them to other women in their families as a bequest.

For medieval married women, childbirth involved many other women. It was an important social occasion. A midwife was called for; midwives were involved with births from all social classes.

Midwife means 'with women' in Old English. A group of neighbours, friends and family members, called gossips, also attended. The mother specifically invited each of the gossips. To be issued an invitation to attend was a compliment; to be passed over was a slight. The origin of the word gossip comes from the Late Old English 'godsibb', a godmother or godfather or baptismal sponsor, literally 'a person related to one in God' from 'God' and 'sibb', a relative. In Middle English the sense became 'a close friend, a person with whom one gossips hence a person who gossips'. By the early 19th century, the meaning became the noun 'idle talk' from the verb, to gossip, which dates from the early 17th century.

St Bridget was an Irish and Celtic saint and we find a number of churches dedicated to her name in the North East of Scotland. According to the legend, St Bridget, Brigid or Bride was miraculously transported to Bethlehem to attend the nativity of Christ and become midwife to Mary. She was also, in Hebridean legend, the foster-mother and wet nurse to baby Jesus. Bridget presided over childbirth for women in Scotland until the Reformation. Among the altars in the parish church of St Nicholas in Aberdeen was one commemorating St Bridget. The patrons of the altar were the magistrates and town council of Aberdeen.

Childbirth was dangerous for all women whatever their status. Both Queens Jane Seymour and Katherine Parr had puerperal fever after childbirth, a septic infection that always resulted in death. Upper class women were more at risk from the dangers of childbirth as they often had more children than working women as they hired wet nurses to feed their babies. So, an upper-class woman would soon be pregnant again whereas a peasant or working woman might have a baby every two years.

Once pregnant, women prepared their birthing rooms or lying-in chambers. When the mother went into labour, the entrance to the lying-in chamber was shut and the windows were sealed to block out light and air. Childbirth was a women's business and a female occasion. Men were conspicuously absent. The art historian Elizabeth L'Estrange has studied childbirth scenes of noble women in Books of Hours, and she argues that the beds, linens and hangings all had pride of place in their lying-in preparations.

From the 14th century women used birthing stools or chairs for most deliveries, believing this put them in the best position to deliver babies. A bed was only for the mother's recovery. After the birth, the mother would remain in her lying-in chamber for a month, during which her only visitors were the midwife and her female companions. Thereafter, she was 'churched'. As *The Catholic Encyclopaedia* notes, churching of women (even until the middle of the 20th century), was

not a precept, but a pious and praiseworthy custom (*Rituale Romanum*), dating from the early Christian ages, for a mother to present herself in the church as soon as she is able to leave her house, to render thanks to God for her happy delivery, and to obtain by means of the priestly blessing the graces necessary to bring up her child in a Christian manner.

However, there was also a dark side to the local practice of midwifery in the Middle Ages, illustrated here in the case history of Margaret Bane, a midwife accused of witchery.

Margaret Bane or Clerk, Midwife and Witch –
'And this thow can nocht deny'

Margaret Bane or Clerk was a local midwife, or 'howdie', who lived at Findrack, in the parish of Lumphanan in Aberdeenshire. On 25 March 1597, she was accused of being a witch at the Commission in Aberdeen when 16 charges, or 'dittays', were brought against her. Some days earlier she had been taken to Aberdeen and held in the former Tolbooth Ward house to await her trial there.

The Scottish Parliament had passed the Witchcraft Act in 1563 making the practice of witchcraft itself and consulting with witches capital crimes, punishable by death. In 1589, James VI had sailed to Denmark to collect Princess Anne, who was about to become his new wife. At the Danish royal court James heard tales of witchcraft and sorcery. When one of the royal ships sank in a violent storm on the return journey to Scotland, James became troubled and feared for his life, believing witches had cast a spell. Shortly after his arrival at Leith, he instigated a Royal Commission that would result in witch trials being held throughout Scotland.

The Commissions set up local hearings to collect evidence from witnesses of a woman's, or more rarely a man's, involvement in witchcraft. Often each of these charges end with the phrase 'And this thow can nocht deny'. Of the 16 dittays that were brought against Margaret Bane, five mention her role as a midwife. The first charge accuses that Margaret, six years previously in 1591, put the labour pains of Elizabeth Sang onto her husband John Jamesoun of Auchinhuiff and that 'by her devilische wytchcraft' John Jamesoun went mad and died.

The next charge accused her that in April 1595, when she had been sent for by the laird of Auchlossin's wife, of casting all the laird's wife's labour pains onto Andro Harper. However, as soon as the laird's wife had delivered her baby the labour pains left Andro.

A further charge relates how, when the wife of Alexander Chalmers of Balnacraig was in her childbed, Margaret Bane was sent for, and Andro Mar came to collect her. During Margaret's journey it was alleged to her that 'thy master the Devil in the likeness of a horse appeared between Tulliheine and Lumphanan and spoke to Margaret for a long time making Andro Mar terrified'.

A charge from three or four years previously, in 1593 or 1594, details how James Braibner in Easter Beltie, his own wife being in labour, had told Margaret that he had been sent by the Lady of Beltie to collect her and take her to the Lady's daughter who was in her child bed. Margaret had told James Braibner that it was not one of Lady Beltie's daughters who was in her childbed, it was his wife and furthermore his wife would not be in need of her services now as she had been delivered of a son before James was half a mile away from his house. The charge states that Margaret had this knowledge from her Master, the Devil.

Yet another charge emerged when Margaret was sent for by the wife of Patrick Gordoune of Kincraigie to be her midwife. Patrick had his best horse and a boy of his own sent to Margaret to bring her to his own guidewife. Margaret being on the horse, behind the boy, at her own door, her Master Satan, the Devil had appeared in the likeness of a grey stag and conveyed the boy and her from her house to Kincraigie. The boy later told his master that he would rather have not seen his horse that day and when asked why had said that the horse was in his stable and doing well enough but the Devil in the likeness of a grey stag was still beside him.

In a further charge Margaret Bane is accused that her sister Jonet Spaldarge, described as the 'mother of all witches' taught Margaret all her art and all the witchcraft she used. Margaret confessed that she knew as much as her sister did. Jonet had already been burnt for a witch in Edinburgh.

Two unsuccessful attempts had previously been made to bring forward charges of witchcraft against Margaret, the first 30 years earlier and the second in 1596. This third attempt was successful, and Margaret was convicted on ten of the points of witchcraft brought against her and found to be 'a sorcerer, practizer and a common witch'. She was strangled then burned on 24 April 1597 at the Heading Hill near today's Commerce Street in Aberdeen.

Tragically, witchcraft charges were also brought against Margaret's daughter Helen Rogie. When Margaret had confessed to taking part with her coven in a devilish dance on Craiglich Hill, she had named all the members including her daughter. Helen, on hearing of her mother's arrest, feared she too would be apprehended and ran away to the nearby Hill of Layrnie to hide but gave herself up after three days to face the same fate as her mother, ten days later.

The practice of midwifery therefore ran its own risks in the Middle Ages.

Monica Green, a historian of medieval medicine, has argued that over the course of the Middle Ages, increasingly greater value was placed on written medical sources, giving men, with their greater access to university training and literacy, increasing authority over women's medicine and health. In 1726, Joseph Gibson was appointed the world's first Chair of Midwifery by the Edinburgh Town Council. William Smellie, a Lanarkshire-born 'man-midwife' who became known as the 'Master of British Obstetrics', published 'A Treatise of the Theory and Practice of Midwifery' in 1752.

By the 1750s, midwives' traditional practice proved no match for the claims of the male midwife, waiting in the wings with his shiny instruments and promise of 'scientific expertise'. By then doctors attended births and midwives were seen as unhygienic and superstitious, and pregnancy might be viewed as a sickness woman would recover from if fortunate enough to survive.

In Aberdeen, poor women were being offered lying-in at the Woolmanhill hospital by Dr David Skene with free board and lodging. He also offered a course of Midwifery lectures in 1758 'particularly intended for the instruction of country midwives'.

Green also states that the establishment of the lying-in hospital was arguably the single most important factor in the demise of the authority and superiority of the female midwife. Charles White, a physician in London in 1773, candidly describes a lying-in hospital in the London area: 'It was instituted for the purpose of instructing young gentlemen.' The close proximity by 1823 of the first 'lying-in institution' at the Guestrow, just across the road from Marischal College, provided easy access for doctors in training to poor, local women, lying in for two weeks after the birth of their children in order to regain their strength.

'Lying-in' hospitals had been established in Edinburgh in 1793 and 1824, and in Glasgow in 1834. All these hospitals were to fall victim to high death rates of mothers and babies from puerperal fever but for the medical profession they provided an environment where 'students could practice obstetric skills' while guaranteeing much-needed bed rest to impoverished women and allowing unmarried mothers 'to deliver their illegitimate babies with no questions asked'. But Aberdeen hospitals is where we carry on this story.

Further Reading

French, K, 'The Material Culture of Childbirth in Late Medieval London and its Suburbs', *Journal of Women's History*, vol. 28, no. 2, 2016.
Green, M, *Making Women's Medicine Masculine: The Rise of Male Authority in Pre-Modern Gynaecology*, Oxford University Press, 2008.
L'Estrange, E, *Holy Motherhood: Gender, Dynasty and Visual Culture in the Later Middle Ages,* Manchester Medieval Studies.
https://www.nrscotland.gov.uk/research/learning/features/safe-delivery-a-history-of-scottish-midwives

PART I

The Places

The first part of this book itemises and highlights the locations of the buildings, hospitals and institutions where the care of women and their babies took place in Aberdeen over the last four centuries. It outlines the changes to the geography of the city over that time period and how that affected midwifery services. The descriptions also place the locations of the original hospitals as precisely as it has been possible, given the fact that most are no longer in existence.

This section refers to those individuals who had the vision and ambition to make these buildings come into existence in order to serve the needs of mothers and babies. Also described are those who were responsible for creating the hospitals, generating the resources to allow the buildings to be constructed, additionally highlighting the purpose and function of each place and why they had come into existence.

1

The Early Aberdeen Hospitals and Lying-in Hospitals

George Youngson and Lesley Dunbar

Before the 1800s

HOSPITALS HAVE BEEN part of the Aberdeen landscape for many centuries. Initially, they were little more than refuges or hostelries for specific (often destitute) groups. One of the first was St Peter's Hospital which was founded between 1172 and 1179 and was built on the Spittal, to sustain 'infirm brethren with sisters subsequently admitted'.

Monastic hospitals had been established from 1211 onwards. The Trinity, Dominican, Carmelite and Franciscan Friars and Knights Templars all had establishments in the town and, in 1459, New Aberdeen had a hospital dedicated to St Thomas the Martyr, founded by John Clat to care for the poor and infirm. This may also have been called Maison Dieu (identified in the cartulary of St Nicholas).

Early health care

By 1333, however, a health-related institution had been developed – the Aberdeen Leper Hospital, built on Spittalhill (Mons Hospitalis) to provide isolation for citizens with leprosy (see p.1 colour section). A leper colony had previously been established halfway between the Gallowgate and Old Aberdeen, but the leper hospital replaced the colony. This also had its own grounds for growing crops and a dedicated graveyard. It was subsequently renamed Hospitale Leprosum, with the last admission being in 1612 and by 1662 it was described as a ruin.

The influence of religious leaders was evident in these early centuries and none more so than through the actions of Bishop Dunbar who, in 1531, had established a hospital with 12 beds which often functioned as an isolation unit during episodes of the plague. St Thomas's Hospital (1459) and the Trades Hospital (1632, developed by Dr William Guild, a minister of the town and son of a former trade deacon) also catered for victims of the plague which had decimated the city during the first half of the 17th century when it killed roughly one in every five people in New Aberdeen. But Aberdeen had no facilities that could cope with the hundreds of plague victims and the leprosy hospital on the Spittal had simply come to be known as the 'sick house' where people with infectious diseases were occasionally sent to die. The exact number of lives lost during the plague epidemic that hit Aberdeen in 1647 is unknown, but New Aberdeen buried 1,600 and a further 140 died in the communities of Torry and Futtie.

Early hospitals were not open to all and in fact treated very few. Their purpose was often simply to give spiritual healing and a safe residence. In 1647, two private hospitals, one for Guildsmen at numbers 20–22 Don Street, known as the Bede House and used as a replacement for the Bishop's Hospital, and one for craft burgesses became retirement homes holding only six men each rather than hospitals as we know them today.

Women's hospitals

Women's hospitals arrived later on the scene and a philanthropist – David Mitchell, who had been born in the city in 1731 and part of a large family – had relocated to London where it was probable that he was a stockbroker with interests in insurance and shipping. Mitchell's Hospital at number 9 in the Chanonry, Old Aberdeen (see overleaf) was founded in 1801 with the following purpose:

> …from a regard for the inhabitants of the city of old Aberdeen and its ancient college, a desire in these severe times to provide lodging, maintenance and clothing for a few aged relicks and maiden daughters of decayed gentlemen merchants or trade burgesses of the said city.

Mitchell had also bequeathed money to the University, and the Principal at Kings College had indicated at the time that an 'unknown gentleman had an intention of founding and endowing a hospital for the maintenance of ten old woman of the city' with the hospital becoming known as the 'The Hospital of Auld Maids'. There were precise conditions set for eligibility to

Mitchell's Hospital, number 9 the Chanonry, founded in 1801 by a bequest from David Mitchell and occupied by women from the Mitchell or Forbes family.
(Image by Ray Oaks. Wikipedia https://en.wikipedia.org/wiki/mitchell % 27s_Hospital_Old_Aberdeen)

become a resident and the ladies were required to be 'of virtuous and good moral character... of the names Mitchell or Forbes (in equal numbers)... and the residents were to 'wear gowns of a deep blue colour'. These residents were known as 'auld maids in blue gowns' and those who were able to earn some money from spinning or knitting were expected to give half to the hospital. The use of the building has been modified twice in the 20th century to provide self-contained flats for elderly ladies.

An earlier hospital for women had been developed in the vicinity of Drum's Lane, off Upperkirkgate. In 1633, Marion Douglas (Lady Drum) had bequeathed a sum of 3,000 Scottish merks (one Scottish merk equalled two-thirds of a pound – 13 shillings and fourpence – 66 pence). This was to provide a 'commodious house for poor widows and aged virgins'. The building began in 1671 and by 1721 the house had also accommodated daughters of burgesses of the Guild. The area was redeveloped, and Drum's Lane was created in 1798 with a plaque now marking the site of Lady Drum's Hospital.

The Poor's Hospital and hospitals of the 1700s

The Poor's Hospital was opened in Aberdeen on 30 October 1741. This was more of a workhouse than a hospital and was located behind the Tollbooth on a site that had once been the burgh's townhouse. There were 25 beds and the people housed were 'old, weak and children under 12 years of age'. It was not

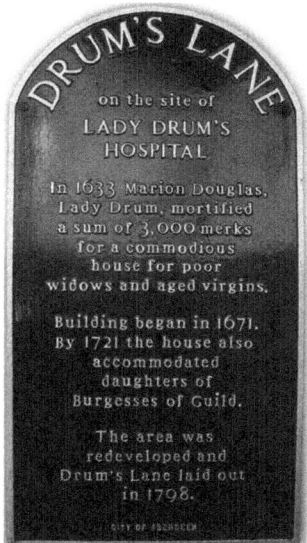

Plaque in Upperkirkgate marking the original site of Lady Drum's Hospital which was the earliest hospital built specifically for women in Aberdeen with a legacy bequeathed by Marion Douglas (Lady Drum) in 1663.

(Courtesy of Aberdeen City Council)

uncommon for poor families to abandon their children at the poor house. Many of the infirmary patients also spent time in the poor house. It was described as 'for the reception of such idle and strolling vagrants should be found in the town'. The town council was responsible for maintaining the institution with help from mortifications and bequests, and by 1742 the number of inmates exceeded the original number of beds, there being 40 old men and women, 51 boys and 13 girls housed in the hospital. By the end of the 18th century only 25 boys remained; all other poor were maintained in their own houses. Children were received into the hospital on the death of a parent, but attempts were made to develop a trade, and rope and net making was an occupation given to the males. Council records indicated the women's lack of skills stating that men would need to train the women as only they had expertise to work the 'muckle wheel' for weaving (though it was in fact the women who then trained the boys to work the wheels).

Another hospital of the time was Robert Gordon's Hospital which, of course, functioned as a school designed especially for the sons and grandsons of merchant and craft burgesses of Aberdeen whose parents were too poor to provide for them. The first boys were admitted on 10 July 1750 after the school had been used to accommodate the Duke of Cumberland's troops after the 1745 Jacobite rebellion.

Aberdeen Infirmary

The first infirmary in Aberdeen was built at Woolmanhill in 1740. The venue was chosen at that time for the 'goodness of the air in that place'. In 1739 the town council had agreed to build an infirmary and William Chrystal was commissioned to draw the plans which were approved for the cost of the hospital to be £480. The foundation stone of the first Infirmary in Aberdeen was laid in 1741 and patients were admitted shortly after completion of building in 1742 on the current Woolmanhill site, previously known colloquially as 'Woman Hill' (see p.28). It was a modest building containing only six beds and in the first year only 21 patients were admitted; nine were cured, ten dismissed as 'uncured after a long trial' and two died. However, a 'West Wing' was proposed in 1758 for

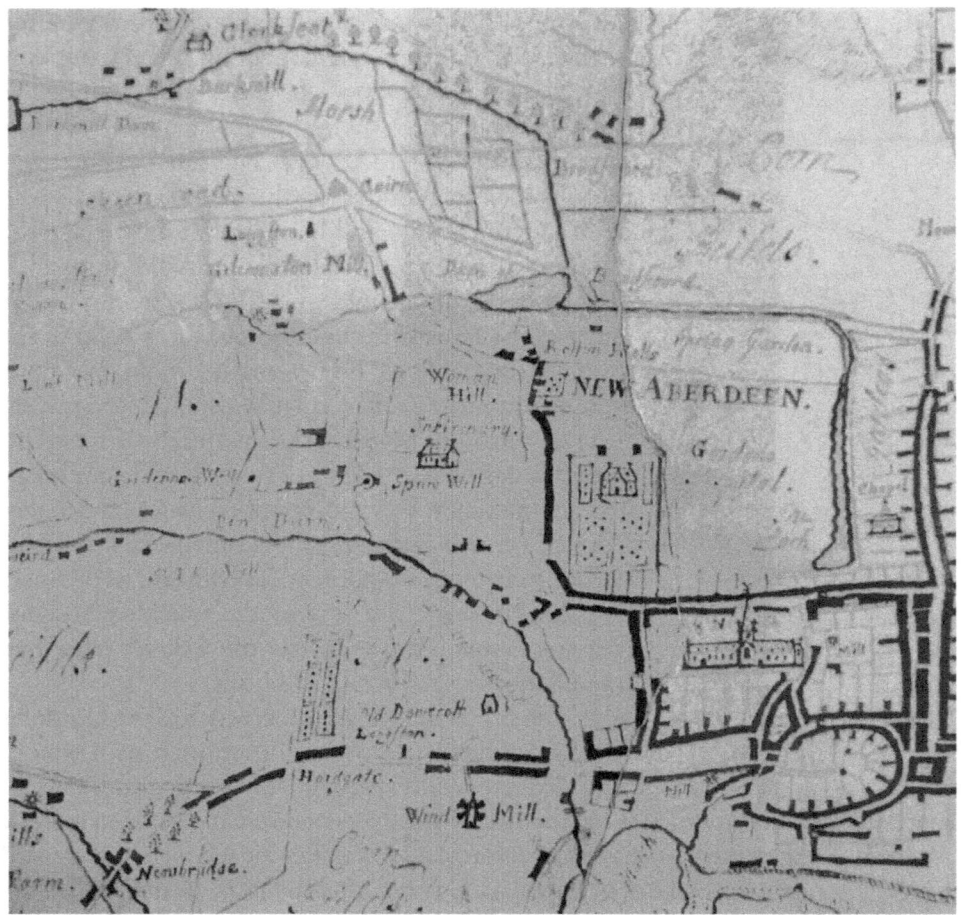

Original map of the site of Woolmanhill hospital in the city (termed 'Woman Hill').
(Reproduced courtesy of the National Library of Scotland)

accommodation of 'poor, distressed lying-in women of the town and country' and an appeal made through Aberdeen's Newspaper for funds, pointing out that 'poor women are often in distress in labour and many of them die for lack of proper care'. A subscription list was established and by the following year £477, 17 shillings and sixpence was accepted for the new building. A major extension took place comprising three floors and an operating theatre.

The West Wing received its first pregnant patient – Margaret Donald – on 5 January 1762, admitted because of Lues Venerea (LV), otherwise known as syphilis. The child was successfully delivered but because of her venereal disease, Margaret was detained in hospital until 17 August that year when she was discharged as 'cured'.

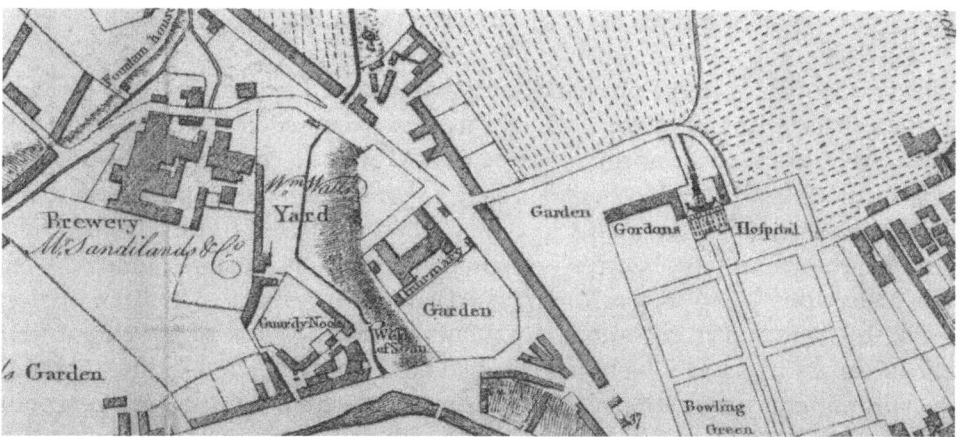

This 1789 map shows the location of Aberdeen Infirmary adjacent to Gordon's Hospital and its garden.
(Reproduced courtesy of the National Library of Scotland)

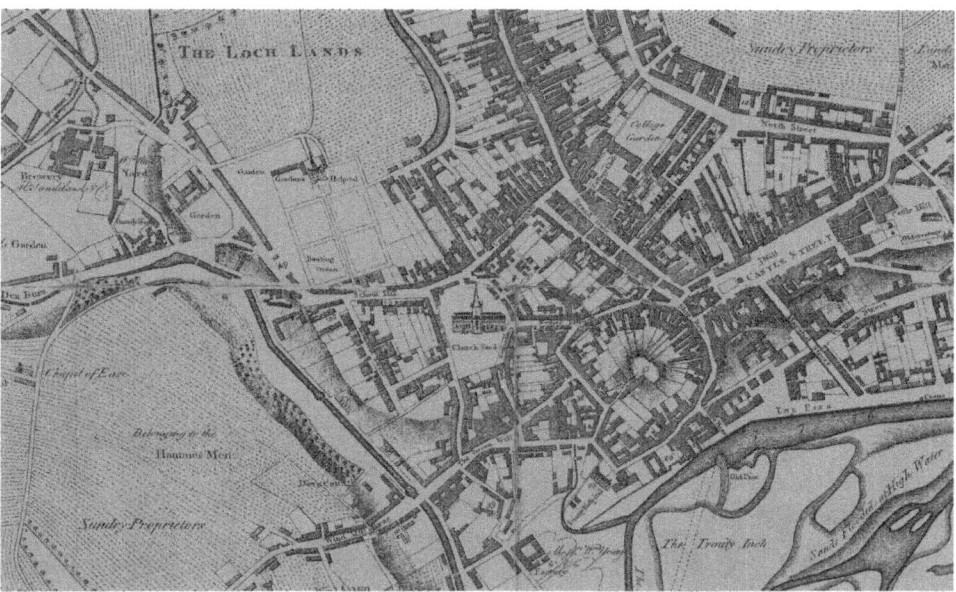

1789 map highlighting Aberdeen Infirmary with its gardens and its relation to Gordon's Hospital and the other streets and buildings within the city centre of New Aberdeen.
(Reproduced courtesy of the National Library of Scotland)

Aberdeen Royal Infirmary in the 1800s

The first Royal Charter for the infirmary was granted as early as 1773 by King George III, but the need for medical care vastly exceeded the capacity of the now 'Aberdeen Royal Infirmary' to deliver. Moreover, funding of the hospital was inconsistent. Church collections were a significant form of income for many hospitals, especially in Scotland, including Aberdeen Royal Infirmary (ARI). The first Sunday in January became known in Aberdeen as 'hospital Sunday' with the collections being sent to the treasurer of the infirmary. The Kirk session were thus allowed to recommend patients for the hospital to the extent that the infirmary checked which parishes had paid or not when deciding to admit specific patients for treatment. As late as 1867, as stated in the annual report of the ARI, the hospital received a total of £954, one shilling and one penny from church collections with various amounts from the Established Churches, the Free Church, the Episcopal Church, the United Presbyterian and other churches. In the same year, the hospital received just £85 from subscriptions and £84 in donations from public bodies and works.

The Infirmary subsequently moved from Woolmanhill to its current site in Foresterhill in 1936.

The early Aberdeen Infirmary building.
(Courtesy of Aberdeen University Archives)

The Dispensary and lying-in clinics

Drawing of the Dispensary and Lying in Clinic in Barnett's Close.
(From *Aberdeen University Review*, vol. 47 no. 160, 1978)

In 1781, the managers of the Infirmary had decided to form a new department to which they gave the name 'the Dispensary' for the treatment of outpatients. It was likely that medical advice was given to expectant mothers from the inception of the Dispensary and in the year 1786, when the managers of the infirmary did not deem it proper to support maternity care any longer in the infirmary, two additional dispensaries were established. In 1790, the Dispensary separated from Aberdeen Royal Infirmary and in the year 1802 the Dispensary,

An extract from the 'admissions book' kept in Woolmanhill, 1762.
(The original document is held in the Sir Duncan Rice Library, University of Aberdeen)

> ### Midwife Wanted
> Qualified midwife, who understands business well, who will be prudent in her walk conversation, and not given to gossip, may hear of the situation, where she may once secure a respectable practice in a thriving town some miles to the south of Aberdeen. Her house rent will be paid for the first year. Apply to the publisher of this paper. Aberdeen, 15th April 1862.
>
> *Aberdeen Press & Journal*, Wednesday 16 April 1862

known as 'the General Dispensary, Vaccine and Lying-in Institution' was planned, coming into place in 1823.

Six medical practitioners had been previously appointed as physicians, each with a separate district in the town, and, prior to 1810, financial support for five local dispensaries appears to have been obtained from the personal friends of the various doctors. In 1822, Dr William Dyce (father of Professor Robert Dyce) was the physician of the dispensary on Marischal Street. Dr 'Sandie' Fraser represented it in the Schoolhill; Dr Campbell in the Nether Kirkgate; Drs Moir and Leslie in the Marine Dispensary, James Street; and Dr Cadenhead in Gilcomston. The maternity work was done by midwives, with the medical officer being called in when required, but in 1824 all the dispensaries were amalgamated at the behest of Dr William Henderson. Its original location is uncertain (probably 66 Guestrow) and in 1826 it was situated in, or close to, the Upper Kirkgate and Broad Street, again supported by voluntary subscriptions and donations. Lying-in institutions were also located at 2 Longacre in 1825–26 and 26 Castle Street 1838–39. Delivery services in these institutions were increasingly dependent upon midwives and those numbers had to be slowly expanded. In 1870, the Dispensary bought two houses in the Guestrow (now demolished) – one of the earliest streets in Aberdeen (1439), which lay adjacent to Flourmill Brae – opposite Marischal College. One of these houses was to serve as a maternity

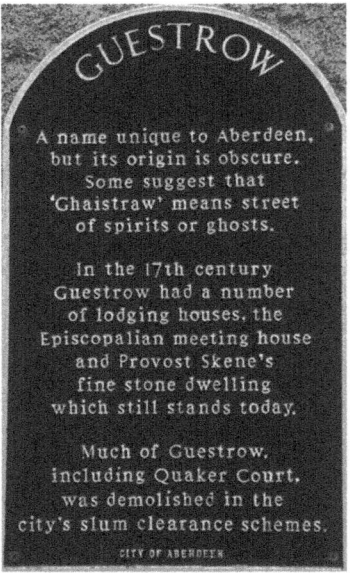

Plaque mounted on the side of a building in Broad Street indicating the origins and site of Guestrow.
(Courtesy of Aberdeen City Council)

> ## Aberdeen Maternity Hospital, 1894
>
> The new maternity hospital, adjoining the dispensary in Bar-
> nett's Close Guestrow, which is to be opened on Thursday,
> compact, yet commodious building with nice, well lighted,
> and cheerful-looking rooms which are situated on 3 different
> floors. The ground floor is to be the committee room, the wall of
> which has already been adorned with engraving of Sir Alexan-
> der Anderson. On the second floor are 5 apartments consisting
> of ward with 4 beds, storeroom for linen, lavatory, delivery
> room and kitchen. On the third floor are a couple of bedrooms,
> the matron's sitting room, and a small ward. A bright aspect is
> imparted in the rooms by the pot plants and cut flowers from
> the public parks disposed here and there under the direction of
> Nurse Jasper, matron of the hospital.
> *Aberdeen Evening Express*, Monday 19 March 1894

or lying-in unit which moved to Barnett's Close in 1893. The Guestrow Street plaque in Broad Street, pictured opposite, reads in part:

A name unique to Aberdeen, but its origin is obscure. Some suggest that 'Ghaistraw' means street of spirits or ghosts.

(It possibly got its name because it could overlook the cemetery at St Nicholas Church!)

In the 17th century, Guestrow was a prestigious part of Aberdeen city and had several lodging houses, the Episcopalian meeting house and Provost Skene's fine stone dwelling which still stands today. However, by the 20th century the street had degraded and much of Guestrow, including Quaker Court, was demolished in the city's slum clearance schemes (1930s). Provost Skene's House is a remaining vestige of Guestrow.

The Aberdeen Dispensary, Vaccine and Lying-in Institution in Barnett's Close opened on 22 March 1894 but no records survive to indicate when the first patient was admitted. The first baby, a girl, was born there on 21 April 1894 at 9.30am and was given the rather unusual name of Johann. This was to be the precursor of a dedicated maternity hospital.

There were in fact only three beds in the lying-in department and in the

A photograph of Marischal College, 1906. The view overlooks the Guestrow area which subsequently became part of a slum clearance scheme in the 1930s. Provost Skene's House is currently the last remnant of the Guestrow area.
(Picture courtesy of Aberdeen City Libraries/the Silver City Vault)

first year some 46 patients were admitted. But numbers had soon grown, and by the end of the century the dispensary managers were forced to look for larger premises – hence the acquisition of the property on the corner of Castle Street and Castle Terrace, and adapting it from the Bank of Scotland to become the new Aberdeen Maternity Hospital. Built adjacent to the Royal Aberdeen Hospital for Sick Children (RAHSC), this became Aberdeen's first dedicated maternity hospital (see p.34).

An extract from the birth certificate of Johnann Farquhar who was born in 1894 in Barnett's Close and resided in the adjacent Guestrow.
(Scotlandspeople ref 1894 164 / 1 604 Copyright National Registers of Scotland)

2

Aberdeen's Maternity Hospitals

George Youngson and Lesley Dunbar

Yesterday afternoon the new maternity hospital, situated in Castle Street, Aberdeen, was opened by Mrs Fleming, wife of Lord Provost Fleming, Aberdeen. Mr A. Walker, LLD, presided and amongst those who commended the object of the institution were Professor Stephenson and Principal Marshall Lang—Dundee Courier, Wednesday, 24 October 1900

THE COST OF the new building in Castle Terrace was covered by donations, including a generous gift of £3,000 from the Trustees of the late Thomas Primrose, Advocate in Aberdeen. A ward was presumably named after this benefactor. There were three wards in 1912: the Primrose Ward, the Alice Ward and a private ward. This hospital grew in its activities to such an extent that it was

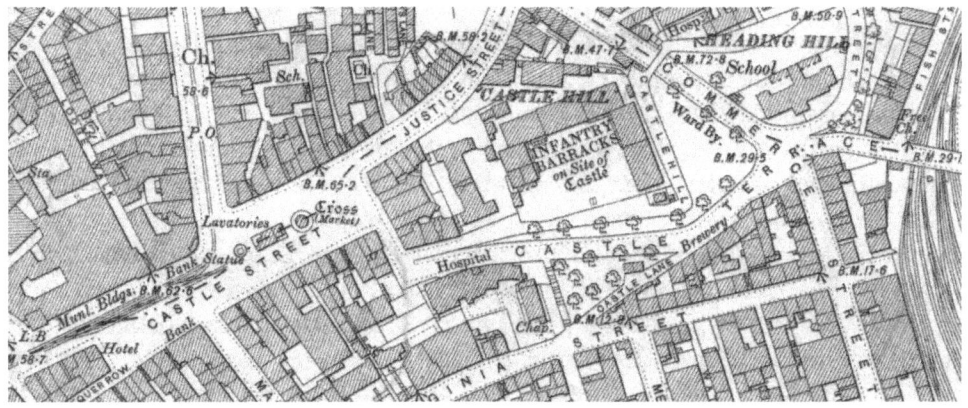

A 1902 OS map of the Castlehill area, showing the adjacent position of the Children's Hospital and the 'new' Aberdeen Maternity Hospital.

(Reproduced courtesy of the National Library of Scotland)

A drawing of Aberdeen Maternity Hospital, Castle Terrace, 1900.
(Picture courtesy of Aberdeen City Libraries/Silver City Vault)

decided to manage it separately from the dispensary and, in 1912, Aberdeen Maternity Hospital was formally established as an independent institution with its own board of directors. Additional facilities were offered in the hospital and, in 1918, 'prenatal clinics' were started with antenatal beds being provided in the neighbouring building the following year. Private paying cases were also accepted.

The perceived need and justification for a dedicated maternity hospital was also changing at this time. Sir Dugald Baird writes in the *Book of Aberdeen* compiled for the 107th annual meeting of the British Medical Association (1939):

> The outlook with regard to the function of the maternity hospital has undergone a complete change, and from simply being a house to accommodate those whose home conditions were very bad, it has become the central point for obstetrics for the area. It occupies the same position in obstetrics that the infirmary occupies as regards general medicine and surgery. It is expected to set a standard of midwifery for the area and must be prepared to treat serious emergency cases sent in by doctors for expert treatment. It must act as a training centre for midwives and doctors and by offering facilities for research work, help to advance our knowledge of the subject.

Aberdeen Maternity Hospital remained a busy place and, despite home delivery still occurring, there was a year-on-year increase in numbers, soon

An aerial photograph of Castlehill area outlining the co-location of Aberdeen Maternity Hospital with the Royal Aberdeen Hospital for Sick Children. (Left: Aberdeen Town House. Centre: Aberdeen Maternity Hospital. Right: Royal Aberdeen Hospital for Sick Children). This was a template for the subsequent co-located development of these hospitals on the Foresterhill site.

outstripping the capacity of the facility. In the year 1928, the number of children born in the hospital was 656 and another 207 mothers were delivered in their own homes. Two hundred and thirty-three cases were treated in the antenatal ward, giving a total of 1,096 cases treated. This increased activity was carried out in the face of financial restrictions, and a deputation visited the city council with a proposal for the development of a maternity home to accommodate the increase in numbers. However, this failed to attract a financial commitment from the city council and AMH remained a poor relation of healthcare spending within the city.

By the year 1937 – the last year of the Maternity Hospital at Castle Terrace – the number of cases treated had risen to 1396 per annum and the accommodation was unable to cope with the demands and the need for a new and larger facility was apparent to all.

When the appeal for the joint hospital scheme at Foresterhill as proposed by Professor Matthew Hay was launched in 1927, it was thought that the new maternity hospital would be sharing in the funds subscribed. But once again, AMH failed to enjoy the same level of financial support as the larger ARI scheme, which seemed to consume all the available funds; so, it was not until 1934 that the start was made for a new maternity hospital entirely dependent on public subscription and which, even then,

Royal Aberdeen Hospital for Sick Children at its initial site in Castle Terrace.

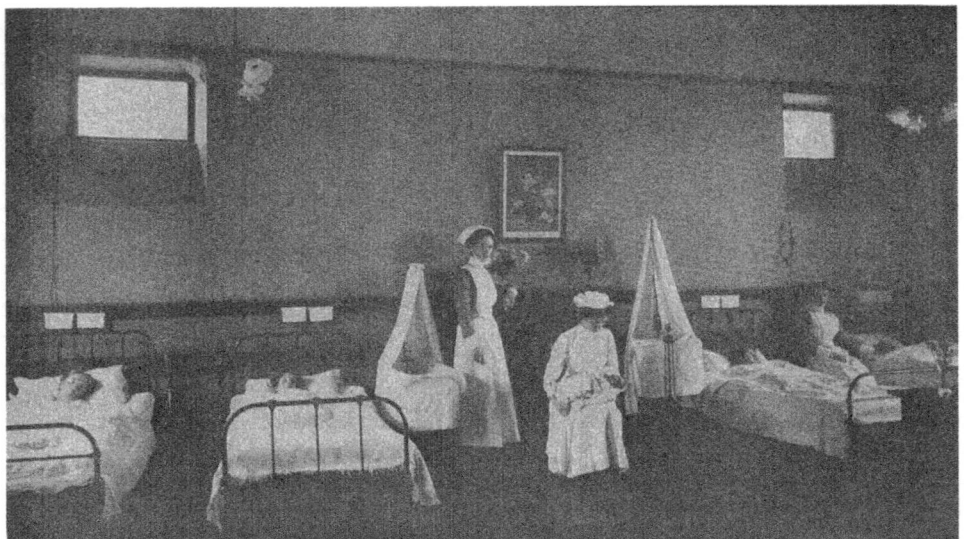

Primrose Ward, Aberdeen Maternity Hospital at Castle Terrace. It shows three nurses looking after several patients in bed and recently born children in cots. After moving to Castle Terrace in 1900 the bed number increased steadily from 18 in 1904 to 32 by the mid-1930s. This image featured on the back cover of many of the hospital's annual reports. Aberdeen Central Library Local Studies hold copies of these reports for the years 1912–47.
(Picture courtesy of Aberdeen City Libraries/Silver City Vault)

had to be downsized from the anticipated 50 beds to 36 beds, even though it was realised it would not meet the demand of the area.

Aberdeen Maternity Hospital, Foresterhill, 1937 onwards

The Aberdeen Maternity Hospital as we now know it was opened on 1 December 1937 at a total cost of £52,000 (all of which had been raised entirely by public subscription because of a lack of available funding from other sources). At the time of opening there were four single labour rooms and a single large operating theatre. There was one host surgeon and one resident registrar. Even then, it was recognised that space was limited and the demand likely to increase. The building had a granite façade, but the ends were built with brick in anticipation of the need for further development.

During the year 1938, there were 733 deliveries booked and 197 emergency cases. The maternity hospital was run (prior to the NHS) by a voluntary board and treatment was free except in the case of patients sent by local authorities from outside the city.

Antenatal and postnatal clinics continued to be provided at Castle Terrace

This oblique aerial photograph (1938) taken facing north, shows the Foresterhill site with Aberdeen Maternity Hospital south of the Polwarth building of Aberdeen University Medical School and adjacent to Aberdeen Royal infirmary.

(Reproduced by permission of Canmore http://canmore.org.uk/collection/1258282)

Aberdeen Maternity Hospital 1938 following its construction on the Foresterhill site.

(Picture courtesy of Aberdeen City Libraries/Silver City Vault) and an antenatal annex was erected adjacent to the new maternity hospital. Lectures on mothercraft, antenatal and postnatal care were being conducted at a variety of venues throughout the city (where mothers received individual instruction in the feeding of infants and management of other ailments). This was until a new antenatal wing at Foresterhill was opened in 1941 which was joined to the maternity hospital by a link corridor.

Haddo Maternity Hospital (Haddo Babies, September 1939 – June 1945)

During World War II, part of Haddo House, near Tarves in Aberdeenshire, operated as an emergency maternity hospital for expectant mothers. Lord and Lady Aberdeen welcomed the use of their ancestral home to provide a safe and tranquil refuge, away from the expected heavy enemy bombings of Glasgow and Clydebank. A total of 1,259 'Haddo babies' were born at the mansion during wartime. Elma Allardyce was in charge.

Expectant mothers arrived at Haddo a month before their due dates and stayed for a month after they gave birth. They came from Glasgow by train and on the final stage of their journey arrived by bus. They were met with a warm welcome from Lord Aberdeen.

With war against Germany being declared on 3 September 1939, the first expectant mothers arrived on 5 September and the first baby was born on 20 September. A total of 27 babies were born there in 1939 but by 1940 the expected bombing of Glasgow had not taken place and only 11 babies were born in Haddo. Glasgow, however, was heavily bombed in March 1941 and consequently there was a huge increase in the numbers of women being transported to Haddo maternity hospital. That year, 239 babies were delivered. The year 1942 saw only 146 babies being born but, in 1943, 426 babies were born, most likely the result of the heavy bombing of Aberdeen on 21 April which saw a huge increase in the numbers of local Aberdeen and Aberdeenshire mothers at Haddo.

In Aberdeen, there was particular concern for expectant mothers after the Aberdeen Blitz (or Mittwoch Blitz) which occurred during the late evening of Wednesday 21 April 1943 when within 44 minutes 29 Luftwaffe (German Air Force) bombers dropped 127 bombs, damaging or destroying over 12,000 homes in Aberdeen and killing 125 people (98 civilians and 27 soldiers). That night a high-explosive bomb of 500 kilos had also been dropped in the grounds of Aberdeen Royal Infirmary at Foresterhill. Fortunately, this bomb had not detonated. At Haddo House, Queen Victoria's Bedroom – named after Her Majesty's visit in 1857 – was used as the delivery room. The grand four-poster

The Marquis of Aberdeen on the steps of Haddo House Maternity Hospital with some of the ward babies, mothers and staff.

(Picture courtesy of archives of Haddo House Estate)

bed, Brussels carpet and portraits of Queen Victoria had been removed and placed in storage. A single hospital bed was used in the delivery room and other beds for the use of expectant mothers were in the nearby Blue Room and Green Room.

The Marquis of Aberdeen (known fondly as 'Uncle Doddie') visited each mother after she gave birth and provided each newborn with a shilling (5 pence). This was the Scottish tradition of giving a newborn baby a silver coin or 'hanselling' to bring it 'good luck'. The belief was, if the baby grasped the coin she or he would be a miser and if the coin was dropped the baby would become an unthrifty spender. Although the emergency maternity hospital had been established for evacuees coming from Glasgow, many babies were also born to local Aberdeen city and shire women, although women came from as far afield as London and one woman came from Finland. All births were registered at the nearby village of Methlick in Aberdeenshire.

In the city, in order to cope with the post-war boom and the increased demand for hospital confinements, two private nursing homes were bought by the town council and adopted for maternity care – Fonthill and Queen's Cross. Summerfield Nursing Home was already being used for maternity cases at this time and, by 1947, the maternity hospital and its various annexes were able to cope with over 3,000 births per annum. Maternity units remained at Summerfield House (previously the infection hospital linked to Woodend Hospital which at that time was outside the city boundary), Queen's Cross Maternity Unit at Carden Place and Fonthill Maternity Unit. Summerfield closed in 1990 to become the Health Board building, Queen's Cross became a bar and Fonthill a block of flats in 1989. (See Part 3 for detail of these and other maternity homes in the city). These midwife-led services were ultimately replaced with a midwives' unit based within the maternity hospital (1990) with NHS Grampian appointing its first consultant midwife in 2007.

Aberdeen Maternity Hospital

In 1948, all these institutions, initially private, had become part of the national health service. The south side of AMH had several additions made to it – the new operating theatre in the 1950s and the West Wing in 1973 including additional labour rooms. A second storey was added to the antenatal block to provide a new research unit and private beds from the Rubislaw Maternity Nursing Home.

A large number of upgrades and modifications have been made to the original 1937 building, including a chapel, but its original structure and design remains, albeit with internal structural and functional changes.

Expansion in the labour suite and antenatal facilities were incorporated, and a new dedicated neonatal unit was added in 1988 (see Part 3).

Further Reading

Aberdeen before 1800: A New History, eds. Denison, Ditchburn and Lynch, Tuckwell Press, 2002.

The Book of Aberdeen, commemorating the 107th Annual Meeting, eds. Dr David Rorie and W Lindsay British Medical Association, 1939.

Hill, Ella, and Roger, Burton, *Aberdeen Doctors at Home and Abroad: The Narrative of a Medical School*, William Blackwood & Son, Edinburgh and London, 1892.

Aberdeen 1800–2000 A New History, eds. Hamish Fraser and Clive Lee, Tuckwell Press Ltd, 2000.

The City and its Worlds; Aspects of Aberdeen's History since 1794, eds. Terry Brotherston and Donald Witherington, Cruithne Press, 1996.

Foresterhill News and Views, June 1994, Fiona Watson, Grampian Health Board.

Milne, GP, 'The History of Midwifery in Aberdeen', *Aberdeen University Review*, Vol. 47, 1978.

PART 2

The People

So many people have contributed to maternity and neonatal care in Aberdeen over the centuries and decades that it would not be possible to record all meritorious contributions. This section of the book is therefore necessarily incomplete; it is not, however, entirely random. Instead, it has sought to identify those individuals from the past who warrant recognition for the sake of posterity rather than all those who carried out valued work for, and care of, mothers and their babies. It lists, in short biographical format, several people who have made significant contributions to midwifery or neonatal care at local, national or international level in the past. With only a few exceptions, these individuals are no longer alive but bringing them together has allowed a collective recognition of Aberdeen's contribution to the care of women and their babies on the wider stage of clinical and social care.

There is also an awareness that the boundaries of influence have changed over these last few centuries. What may have been considered as having a local impact on the 18th and 19th century would today, with the benefits of modern communication platforms, perhaps now have much wider recognition and impact upon care beyond the limits of North East Scotland.

The following is, therefore, a sample of those who have contributed socially and clinically to the community of women and their babies. Omission has no implication, and this restricted list tends to identify the historic, rather than the contemporary contributors. That bias of selection apart, neither does it attempt to be comprehensive nor exhaustive.

3

The Early Practitioners

George Youngson, Lesley Dunbar and Alison McCall

Dr David Skene (1731–70)

ONE OF THE first doctors chronicled to have an interest in and make contributions to midwifery was Dr David Skene. He was born in Aberdeen on 13 August 1731 to Andrew Skene and his wife Mary Lumsden. Dr Andrew Skene was physician to Aberdeen Royal Infirmary between 1743 and 1745.

David studied at Aberdeen Grammar School and graduated with an MA from Marischal College in 1748. From 1751 to 1753 he studied medicine in Edinburgh, London and Paris, also studying botany under Dr Alston of the University of Edinburgh at the same time. He received his MD from King's College in Aberdeen and joined his father in medical practice in Aberdeen the same year.

David Skene was described as a polymath who was a significant figure in the Scottish enlightenment of the 18th century. He took an interest in a range of

THat on Monday the 6th of November, a course of MEDICAL LECTURES will be begun by Dr. *John Gregory*, and Dr. *David Skene* ——— And on Monday the 4th of December, Dr. *David Skene* begins a course of LECTURES on MIDWIFERY, particularly intended for the inftruction of country midwives.

Advert for Dr David Skene's lectures on midwifery published in *Aberdeen's Journal*, 1758. (Reproduced courtesy of Aberdeen Journals)

'Dr David Skene begins his Lectures on the Practice of MID-WIFERY; and he uses this Opportunity of giving Notice that any lying-in women, by applying to him will be carefully attended to gratis in their own Houses by suffciently skilful Midwives and such as are poorer will not only be attended to, but maintained in Bed and Board at his Expense till their Recovery'
Aberdeen's Journal, Advertisements, 29 September 1760

The text of an advert for Dr David Skene's lectures on midwifery published in *Aberdeen's Journal*, 1758.
(Reproduced courtesy of Aberdeen Journals)

subjects, including botany, philosophy, geology and Russian history. He was a correspondent of Carl Linnaeus, the Swedish botanist. He studied medicine in Edinburgh, and then moved to London where he studied anatomy and obstetrics under Dr William Smellie, who was significant in introducing the safe use of forceps into obstetric practice. He accompanied Smellie on his deliveries (often in the wee small hours of the morning) and also introduced simulated manikins (or 'machines' as he called them), as used by Smellie in the practical aspects of his lectures.

Skene travelled to Paris where he had further opportunity to pursue his interest in obstetrics by observing the work of French midwives. After his travels he returned to Aberdeen and took up practice with his father in 1753. He became Director of the Infirmary and Dean of Faculty at Marischal College. He campaigned for the proper training of midwives and one of his contemporaries, Dr Thomas Reid, gave the following account of David Skene and his work:

Dr Skene likewise instructed young women in midwifery who by subscription in country parishes were trained to the practice of that art in the parish that supported their education. By this means the poor in many parts of the country were furnished with midwives who knew what was to be done to mother and children in ordinary cases and who would consult a physician in cases of difficulty, in place of midwives who by their ignorance, temerity and self-conceit did more hurt than good.

By way of inducement for potential patients upon whom midwives attending his lectures could develop their skills (he named them 'touching lectures'), he advertised in the local newspapers with an offer of free 'bed and board' for the 'poor women lying in'.

There was general public approval of this initiative and by 1758 Dr Skene offered a two-year course in midwifery. The cost for the first year was two guineas and one guinea for the second year. The course was both theoretical and practical. The Kirk session in Kintore recorded that 'women educated at public expense might, under God, prove the means of saving the lives of many women and children…' The Session were unanimously of the opinion that 'their publick money could not be more properly disposed of than to such a valuable purpose' (than to send a woman to attend Dr Skene's course).

From 1767 until his death, he was elected annually as Dean of Faculty in Marischal College. During this time, he was also a manager of Aberdeen Infirmary and acted on behalf of the Commissioners for Sick and Wounded Seamen. He was one of the co-founders of the Aberdeen Philosophical Society (1758), whose members included James Beattie, a poet and philosopher, and Thomas Reid, a philosopher. He also undertook a great deal of research into all areas of natural history and the sciences and corresponded with leading contemporary scholars in these fields.

He died in the prime of his life, 'unmarried and very much regretted', aged 39, surviving his father by just three years.

Dr Alexander Gordon (1752–99)

Another of the earliest and most seminal contributors to maternity care to come from Aberdeen was Alexander Gordon. Alexander Gordon was born in 1752 at Milton of Drum, Peterculter, near Aberdeen and was one of twins. His father was a tenant farmer. He took a degree in MA at Marischal College in 1775 and started studying medicine, continuing at the University of Edinburgh for clinical experience (as was often the case at that time) before travelling to Leiden University to continue his medical education. He graduated in medicine in Aberdeen in 1780 and served in the Royal Navy as a surgeon until 1783. He thereafter trained in midwifery in London. In 1785, he returned to Aberdeen where he became physician to the Aberdeen Dispensary in 1786. He practised obstetrics and lectured on the subject at Marischal College. He gained an MD from Marischal College in 1788.

From 1789, Aberdeen suffered a series of epidemics of puerperal fever – an infection caused by the germ beta haemolytic streptococcus transmissible from mother to mother and mother to baby – a major one happening in Printfield, Woodside. Gordon carefully gathered statistics on these cases and published the results in A Treatise on the Epidemic Puerperal Fever of Aberdeen in 1795. Semmelweis, an Austrian doctor, is widely credited with discovering this condition but, 50 years before, Gordon showed that the condition was not caused by 'a noxious constitution of the atmosphere' as doctors then believed, but only 'seized such women only as were visited, or delivered, by a practitioner or taken care of by a nurse who had previously attended patients affected by the disease'.

In other words, the disease was transmitted by the attending clinical staff. Gordon recognised that he, himself, was not blameless.

'It is a disagreeable declaration for me to mention that I myself was the means of carrying the disease to a great number of women.'

He argued that spread could be prevented by attendants carefully washing their hands and wearing clean clothes after attending patients with the disease. His views were ridiculed by medical and nursing colleagues and his theories received a hostile response both locally and elsewhere. Gordon, however, also argued that the disease could be cured by venesection (bloodletting), a view that was accepted and widely quoted at the time, unlike his first conclusion that the disease was contagious (which was ignored until it was rediscovered many years later).

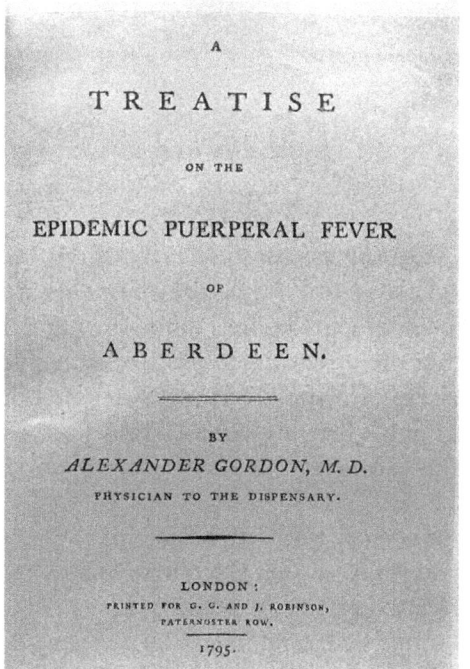
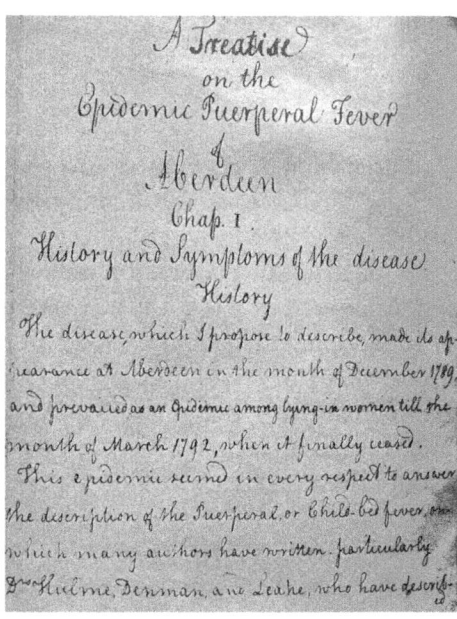

Left: the title page of Dr Alexander Gordon's treatise on the epidemic of puerperal fever in Aberdeen published in 1795, several decades before Semmelweis of Vienna.

Right: The opening page of the MS.

(Reproduced from Alexander Gordon, MD of Aberdeen 1752–99 by Ian A Porter. *Aberdeen University Studies* no. 139. Oliver and Boyd)

When taken ill	№	Name	Age	Residence	Cured	Dead	By whom delivered
D°	25	Ann Smith	24	Denburn		5th day	Mrs Elgin
D°	26	Mrs Malcom	25	Green		1 —	D°
D°	27	Wm Hobson's wife	30	Gilcomston		5 —	Mrs Emslie
October	28	Jean Webster	17	Justice port	12		Mr Anderson
November	29	Ann Cumming	29	North street	13		D°
D°	30	Mrs Still	25	D°	14		D°
D°	31	Janet McKay	38	Gallowgate	15		Mrs Clark
D°	32	Jean Laing	32	D°		7 —	Dr Gordon
D°	33	Mrs Leitch	40	Carnegie's brae	16		D°
D°	34	Ann Barclay	20	Tannery street	17		Mrs Clark
December	35	Mrs Muffart	36	Harrogate	18		Mrs Davidson
D°	36	Jean Galloway	27	North street	19		
D°	37	Janet Anderson	25	Putachy side		5 —	Mr Harvey

Some of the patients Gordon records as having contracted Puerperal Fever. Note age range and outcome.

Later, he was appointed as a physician to the Dispensary and was known to hold classes – one for 'gentlemen' and another for 'women' on 'the Theory and Practice of Midwifery'.

Soon after the publication of his book, Gordon was recalled to the Navy. He left Aberdeen in 1795 amid strong disapproval from the populace of the city who were hostile to him as a result of the statements he had made during the epidemic of puerperal fever and identifying the attending staff as responsible for transmitting the germ. Midwives strongly disapproved of his treatment and instead of acclaim, there was abuse from his fellow citizens Iain A Porter's biography of Alexander Gordon details this moment of his life:

At the end of 1795 Gordon, no doubt in sorrow but with a tinge of relief, left Aberdeen and made his way south to re-join the Navy. His anguish at leaving behind his wife and daughter, the Dispensary for which he had worked so hard and his pupils who held in so high esteem, would be partially relieved by the fact that he would no longer have to live in a city whose inhabitants had abused him so cruelly and scorned so pitilessly his wonderful discovery. Gordon never practised obstetrics again… Let us now remember Gordon of Aberdeen and give him the

TO MIDWIVES.

On Monday the third day of November,

DR. GORDON will begin a courfe of LECTURES for the inftruction of Midwives, to which, thofe already in practice, who wifh for further improvement, may have accefs on very reafonable terms. Application to be made at his houfe in Queenftreet.

An advertisement in *Aberdeen's Journal*, October 1795, outlining Alexander Gordon's lecture course for established midwives to assist in their professional development.
(Reproduced courtesy of Aberdeen Journals)

credit which is his due for the discovery he made. He suffered because its importance was not realised by his contemporaries. He had erred in only one respect-that his outstanding contribution was made too soon in history.

In 1799 he developed tuberculosis from which he died. He is commemorated by a plaque at his first home in Aberdeen –17 Belmont Street (see Appendix 1).

4

Professors of Midwifery

George Youngson, Lesley Dunbar and Alison McCall

Professor Robert Dyce (1798–1869, appointed 1860)

Portrait of Dr William Dyce (father of Prof Robert Dyce) painted by William's other son – also William Dyce. Dr William Dyce was lecturer in midwifery at Marischal College prior to his son's subsequent appointment as Professor of Midwifery.

(Reproduced courtesy Aberdeen Medico-Chirurgical Society)

IT APPEARS THAT maternal and women's health elicited little interest from the medical profession after Alexander Gordon. However, an exception and an early proponent and advocate of obstetric care was Dr Robert Dyce. The Dyce family had been a distinguished one in Aberdeen. In the beginning they were landed proprietors, bishops and doctors. The early charters refer in 1457 to John de Diss and there is good reason to believe that the Dyce family gave the name to the current suburb of Aberdeen.

Robert was born in Aberdeen on 30 November 1798 and lived with his parents and his artist brother, William, at 48 Marischal Street (A plaque commemorating the contributions of his brother to art marks this address). Robert's father, William, was a

MIDWIFERY.

ON Tuesday the first of May, Dr. DYCE will o-
pen a Class for the Instruction of MIDWIVES.
—Particulars may be learned by applying to Dr. Dyce,
Litttlejohn's Street,

This advert appeared in *Aberdeen's Journal* on 10 April 1798 outlining classes for midwives to be
held on Tuesday 1 May 1798.
(Reproduced courtesy of Aberdeen Journals)

physician to Aberdeen Royal Infirmary and president of the Aberdeen Medico-
Chirurgical Society. He, too, had a commitment to midwifery and was a teacher
of both students and midwives. He succeeded Alexander Gordon as physician
to the dispensary and in 1811 was appointed lecturer in midwifery at Marischal
College.

Robert took his degree at Marischal College in 1816, studying medicine
in Aberdeen and, like others, in Edinburgh and London. In the early part
of his career, he was attached to the Military Hospital at Chatham. After a
distinguished career in Mauritius and the Cape, he was appointed lecturer in
Midwifery at Marischal College in 1841, and, on the union of Kings College
and Marischal College into the University of Aberdeen in 1860, his lectureship
was converted into professorship – the first Professor of Midwifery.

The following is an extract from *Aberdeen's Journal*, Wednesday 13 January
1869, referring to his death:

> Our readers will observe with sorrow, in our obituary of this day,
> the death of Dr Dyce, one of our senior physicians, and Professor of
> Midwifery in the University of Aberdeen. He had been ailing for some
> weeks, but intermitted none of his duties, not even night work, which
> probably overtasked his strength... Dr Dyce was the eldest son of the
> late Dr William Dyce of this city.
>
> In 1841, he was appointed Lecturer on Midwifery in Marischal
> College, and, on the union of the two Colleges and their erection into
> the University of Aberdeen in 1860, this Lectureship was converted
> into a Professorship, and Dyce was appointed first Professor. His large
> experience and skill in the special department to which his Chair
> related gave him great weight, and caused him to be looked up to as
> an authority, while his gentlemanly bearing and winning manner were
> everywhere recognised. How much he gave away to the poor, in the
> shape of gratuitous attendance, was known only to his family and

immediate friends.

We may add that, as a Professor, we have reason to know he was much beloved by the students, who admired his perspicuous style of lecturing, while they felt the kindness with which he uniformly treated them. We understand that in his special branch he contributed valuable papers from time to time to the medical periodicals. From the commencement of his practice in Aberdeen, Dr Dyce acted as Physician to Gordon's Hospital, and up to within the last few years he held the important position of Physician to the Royal Infirmary, on his retirement from which he was appointed Consulting Physician.

Professor Andrew Inglis (1837–75, appointed 1869)

The successor to Robert Dyce was Andrew Inglis who was born in Edinburgh in 1837 and who died prematurely in 1875. He occupied the Regius Chair of Midwifery in Aberdeen from 1869 to 1875. As the son of an Edinburgh surgeon (Archibald Inglis, who had been President of the Royal College of Surgeons of Edinburgh from 1853 to 1855), Andrew started his practice in Edinburgh in 1860 and in 1867 became one of the lecturers in midwifery in connection with the University of Edinburgh. His inaugural lecture on appointment to the chair in Aberdeen is to be found in the Special Collection at the University of Aberdeen's library. He was described as an 'able and well-loved obstetrician' but he did not contribute to medical journals and during his tenure he was unwell and took a leave of absence for two years. In 1872, a small maternity hospital had been commenced in connection with the Dispensary. His obituary quotes:

> His main contribution to obstetric clinical teaching was in getting a limited number of maternity beds provided at the Aberdeen General Dispensary at the Guestrow, which already provided a domiciliary midwifery service that students attended… In 1869 the Dispensary directors reported that additional premises had been purchased making it possible to establish a lying-in branch within the building with Prof Inglis as physician accoucheur. The setting up of the lying-in ward, despite local opposition, was entirely due to Inglis's efforts.

It ceased operation in 1874 during the time that Professor Inglis was on sick leave and the closure of these beds may have been associated with his illness. He was succeeded by Professor William Stephenson, a more formidable individual and one who amongst several of his fundamentally important initiatives for the city, fostered the development of the first Children's Hospital in Aberdeen in 1877.

Professor William Stephenson (1837–1919, appointed 1875)

Professor Stephenson became the main advocate for women's health and although initially registered as a paediatrician and obstetric physician, he continued pleading for maternity beds and beds for diseases of women. William Stephenson was born in Edinburgh on 2 July 1837. He was educated at the High School in Edinburgh and graduated from the University of Edinburgh in 1861. He practiced there for 13 years and was subsequently appointed as Professor of Midwifery at the University of Aberdeen in 1875. Stephenson held the chair in midwifery until 1912 when he was succeeded by Professor Robert G McKerron – also a paediatrician who remained in post until 1936.

Professor William Stephenson who was responsible for the creation of the first children's hospital in Aberdeen, the Royal Aberdeen Hospital for Sick Children. He was appointed Professor of Midwifery at the University of Aberdeen in 1875.

(Image held by and reproduced with permission of Aberdeen Medico-Chirurgical Society)

Unlike his predecessor, Stephenson contributed extensively to medical and scientific journals and enjoyed a national reputation. He was on the council of the Obstetric Society of London and became president of Edinburgh Obstetric Society in 1908. His scientific interests were particularly in diseases of children and the mechanisms of labour.

Professor Stephenson was a staunch advocate for the health and wellbeing of women and children and was instrumental in establishing the first Children's Hospital in Aberdeen in 1877, subsequently adjoining the old maternity hospital in Castle Terrace. In his inaugural lecture he made a plea for midwifery beds to be established in Aberdeen, although he did not get these beds till 1894 until the opening of the Dispensary in Barnett's Close, the unit moving to Castle Terrace in 1900. It was, however, he who persuaded the Dispensary to have inpatient beds, or 'lying-in' beds as they were called, for maternity cases. These were placed in a house adjoining the Dispensary in Barnett's Close at the Guestrow.

In his inaugural lecture he states:

It is the duty of a professor not only to teach what is already known, but also, to help on the advance of our knowledge. If I succeed in so training and inspiring you with enthusiasm for our art that you will be able to become the observant scientific practitioners I have indicated, I feel I shall be contributing more to the progress of midwifery than I can ever aspire by personal research. It will be the lot of most of you to be country practitioners – and so at the beginning of their career with the fathers of obstetrics, Smellie and William Hunter... Surgery and Medicine have each their clinical wards and clinical lectures; none exists for the diseases of women and children. Such is the defect. But it does not lie in the power of the profession or university authorities to remove it. It is the public alone that can do it. They must put their hands into their pockets and furnish the means by the establishment of separate institutions, or, better still, additional wards in the infirmary.

He retired in 1912 and died in 1919 having achieved his dual goal of creating institutions for both children and for women.

Professor Robert McKerron (1862–1937, appointed 1912)

Robert Gordon McKerron was Professor of Midwifery at the University of Aberdeen from 1912 to 1936 as successor to Stephenson. McKerron had been a student of Stephenson who was celebrated for his lecture style and as being a great raconteur. McKerron was likewise known for his enthusiastic lecture style and was very popular with the students since his lectures were delivered with wit and enthusiasm. He had been born in 1862 at Auchindoir beside Huntly, where his father was the parish minister. He graduated MA with honours in 1884, MB CM in 1888, and MD with honours in 1898. During the First World War he served with the Royal Army Medical Corps attached to the 1st Scottish General Hospital with the final rank of Major. He was a foundation fellow of the Royal College of Obstetricians and Gynaecologists.

He had entered general practice initially, but his reputation rapidly spread by virtue of his expertise in paediatrics and midwifery. Students at the University of Aberdeen knew McKerron as 'old Howds', or 'Clachnaben' – a reference to the large cyst on top of his bald head which resembled the shape of the hill of that name.

He was known to be very conservative in his practice and reticent to perform caesarean sections but was otherwise an astute clinician. His textbook *Pregnancy, Labour and Child Bed with Ovarian Tumour* became known as a classic, having collected 1,290 cases. He was the last of the well-known triumvirate of the early part of the 20th century: Professors Marnoch, Macintosh and McKerron, who occupied the chairs of Surgery, Medicine and Midwifery respectively.

Professor Sir Dugald Baird (1899–1986. Appointed 1937)

McKerron successor was the irrepressible Sir Dugald Baird. Baird was born in Beith, in Ayrshire, in 1899, and after being schooled in Greenock Academy went on to read science at Glasgow University. He graduated MB ChB in 1922 and undertook further training at the University of Strasbourg. He proceeded with his MD with honours and was awarded the Bellahouston Gold medal in 1934 and fellow of the Royal College of Obstetricians and Gynaecologists in 1935. His earliest appointments were at Glasgow Royal Maternity and Women's Hospital, Glasgow Royal Infirmary and Glasgow Royal Cancer Hospital, being senior assistant to the Muirhead Chair of Obstetrics and Gynaecology at the University of Glasgow. He had already built up a reputation as being a rigorous scientific investigator by the time of his appointment as Regius Professor of Midwifery in Aberdeen in 1937. This was at a time which coincided with the move of the AMH from the Castle Terrace site to the new site at Foresterhill. Before moving from Glasgow, he was warned about how 'thrawn' the people of Aberdeen could be, but he saw many opportunities. He was very aware of the wide discrepancy in health and reproductive efficiency of women in private and hospital practice and was acutely aware of the importance of social factors in obstetrics. Consequently, he undertook the unprecedented step of introducing dieticians, sociologists, psychologists and statisticians to his department and persuaded the Medical Research Council to support his research, allowing him also the opportunity to define and classify the causes of maternal and perinatal deaths.

Throughout the 1940s, he placed emphasis on influencing these parameters and in 1951 he established the Aberdeen Maternity and Neonatal Databank (see Part 3) to link all the obstetric and fertility-related events relating to women from the defined population of the North East of Scotland. Patient management was based on these data. Having established this 'Obstetric Medicine Research Unit' he went on to attract and develop many academic clinicians to work with him. He identified the problems of high parity (multiple pregnancies) and was instrumental in developing policies and fertility control, bringing about the changes identified in the act of 1967 which dealt with sterilisation and abortion reform.

His approach to women's health was holistic at a time when the aim of obstetric care was safe delivery of the baby and an 'intact mother', hopefully alive and undamaged. He named freedom from excessive fertility with a high parity risk to many women as 'the Fifth Freedom'. The 'Four Freedoms' were goals articulated by United States President Franklin D Roosevelt in 1941, indicating that people everywhere ought to enjoy: freedom of speech; freedom of worship; freedom from want; freedom from fear.

Baird added this 'Fifth Freedom' – freedom from excessive fertility. This was crucial in influencing the reform of the abortion law in 1967. He also encouraged women who had completed their family to be sterilised. Along with his wife, Lady May Baird – a member of the Health Board – he set up the first free family planning clinic in Aberdeen, as well as sterilisation and safe abortion. He led on major initiatives in clinical practice, service provision and health policy in reproductive health, perinatal and maternal mortality and social obstetrics.

His support for the termination of pregnancies for socio-economic reasons, with the service being offered as part of the NHS in the 1950s, created the impression that abortion was rife and was available 'on demand'. This, however, was far from the truth, and it was simply his emphasis on the need to liberate women from the burden of frequent childbearing that motivated his work in this aspect of women's health.

He recognised the importance of public health, diet and social housing in a population who 'lived on chips and beer' – a very different description to the perceived affluence in Aberdeen following the emergence of the oil and gas industry in the 1980s. He worked with Boyd-Orr at the Rowett Institute on diet and nutrition of mothers. In the 1950s, he encouraged Dr Betty Macgregor to learn cervical cytology and establish a cervical screening programme with North East Scotland as one of the first regions in the UK to offer cervical screening. The screening programme was able to demonstrate reduction in cervical cancer deaths. At that time, however, family planning and cervical screening were only available to married women.

His multidisciplinary approach to clinical care and research contrasted with other university units in the UK, and he had the foresight to recognise that this was the means to improving obstetric care and reproductive performance. With the previously mentioned support from the Medical Research Council to develop the Obstetric Medicine Research Unit (OMRU), situated in the top floor of AMH along with the MRC Medical Sociology Unit which he had established, research conducted in 1955 within these units was able to exploit the two unique features of North East Scotland – a region with a stable population and a centralised medical service which allowed long term follow-up of women and their families. As honorary director, he created 'social obstetrics', and much of what he pioneered later became commonly accepted practice. Many of those attached to the Obstetric Medical Research Unit went on to achieve professorial status throughout the UK and his mentorship and collaboration with individuals such as Raymond Illsley, (MRC Medical Sociology Unit), Angus Thomson (nutritionist), and Frank Hytten, (clinical physiologist). He thus produced a diverse but inclusive and comprehensive approach to maternal health as had never been seen before.

He became Dean of the Medical School and his contributions to obstetrics and reproductive medicine were recognised by a knighthood in 1959. He was also given honorary degrees by six universities (including an honorary LLD from his alma mater, the University of Glasgow) and the Royal College of Physicians and Surgeons of Glasgow. He was made a Freeman of the City of Aberdeen in 1966. His international fame had spread and while he served on many local medical and charity committees he was also a consultant to the World Health Organisation and travelled extensively. He died in November 1986, aged 86 years. (See appendix 1 for details of his commemorative plaque).

Professor Ian MacGillivray (1920–2021, appointed 1965)

The next Regius Professor of Obstetrics and Gynaecology was Ian MacGillivray, who was educated at the Vale of Leven Academy, Alexandria and who was also a Glasgow graduate. He graduated MB ChB from the University of Glasgow in 1944. After qualifying he served as a naval surgeon in troopships in the Far East. On his return he trained in general medicine and Obstetrics and Gynaecology in Falkirk and in Glasgow.

In 1948 he was awarded Gardiner Research Scholarship by Glasgow University. In 1950 he was appointed as lecturer in midwifery. Having worked on problems in obstetrics he obtained an MD degree in 1953 and was appointed senior lecturer in obstetrics and Gynaecology at Bristol University.

He first came to Aberdeen in 1955 as a senior lecturer in Sir Dugald Baird's department

Prof Ian MacGillivray, Regius Professor of Obstetrics and Gynaecology, University of Aberdeen, a major contributor to research into hypertension in pregnancy.
(Photograph reproduced from *Aberdeen University Medical Students Final Year Book*, 1973)

where he remained till in 1960 he was appointed to the newly created Chair of Obstetrics and Gynaecology at St Mary's Hospital Medical School in London.

He chose to return to Scotland as Regius Chair of Obstetrics and Gynaecology at the University of Aberdeen as he considered there were more opportunities to pursue his main interests there. He held the post from 1965 to his retirement in 1985.

His research focused on twin pregnancies, pre-eclampsia and other hypertension disorders in pregnancy, and the sequelae of termination and sterilisation amongst other things.

As a father of twins himself, he had a deep personal understanding of the significance of multiple pregnancy and he established the working group on multiple pregnancy in 1978 as part of the International Society for Twin Studies, becoming its president in 1981. He hosted the fourth International Congress in London in 1983. In 1976, at a meeting in Munster of worldwide scientists with a major research focus on pregnancy hypertension, he was chosen by his peers to be the first president of the International Society for the Study of Hypertension in Pregnancy, serving 1978–1980.

He was appointed to represent the University of Aberdeen on the General Medical Council in 1979 and retired from the chair in 1985.

The MacGillivray Academic Centre, which was opened in AMH in 1999 to provide future doctors and midwives, as well as current staff, with the best and most up-to-date support for their continuing education, is named in his honour.

Throughout his career he continued to play a full role in the clinical work of Grampian Health Board as well as his role as an academic both in research and teaching. Despite his very full schedules he always was available to all – patients, staff and colleagues – to listen to their problems and give advice as deemed appropriate.

Professor A Allan Templeton (1946—, appointed 1985)

Professor Allan Templeton was born in Glasgow but moved to Aberdeen when he was one year old. His father was a chiropodist who established the Aberdeen Foot Hospital and Templeton was educated at Aberdeen Grammar School. He entered Aberdeen University Medical School at the age of just 16 years and it was during his elective year as an undergraduate which he spent in Kenya as part of a student exchange programme, that he became interested in the specialty of obstetrics and gynaecology. Professor Templeton graduated in 1969 and obtained MD with honours from the University of Aberdeen in 1981. He moved to Edinburgh 1975, where he was introduced to the field

Professor A Allan Templeton CBE Appointed Regius Professor in Obstetrics And Gynaecology, University of Aberdeen 1985. He is considered a pioneer in the field of infertility, fertility control and reproductive health.

(Photograph reproduced with permission of Professor Templeton)

of infertility. After working ten years in Edinburgh he returned to Aberdeen in 1985 as the University Regius Professor of Obstetrics and Gynaecology. He assembled a multidisciplinary team to pioneer many techniques in assisted conception and was considered a pioneer in the field of infertility, fertility control and reproductive health.

Out of Aberdeen, he adopted the role of honorary secretary at the Royal College of Gynaecologists and Obstetricians for seven years before becoming President of the College (2004–2007). He had founded the Aberdeen Fertility Centre in 1985 to provide fertility services within the North East of Scotland. The centre initially provided donor insemination treatment and the first baby was born in 1986. Several innovative research projects led to the creation of an in-vitro fertilisation (IVF) service in 1988, leading to the first IVF baby being born in 1989.

He was awarded a CBE in 2008 for services to medicine. In addition to his clinical activities, he went on to work with the Academy of the Medical Royal Colleges, the Academy of Medical Sciences (2002), the Postgraduate Medical Education and Training Board and the Royal College of Midwives.

Professor Marion Hall (1939—)

Marion Hall (MacLennan) was brought up in Blairgowrie where she attended Blairgowrie High School. Following in her mother and father's footsteps north she came to the University of Aberdeen to study medicine and graduated in 1963. During her undergraduate years she met and married Peter Hall, who became a physics teacher in 1959. Marion could sing many a folk song and she and Peter did folk music tours together as students.

They had two children born in 1969 and 1971. Sadly, Peter died before she retired.

She was strong-willed and always fought her corner, bringing up her two children during her training years. She was the first woman to become a Consultant Obstetrician and Gynaecologist in Aberdeen.

She remained in Aberdeen, doing all her training there, which led to her MRCOG in 1969, during which time she developed an interest in clinical research. She was appointed as lecturer in Obstetrics and Gynaecology by the University of Aberdeen in 1969 and following her conducting of one of the first double-blind controlled trials in a total population of pregnant women in Aberdeen was awarded an MD degree in 1971 entitled 'Assessment of the effects of folic acid deficiency in pregnancy'.

In 1973 with support from Professor Ian MacGillivray she fought off male opposition and was appointed as a consultant by Grampian Health Board, a post held until her retiral in 2004. Although her appointment was to an NHS post, her research interest was maintained and her academic output outstanding.

Following the lead of both Professors Baird and MacGillivray she played a major role in the continuation and further development of Aberdeen Maternity and Neonatal Databank (AMND) becoming the chair of its Steering Committee in 1984 until her retiral. During this time her publications in the field of obstetric epidemiology were many: topics included antenatal care,

Professor Marion Hall was the first woman to be appointed Consultant Obstetrician and Gynaecologist in Aberdeen in 1973 and subsequently bestowed a personal chair by the University of Aberdeen.

(Reproduced from *Aberdeen University Medical Students Final Year Book*, 1973)

maternal morbidity, outcome of pregnancy after operative delivery. She along with colleagues began intergenerational studies from AMND and initiated 'The Aberdeen Children of the 1950s Cohort' and other cohorts, all of which has led to significant findings in the field of obstetric antecedents of adult disease.

She was clinically very competent in both obstetrics and gynaecology with a wide range of gynae operative skills, including cancer surgery before it became a subspecialty. She recognised familial breast and ovarian cancer in Scottish families long before the BRACA gene was identified (which determines susceptibility to certain cancers).

She stood up for woman's rights, following in the tradition of Dugald Baird by advocating the 'demedicalisation' of pregnancy with less hospital care/intervention for women with healthy pregnancies. Keeping women safe during pregnancy was paramount and for several years she was a member of the Confidential Enquiry into Maternal Deaths following from its beginning from smaller, local enquiries dating back to 1917 in Aberdeen, with national enquiries across England, Scotland and Wales following in the 1920s and 1930s.

Throughout her career she contributed fully to teaching both undergraduates and trainees. One trainee commented as follows:

She was one of the best teachers. All of her operating lists were planned in a little diary right down to a teaching case for Registrar and her Senior House Officer. Although it could be hair-raising for her Registrar being taught on the car journey all the way to the Banff clinic while she was driving.

She was always very supportive to women pursuing a career in Obstetrics and Gynaecology. She was made an honorary professor by the University of Aberdeen and continued her research after retirement, including spending six months in Burkina Faso on Professor Wendy Graham's IMMPACT project into maternal mortality as part of her study for a degree in French and Spanish. She graduated with honours in 2009.

Further Reading

'Aberdeen Maternity Hospital', Prof W Stephenson, in *British Medical Association Handbook and Guide,* Aberdeen 1914, J Scott Riddell Ed.J. Burrow Co. Ltd., Cheltenham 1914.

Aberdeen Medico-Chirurgical Society, A Bicentennial History. Ed. George P Milne. Aberdeen University Press, 1989.

Aberdeen Royal Infirmary, The Peoples Hospital of the North-East. Eds. Iain Levack & Hugh Dudley. Bailliere Tindall, 1992.

Chambers Scottish Biographical Dictionary Ed. Rosemary Goring 1992

Lesley Diack in *The City and its Worlds* pp 125–26 Ed. T Brotherstone and Donald J Witherington. Cruithne Press Glasgow 1996.

Iain A. Porter in 'Alexander Gordon, MD of Aberdeen. 1752–99', in *Aberdeen University Studies* 139. Oliver and Boyd Ltd, Edinburgh, 1958.

The Book of Aberdeen. 107th Annual meeting, The British Medical Association by David Rorie. 1937

5

The First Neonatal Surgeons

George Youngson, Lesley Dunbar and Alison McCall

Professor Andrew Wilkinson (1914–1995)

ANDREW WOOD WILKINSON was born in Taunton and was to become the first Professor of Paediatric Surgery in the United Kingdom. Schooled in Weymouth and graduating from the University of Edinburgh Medical School, he went on to become a lecturer in surgery in Edinburgh before moving to Aberdeen in 1953 where he was appointed as a senior lecturer and junior surgeon at Aberdeen Royal Infirmary and Royal Aberdeen Children's Hospital. It was here that he was to establish his reputation as a global expert on fluid and electrolyte management in surgery, going on to publish his seminal work *Body Fluids in Surgery* and this contribution made an impact on the clinical care of patients, including surgical neonates, worldwide. He went on to become the Nuffield Professor of Paediatric Surgery at the Institute of Child Health at the University of London and consultant surgeon working at Great Ormond Street Hospital. He was elected as President of the Royal College of Surgeons of Edinburgh in 1976.

Professor PF Jones (1920–2009)

Peter F Jones ('Puffy') was educated at St Bartholomew's Hospital Medical School and was registrar at the Central Middlesex Hospital in London from 1953 to 1957. He was appointed as consultant surgeon to Woodend General Hospital and the Royal Aberdeen Children's Hospital in 1958 and he continued to hold both these posts until his retirement in 1985. He made the surgery of children and infancy his interest and taught and published widely on emergency abdominal surgery in adults, children and the newborn. Not only did he practice paediatric surgery and gastrointestinal surgery to a high standard, but he also made considerable original contributions to both specialties. As a paediatric surgeon, the mismatch between his substantial hand size and dimension of the neonatal abdomen was of no consequence given his sureness and lightness of touch. He worked hard at his craft, becoming very skilled and seemingly able to understand the difficulties which some trainee surgeons experienced in learning the craft aspects of surgery, indeed, becoming a teacher of operative technique without peer. He was highly productive academically and published many papers in surgical journals as well as several books on operative surgery.

He was noted for his commitment and dedication to patient care and could be seen cycling from his home in Cults to the Children's Hospital and Woodend at all hours of the day and night.

6

Major Local Contributors to Midwifery and Neonatal Care

James Matthews Duncan
(1826–90)

JAMES MATTHEWS DUNCAN was born in Bon Accord Square, Aberdeen in 1826, the son of a shipping merchant. He was educated at Aberdeen Grammar School and at Marischal College where he undertook a Master of Arts degree. He went on to study medicine in Aberdeen, Edinburgh and Paris and in 1846 he obtained a Doctorate in Medicine from the University of Aberdeen. While working in Edinburgh, he became acquainted with James Young Simpson, professor of midwifery who adopted Matthews Duncan as a collaborator in his discovery of the anaesthetic properties of chloroform. Matthews Duncan began practice in Edinburgh and in 1853 ran a course of lectures on midwifery at the Extramural School. Simpson, Matthews Duncan and Dr George Keith used to research and self-experiment in Dr Simpson's dining

James Matthews Duncan was renowned for his contributions to the discovery of chloroform along with James Young Simpson and for his contributions to the understanding of diabetes and pregnancy, and his subsequent position as President of the Edinburgh Obstetrical Society and Fellow of the Royal Society (1883).

(Picture reproduced from https://en.wikipedia.org/wiki/James_Matthews_Duncan#Life)

room to evaluate the anaesthetic properties of chloroform. They were known to inhale chloroform to the point of loss of consciousness!

He was elected Fellow of the Royal Society and fellow of the Royal College of Physicians in Edinburgh and in 1861 was appointed physician to the Edinburgh Royal Infirmary, being instrumental in the founding of the Royal Hospital for Sick Children in Edinburgh. He published many lectures and books on his research, which included the mechanisms of childbirth and diseases in women.

On the death of Sir James Simpson in 1870, it was expected that Matthews Duncan would be Simpson's successor. However, he was not appointed to that post and later became obstetric physician to St Bartholomew's Hospital in London, where he became recognised as the leading obstetric authority of his day. He acquired several honours, including FRS, FRCP of London, LLD's of Edinburgh and Cambridge and an honorary degree from the University of Dublin. He was an honorary member of the medical societies of America, Russia, Austria, Germany and Norway. At the age of 60 he retired from obstetrics, developing angina two years later, and suffered a fatal heart attack in Baden-Baden in 1890. On his death, Queen Victoria sent a telegram to his widow in which she wrote 'the country and Europe at large have lost one of their most distinguished men, and one who will be sorely missed'.

Rachel Frances Lumsden (1835–1908)

Rachel Lumsden was born in Ferryhill on 17 April 1835. She was the second youngest daughter of Clements Lumsden, who was an Advocate in Aberdeen, and Jane Forbes of Echt. In her early childhood and youth Rachel didn't seem a likely or promising candidate for nursing – unlikely due to her family's social standing, and not promising, given that she was described as 'not strong'. Rachel and her youngest sister Louisa were the first female members of their family to seek careers.

At the age of 35, she shocked her family when she announced she would train as a nurse at the Hospital for Sick Children on Great Ormond Street in London. She probably went as a paying probationer. Her health and strength improved. In 1877, she returned back home to Glenbogie, just as the new Royal Aberdeen Hospital for Sick Children at Castle Terrace was about to open. She accepted the post and was appointed as the Lady Superintendent on condition she would not accept a salary.

In fact, she loaned £600 of her money to the hospital. While at the Children's Hospital she introduced a form of nurse training for lady probationers. In 1885, she put herself forward and was appointed as superintendent, head nurse and housekeeper-matron of the Aberdeen Royal Infirmary at Woolmanhill. Her sister Katherine, although not trained as a nurse, was appointed as the Lady Superintendent at the Royal Aberdeen Hospital for Sick Children when Rachel left her post there.

By December 1886 she had initiated a system of nurse training which included three courses of lectures, general nursing, elementary anatomy and surgical nursing as well as elementary physiology and medical nursing. Five years later, she pioneered a three-year nurse training course. In 1889, she became a member of the Provisional Committee of the Scottish Branch of the Queen Victoria Jubilee Institute for Nurses and in 1891 was one of the eight members appointed by the Queen. Rachel was one of the signatories of the Petition for State Registration of Nurses in 1892 and that same year one of the new wards at the

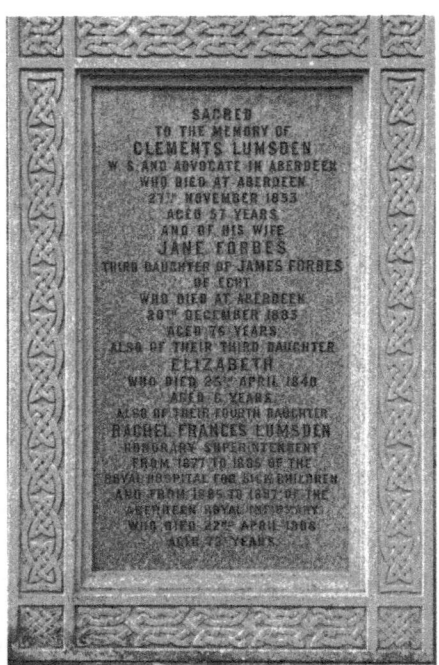

The family gravestone of the Lumsden family can be found in St Nicholas Churchyard, Union Street, Aberdeen.

Aberdeen Royal Infirmary was named after her, as she had been heavily engaged in all the arrangements for their Jubilee Extension Scheme. When she retired in 1897, she received a message from Queen Victoria and an album signed by 63 Aberdeen doctors. She moved back to her family home at Glenbogie.

In 1906 she travelled with her sister Louisa to Egypt. She died on 22 April 1908 at her sister Katherine's house at 17 Richmondhill Place and was buried in the family burial ground at St Nicholas Churchyard, off Union Street, Aberdeen. Her name is included on a tablet at the Rotunda at the Aberdeen Royal Infirmary at Foresterhill that commemorates the names of pavilions and wards in the Royal Infirmary when it was situated at Woolmanhill.

Dr Agnes Thomson (1880–1952)

Agnes Thomson was born in Brechin, attending the University of Aberdeen to become a teacher before changing her course to medicine, and was the first woman to attain triple degrees, graduating MA 1902, BSC 1905 and MB ChB in 1907. Ultimately, she became anaesthetist, lecturer in midwifery, and general practitioner at Royal Aberdeen Hospital for Sick Children in Castle Street. In 1907 she married Benjamin Thomson, a schoolmaster who later became the Rector of Forfar Academy. He died in 1934. Their two daughters both graduated in Medicine. Ann was a senior Medical Officer when she retired in 1974, and Sheila was senior Medical Officer for maternity and child welfare in Renfrewshire.

Dr Agnes Thomson was a Burgess of the City of Aberdeen and has a plaque commemorating her many contributions to women's health and child welfare in Aberdeen. She obtained three degrees from the University of Aberdeen.

(Picture courtesy of Aberdeen City Libraries/Silver City Vault, previously published with her obituary in the *Press & Journal*)

She was active during the first half of the 20th century and was a founding Member of the Medical Women's Federation, as well as being instrumental in establishing Aberdeen's Mothers and Baby Home. She served as President of Aberdeen Women's Citizens Association, becoming President of the Scottish Council of this association in 1945, and supported many other agencies in the city, including the Soroptimist Club, St Katherine's Club, Aberdeen Old People's Welfare Council and the National Council for Women. From 1914 onwards she acted as medical officer to the Mother and Child Welfare Association at Holburn Clinic. In 1945 she became president of the Scottish Council of Women's Citizens Association. Her honours included being Burgess of the City of Aberdeen and having a plaque at her previous residence in 13 Albert Street.

In the *Press & Journal* of 11 April 1942, there is a report that Thomson chaired the committee which worked to open the Aberdeen Mother and Baby Home at 25 Westfield Terrace 'to give young friendless girls a second chance and their babies the best possible start in life'.

Dr Laura Stewart Sandeman (1862–1929)

Dr Laura Sandeman was born on 2 January 1862 in Bradshaw, Lancashire. Her father was Colonel Frank Stewart Sandeman and her mother was Laura S Sandeman. Laura was the eldest of seven brothers and three sisters. Her father owned the mill at Stanley, Perthshire, where Laura grew up. She studied at the University of Edinburgh, graduating with a Bachelor of Medicine and a Bachelor of Surgery in 1900 and became a Doctor of Medicine in 1903, making her one of the earliest women to graduate in Medicine. She then came north to Aberdeen and started a medical practice at 22 Waverley Place with Dr Anne Mercer Watson. She also opened a practice in Victoria Road, Torry where she worked with women and their families.

Fees were to her a minor consideration and from poor patients, she would have no fee. She was really the moving spirit in the establishment of the Child Welfare Centre in Torry, of which she was Medical Officer. She regularly visited mothers, their babies and children. Her name was a household word in the East End of the city and Torry.

At the beginning of the First World War in 1914, she placed herself at the disposal of the country. She went to France with the Scottish Women's Hospitals for Foreign Service and was the first Chief Medical Officer from May to September 1915 at Troyes. She served alongside Louise McIlroy at the Girton and Newnham Second Unit, 'under tents'. Dr Elsie Inglis from Edinburgh, who had set up the Scottish Women's Hospitals, also served at the Second Unit as a Bacteriologist. Later, Dr Sandeman became Controller of Medical Services to Queen Mary's Army Auxiliary Corps and was also Mentioned in Dispatches. She then served in the War Hospital in Leith in 1916, which was previously the Eastern General Hospital. In June 1916, Dr Sandeman presided over a meeting held in Edinburgh to form the Scottish Midwives Association where 'steps were taken to make the initial arrangements'.

Dr Sandeman returned to Aberdeen and her general practice, where her colleague Dr Anne Mercer Watson had carried on their work in her absence. Dr Sandeman and Dr Watson continued their work together with the city's East End and Torry 's disadvantaged families until her death. After 1919, Dr Sandeman also served on the Scottish Board of Health Consultative Council - a precursor to the NHS. In 1924 Dr Sandeman stood for election as a Member of Parliament as a candidate for the Conservative and Unionist Party for the North Aberdeen seat but only came second, behind the Labour Party candidate, William Wedgewood Benn. She ran again unsuccessfully as a candidate for this seat at the by-election in 1928. Dr Sandeman died at her home in Waverley Place on 22 February 1929 from pneumonia, following a bout of flu. There had been an epidemic in the city in the previous weeks affecting many of Dr Sandeman's patients.

Professor Alexander Low, President of the Aberdeen Medico-Chirurgical Society which Dr Sandeman had been a member of since 1905, paid the following tribute to her in the *Press & Journal*, 23 February 1929:

> The death of Dr Laura Sandeman leaves a deep sense of personal loss among all her medical colleagues with her robust common sense, wide sympathy, and large outlook on life, she filled a place in the regard and esteem of the members of her profession not often attained. The full range of her activities and influence was known to few. It can be truly said that, for the greater part of her life, she had lived for her profession. Her conspicuous ability and devotion is a tribute to the advance in medicine that has followed the entry of women into its study and practice.

Dr Matthew Hay (1855–1932) MB CM (Hons) MD Edin

Portrait of Professor Matthew Hay who was Professor of Forensic Medicine at the University of Aberdeen and the city's Medical Officer of Health. He was the major driver behind the development of the Foresterhill campus which could contain all medical services for the city and which was named the Joint Hospital Scheme.

(Reproduced by permission of University of Aberdeen Special Collections and Museum. Displayed in the council chamber of Aberdeen Medico-Chirurgical Society)

Much is written about Professor Matthew Hay elsewhere and although he may have become the 'best known medical man in the Kingdom', when he was young, his career could have taken a different direction on one or two occasions. He was born in 1855 in Slamannan, Stirlingshire into a coal mine owning family and was educated at Dollar Academy. When Hay was still at university, his father bought an iron foundry and Matthew considered leaving his medical studies to work in the family business, designing improvements to the coal and iron industries. However, he chose to study medicine in Glasgow and Edinburgh from where he graduated with distinction in 1878. Matthew Hay continued his medical career working in Materia Medica in Edinburgh and studying in Europe. He obtained his MD with honours in 1881.

His next life-changing decision occurred when he was appointed to the Chair of Pharmacology and Therapeutics in Johns Hopkins University, Baltimore. William Osler, whom Hay had met in Berlin, had become Professor of Medicine at this American University, but Matthew Hay declined the position and instead took the Chair of Medical Logic and Jurisprudence in Aberdeen. Here, he spent the rest of his life working to improve conditions in North East Scotland. His first contribution was to develop the Aberdeen Improvement Scheme (Housing of the Working Classes) which, from 1894, resulted in a massive slum clearance programme.

His second contribution was his role as the driving force behind the Aberdeen Joint Hospital Scheme which put together Aberdeen University and the governors of the voluntary hospitals in the town council. He thus developed an integrated health campus on the Foresterhill site incorporating clinical services, medical education, and research. This was to be the site of the current Aberdeen Maternity Hospital, opened in 1937. However, the re-siting of the maternity hospital within the Baird Family Hospital brings Matthew Hay's vision of one collocated site even closer, with the new hospital being developed alongside and connected to the Royal Aberdeen Children's Hospital and, through it, to Aberdeen Royal Infirmary.

Amongst his many contributions to the city, he was key to the fundraising for the development of the current granite façade for Marischal College, added in 1906.

In 1917, Hay resolved to initiate a systemic investigation of all maternal deaths occurring in Aberdeen because of the unduly high maternal death rate in the city. He, along with his successor Dr J Parlane Kinloch, published a report, the outline of which became the forerunner of the National Maternity Mortality Committee reports. The design of these confidential enquiries into each maternal death adopted the format described by Hay and his colleagues. The report was a damning indictment of hospital maternity services of the day, especially in relation to the spread of infection and sepsis and acted as a driver for re-evaluating both clinical practice in midwifery and ward design in maternity hospitals.

Lady May Baird (1901–1983)

Matilda (May) Deans Baird was born on 14 May 1901, elder daughter of Matthew and Matilda Tennant, Newton, Lanarkshire. She graduated BSc in 1922 and then in medicine from the University of Glasgow in 1924. She married Dugald Baird in 1928 and she and her husband moved to Aberdeen on his appointment to the chair of Midwifery in 1937. The next year, she was elected to the town council, featuring prominently in local politics and was soon made Chairman of the City Council's Public Health Committee.

In 1947 she was appointed Chairman of the North Eastern Regional Hospital Board, the first woman to gain such a post, which she held for 18 years. She served as a member of the Royal Commission on the Law of Marriage and Divorce in 1951. She also served as a member of the Maternity Services Review Committee of the Department of Health and was a Governor of the BBC from 1966–70. Known as a social pioneer, she, like her husband, received Freedom of the City of Aberdeen (1966) and was awarded an honorary LLD from the University of Aberdeen. She received a Commander of the Most Excellent Order of the British Empire (CBE) in 1962. A number of Aberdeen streets were named in her honour. She is commemorated by a plaque at 38 Albyn Place. (Appendices 1 and 2).

Dr Mary Esslemont (1891–1984)

Dr Esslemont was born in Aberdeen into a notable family, both parents being politically active. Her father, George was a Liberal MP for South Aberdeen, as had been her grandfather. Her mother, Clementina Esslemont, was one of the founders of the Aberdeen Mother and Child Welfare Society and was involved in many initiatives to improve the lives of women and children in Aberdeen. Having initially studied and graduated botany at the University of Aberdeen, Mary Esslemont entered medical school as a mature student, graduating in 1923. She had been appointed as the first woman president of the University's Student Representative Council. She was initially Assistant Medical Officer of Health in Yorkshire but returned to general practice in Aberdeen for over 30 years.

Esslemont was the only woman to sit on the committee that negotiated on behalf of the British Medical Association (BMA) with Aneurin Bevan over the development of the National Health Service. She had served on the University General Council for 40 years and was president of the Women's Medical Federation in 1953. She was the first woman to be elected to the University Court and in 1955 she was made a CBE. She became a Justice of the Peace and was subsequently awarded the Freedom of the City of Aberdeen in 1981. It was her role

Dr Mary Esslemont CBE worked as a gynaecologist at the Dispensary in Barnett's Close, Guestrow. She was the only woman to sit on the committee that negotiated on behalf of the British Medical Association with Aneurin Bevan on the development of National Health Service. She was awarded the Freedom of the City of Aberdeen in 1981. She was president of the Federation of Soroptimist Clubs of Great Britain and Ireland.

(Photograph by permission of Aberdeen City Council)

as a GP, however, where she made a substantial contribution to the health of women and their babies, having been appointed gynaecologist at the city's Free Dispensary in Barnett's Close, Guestrow, where for many years she ran a clinic for the diseases of women twice weekly. She was a keen Soroptimist and in 1961 became president of the Federation of Soroptimist Clubs of Great Britain and Ireland. In that capacity, she went out to Africa to establish the first Soroptimist Club on the continent and was made a vice president of the United Nations Association.

Mary Esslemont was also a key advocate of sex education and was keen that sex education should start early. She contributed to a pamphlet, 'Telling Children about Sex', published in the 1950s which was sent to GPs across the UK to distribute to their patients. Esslemont's practice at 20 Waverley Place was the first to employ an all-female workforce and her surgery was the one to which women were referred with abortion or family planning concerns.

Her obituary in the *British Medical Journal* reports:
Dr Mary was a firm believer in the importance of the home and the family unit in healthcare and in the formation of character. She was held in great affection by all her patients of several generations... An inveterate traveller, she visited the Far East in the 1920s and Eastern Europe in the late 1930s. During the 25 years 1950–75 she was a frequent visitor to all five continents, usually as a member of an official delegation or medical party... Dr Esslemont was blessed with a strong constitution. Humorous and with a twinkle in her eye, she loved people and especially children, who were always comfortable with her. She was a great Trooper who lived her long life to the full...

Throughout her long life, Dr Mary remained a steadfast supporter of the Liberal party. She died sitting in her armchair beside the window while outside in her garden the local Liberal fete was in full swing.

Fenella Paton (1901–49)

Fenella Paton was instrumental in establishing family planning clinics in Aberdeen and being an advocate for birth control. She funded the service from her own personal funds.
(Picture courtesy of Aberdeen City Libraries/ Silver City Vault)

Fenella Paton (née Crombie) was born in Kensington, London in 1901. Her father, John W Crombie was the Liberal MP for Kincardineshire and the Crombies were part of the Aberdeen family noted for their woollen mill and the 'Crombie Coat'. She married John Paton of Grandhome in 1923 and became an active member of the Women's Liberal Association.

Paton was inspired by the work of the birth control pioneer Marie Stopes, who had opened the first birth control clinic in Britain – the London Mothers Clinic in 1921. Paton founded Aberdeen's first birth control clinic for married women, the Woman's Welfare Centre in 1926 (amidst a storm of controversy) which she financed from her personal funds. The clinic opened initially three days a week and the staff, consisting of a qualified nurse and a general practitioner, gave their services voluntarily. The clinic did not have universal approval, with one doctor denouncing the initiative in the press as an affront to the city's civic morality. Nonetheless, it gained acceptance within the community and a reduction in pregnancy terminations by 'unqualified persons' in the city.

In 1935, Aberdeen Council started to partially fund the clinic (an annual grant of £20 in 1935, rising to £50 by 1940), with Paton transferring it to the National Health Service in 1948. She died of cancer at Grandholme in 1949, leaving a widower, two sons and four daughters. Her death was a huge loss to Aberdeen for, in addition to founding the clinic, she had founded the District Nursing Association at Old Machar, been a president of the St Katherine's Club, a prison visitor, a president of the Women's Liberal Association of Central Aberdeenshire and a director of both Aberdeen Maternity Hospital and Aberdeen Royal Infirmary. She was also the person who organised a Greek tutor for Prince Philip whilst he was a pupil at Gordonstoun.

Maggie Myles (1892–1988)

Margaret (Maggie) Fraser Myles (née Findlay) was born in Aberdeen at 52 Spital, on 30 December 1892. She was the daughter of a house painter, Robert Findlay and Mary Findlay, a domestic servant. She spent her childhood in Aberdeen but emigrated to Canada before World War I where she met her future husband, Charles James Myles, a Canadian farmer. Her husband served in the Canadian Army during the First World War but died in France in 1920, the same year as the birth of her son, Ian. As a young widow, she returned to her parents' home in Aberdeen where she trained as a midwife and practised as a district nurse in Alford. However, her young son died of pneumonia in 1924 and Maggie left Alford to undertake further nursing training in Edinburgh Royal Infirmary before returning to Canada to study at McGill University in Montréal. She next worked as Director of Midwife education in Philadelphia and Detroit but returned to the UK to study for a midwife teacher's diploma in London. In 1939 she was appointed Midwife Tutor at the Simpson Memorial Maternity Pavilion in Edinburgh – a post she held for 17 years.

The first edition of her book, *Textbook for Midwives*, the most successful, widely acclaimed and widely read textbook on the practical aspects of midwifery, was published in 1953 and edited versions are still in use today, with over 20 reprints translated into numerous languages. It has been considered the seminal textbook for midwifery for over 60 years and this, along with her other contributions to midwifery and its practice, have received and continue to receive international acclaim to the present day.

After her retiral (1954), she continued to examine and act as a tutor. She received many accolades and honours. She was greatly pleased by the conferment of an Honorary Fellowship of the Edinburgh Obstetrical Society. She died age 95 in Banchory.

Dr Elizabeth 'Betty' Macgregor (1920–2005)

Dr Betty Macgregor, OBE, was closely associated with Sir Dugald Baird and established a screening programme for cervical cancer which subsequently gained worldwide recognition and became established practice globally.
(Photograph courtesy of NHS Grampian)

Janet Elizabeth Macgregor was a pioneer of cervical screening and was born in Glasgow on 12 January 1920 to Jean (née Craig) (1886–1929) and Andrew MacPherson (1888–1946), a company secretary. She attended school at Bearsden Academy, going on to study medicine at the University of Glasgow, graduating in 1943. After qualifying, she served in the Royal Army Medical Corps, rising to the rank of captain. She completed her training at Glasgow Royal Infirmary and Western General Hospital. She worked in Sheffield and Edinburgh before moving to Aberdeen in 1958 with her husband Alistair Macgregor, when he took up the position of Regius Professor of Materia Medica.

In 1960, Macgregor became a research assistant in Sir Dugald Baird's department and worked with his team to establish a trial screening programme for cervical cancer. Macgregor took exfoliated cell smears using the Papanicolaou stain (the Pap smear), interpreted them, and trained the team in the technique. In 1963, she received an MD thesis for her work. In a co-authored article in the *British Medical Journal*, Macgregor and Baird stated that cervical cytology

has now passed beyond the 'experimental stage' and that cervical cancer could largely be prevented by cytological detection and treatment of a pre-invasive stage. She spoke with general practitioners, convincing them that their patients should be screened. She and the team at the University kept careful records of the screenings, and she collaborated with statisticians to evaluate its effectiveness. Within five years of the screening service being established, there was a significant decrease in cervical cancer in the Aberdeen area. Such was the success of the programme in Aberdeen that it led to cervical screening services being introduced throughout the UK. The research and programme were recognised worldwide, leading to the development of cervical screening all over the world. She was awarded an OBE in 1984.

Macgregor retired from the University of Aberdeen in 1985. She continued to work part-time as Director of Harris Birthright Research Centre in Aberdeen. She died in 2005.

Professor Arnold Klopper (1922–2014)

Arnold Klopper was Professor of Reproductive Endocrinology at the University of Aberdeen. He made fundamental advances in research on human fertility, which earned him an international reputation. At the same time, he was a caring doctor, and a lifelong socialist dedicated to the National Health Service.
Arnold was born in South Africa, the only child of an Afrikaner policeman and a mother of English parentage. As a child, he accompanied his father on rounds in rural areas, during which he witnessed poverty and ill health.

Klopper entered the University of Witwatersrand in 1943 to read medicine. During his second year, he was outraged by the exclusion of a black student from an anatomy class while white women were present. He organised a strike of medical students and slowed the creeping apartheid in the university. He continued his human rights activities, and in 1945 became president of the National Union of South African Students.

Klopper graduated in 1947 and specialised in obstetrics and gynaecology and was appointed to the British Hospital for Mothers and Babies in south London and research staff member at the Medical Research Council in Edinburgh 1950–55 and in 1960 he was appointed as a senior lecturer in obstetrics and gynaecology at the University of Aberdeen. In 1956, Sir Dugald Baird set up the Medical Research Council Obstetric Unit at Aberdeen University Hospital and invited Arnold to take a leading role. From 1962 to 1970 he was the Professor of Reproductive Endocrinology.

Dr Michael Tunstall (1928–2011)

Michael (Mike) Eric Tunstall was born (into a bucket!) in Assam, India, where his father was a tea planter. He spent his early childhood there before being sent to school in the north of England and then educated at a public school in Monmouth, subsequently graduating in medicine from University College Hospital, London in 1952. He served as a medical officer in the Artillery Regiment in Germany in 1956 and, after a short career in general practice, he entered anaesthesia, becoming a registrar in Portsmouth, Oxford and the Middlesex Hospital. He was subsequently to go on to become one of the greatest contributors ever to obstetric anaesthesia.

He made several seminal contributions to the clinical care of women in labour, but it was his research on anaesthetic gases that led him to discover Entonox – the mixture of oxygen and nitrous oxide (also known as gas and air) which is now used universally in not just obstetric care, but for pain relief across a wide range of specialties in both childhood and adult medicine. He was uninterested in commercial gain, but his 1961 description of the 50/50 gaseous mixture published in the Lancet, went on to transform pain management in labour across the world. Additionally, he invented the 'isolated fore-arm technique' which allowed doctors to detect whether the patient remained aware of delivery by caesarean section, as well as devising an airway management drill (Tunstall drill) to be followed when airway intubation (as part of anaesthetic for caesarean section), had failed. He helped devise a topical anaesthetic cream for children and was involved in establishing ventilatory support for newborns, establishing one of the UK's first neonatal intensive care units in Aberdeen Maternity Hospital.

His work in obstetric anaesthesia had been identified by Sir Dugald Baird at an early stage and it was Baird who enticed Tunstall to come to work in Aberdeen, where he was appointed consultant anaesthetist. He was active in the Obstetric Anaesthetists' Association, of which he was its president 1987–90 and received its gold medal 1990. He received an honorary doctorate from the University of Aberdeen, but despite his enormous talent and innovative contributions to the childbirth experience of millions of women around the world, he remained typically modest and committed to clinical research throughout his lifetime. A street in Newtonhill is named after him (Michael Tunstall Place, see Appendix 2).

Trish Lively (1948–2019)

Lively was one of the founders and leading members of the Friends of Special Nursery – a charity which campaigned for and raised funds to build a new facility in Aberdeen Maternity Hospital which would be its first purpose-built neonatal unit (Special Nursery). She served as the publicity coordinator for the campaign to raise funds and her help and efforts raised more than £900,000, allowing a new unit to be built in 1988. She was born in Ellon and spent much of her life in Aberdeen before relocating to Dubai and Cyprus. She was recognised for her energy, focus and powers of persuasion in achieving the target for the fundraising campaign which allowed the opening of the neonatal unit adjacent to and co-located with Aberdeen Maternity Hospital in 1988.

Further Reading

Diack, Lesley, in *The City and its Worlds*, eds. T Brotherstone and Donald J Witherington. Cruithne Press, Glasgow, 1996.

Levack, I, and Dudley, H, 'Aberdeen Royal Infirmary', *The Peoples Hospital of the North-East*, ed. Bailliere P Tindall, 1992.

Milne GP, and the Aberdeen Medico-Chirurgical Society, *A Bicentennial History*. Aberdeen University Press, 1989.

Porter, IA, in 'Alexander Gordon, MD of Aberdeen 1752–1799', *Aberdeen University Studies* No. 139, Oliver and Boyd Ltd, Edinburgh, 1958.

Riddell JS, 'Aberdeen Maternity Hospital', *British Medical Association Handbook and Guide Aberdeen,* J. Burrow Co. Ltd, Cheltenham 1914.

Chambers Scottish Biographical Dictionary, ed. Rosemary Goring, 1992.

Rorie, D, *The Book of Aberdeen,* 107th annual meeting, British Medical Association, 1937.

PART 3

The Services

The medical care of newborn babies and women during pregnancy is in many ways a microcosm of the whole of medicine. In that regard, and in keeping with the rest of medicine, sub-specialisation has been an inexorable trend. This section details some of the important subspecialties within the domain of midwifery and neonatal care. As in the rest of the book, there is no attempt made to be exhaustive in this review. Instead, an attempt is made to focus on the individuals and specialty areas where Aberdeen has contributed, be that in a local context, or at a national and international level.

This section contains contributions written with varying levels of technical language and terminology, as well as clinical complexity. This has been retained intentionally in order to provide for the differing background knowledge and level of interest of the readership. Some contributions refer to past practice, but others represent the recent past, particularly when scientific progress has been a more modern development or a new event.

7

An Obstetrician's Perspective on the Period from the 1960s to the 1990s

Dr Hamish Sutherland

IT WAS THE 1960s that saw the widespread use of the oral contraceptive pill (OCP) develop in western societies, heralding great changes in women's lifestyle and work, clearly with the prospect of permanence. The OCP put women in control of their lives as never before.

Independently, in medical science, there was renewed thirst for new knowledge predominantly to explore and influence the evidence-base for justifying clinical advice and interventions. For those in the field of human reproductive medicine, the focus was on 'the quality of the child produced' in affecting, at the core, the stubborn cycle of deprivation.

High parity often coincided with poverty with many of the pregnancies being unwanted. Neither were there accessible family planning services or the prospect of parents starting conception, as far as possible, in maximal good health. It is not hard to believe this dawn of enlightenment arose from the Glasgow experience of Sir Dugald Baird and was further promoted enthusiastically in Aberdeen by his influential younger academic colleagues, many or all of whom worked with him in his department, including his successor to the Aberdeen Regius Chair of Obstetrics and Gynaecology, Professor Ian MacGillivray, along with Regius Professor James Walker (Dundee), Professor (later Sir) Alec Turnbull, appointed to Cardiff and subsequently Oxford, and Professor (later Sir) Malcolm (Callum) McNaughton in Glasgow.

In specialist and general obstetric practice, two other exceptional competencies buttressed confidence in the decision making. These were the widely acclaimed expertise in induction and management of labour developed by Dr Alec Turnbull, Senior Lecturer, Dr Anne Anderson and the antenatal and labour ward midwives, led respectively by Sister Isobel Leet and Sister McKay. Secondly, there existed at AMH an outstanding obstetric anaesthesia service, led by the internationally acclaimed consultant anaesthetist Dr Michael Tunstall who was an exceptional leader in the field of analgesia and anaesthesia for every aspect of labour and operative delivery. This approach provided the highest standard of clinical care and optimised outcomes for both mother and baby.

To illustrate the changes made in the 1960s, the clinical practice for women with diabetes in Aberdeen Maternity Hospital changed with the arrival of Dr (later Professor) John Stowers, and, as previously outlined, a cohort of clinicians grew within this forward-looking obstetric department. When the antenatal clinics moved from Castle Terrace, a physical accommodation was built to facilitate modern obstetric care and a new antenatal service was created. The new clinic was widely considered 'Baird designed', nearly adjacent to the AMH labour ward corridor and lying-in wards and had two changing rooms per consulting room that enabled all women to be weighed and blood pressure measured by the midwife in the consulting room at every clinic visit. This was found to be important in raising the early suspicion of foetal morbidities relating to foetal growth aberration and, also, the early detection of the development of pre-eclampsia as well as the possibility of dietary mismanagement.

The author of this perspective, Dr Hamish Sutherland, until his retirement in 1995, consistently provided the obstetric input at the combined clinic for nearly three decades, including methodical palpation, foetal heart auscultation, fundal height, and kick chart assessment and, as required, blood sampling. In conjunction with the agreement of each woman with diabetes and the diabetes specialist, along with the Special Hospitals dietician, a plan for mode and potential date for delivery was devised in what was described from first clinic attendance as 'partnership of care'. The carefully monitored foetal development was the determining trigger, taking into consideration the potential for avoiding the clinical consequences of premature delivery. A detailed evaluation of degree of adherence to the policy of blood sugar control to 'Stower's standards', along with the obstetric decisions to keep the foetus maturing in utero to as near term as possible, were rewarded by good intrapartum and neonatal outcomes.

When Ian MacGillivray returned to the Department to take the Regius Chair in 1964, more attention was Focused on the foetus, particularly because ultrasound scanning had just been developed by Professor Ian Donald in Glasgow for use clinically. Thanks to Professor John Mallard and Mr Sandy Christie of the Medical Physics University Department, and to a young in-training career obstetrician, Dr Sandy McIntosh, ultrasound scanning soon became available at AMH. Also, early on, it became clear that ultrasound scanning offered the potential of a readily available, non-invasive way to monitor foetal presence, size, maturity, growth, anatomical detail and aspects of physiological normality, along with some critical placental issues. Dr Valerie Farr, who joined the obstetric department from the Neonatal paediatric unit, took over the expanded role to meet the expectations and the greatly increasing number of referrals to the AMH scanning department through the '70s and '80s. As an example, at the combined clinic the midwife's role was developed to ensure that those in need in the waiting area were supported and ad hoc ultrasound scans carried out as required.

Dr Farr's successor, Dr Pat Smith, was to bring distinction to ultrasound scanning at AMH, not least through her book. Additionally, Dr Bill Sinclair, obstetrician, was tutored in the methods and potential clinical value of laparoscopy, observing its clinical use by the pioneering obstetrician Dr Patrick Steptoe. Thus, Aberdeen gained very early experience in both these seminal advances.

Research was often the driver for service improvement. Sir Dugald had established a Medical Research Council funded unit in AMH with the physical presence of a research ward, a well-equipped and funded endocrine research laboratory and an eminent research group of leaders in a variety of aspects related to human reproduction. These included:

- Professor Angus Thomson, who developed and was curator of, and regularly audited, the valuable comprehensive data bank of demographic and clinically significant information of all registered pregnancies in AMH and the three midwife-led maternity 'homes' in Aberdeen, namely at Fonthill, Queens Cross and Summerfield.
- Professor Frank E Hytten, whose studies informed his classic book *The Physiology of Human Pregnancy* and who was to become a pioneer and widely published author in the physiology of pregnancy relevant to the care of pregnant woman.
- Professor Arnold Klopper who enjoyed international recognition and who would later set up the AMH sperm bank.
- George Wilson, a scientist, and methodology guru for assessing the value of estimating maternal urinary and plasma oestrogen and progesterone in the assessment of foetal growth and wellbeing in pregnancy, as well as the endocrine aspects of infertility.
- Professor Raymond Illsley, who was a highly regarded medical sociologist and first director of the Aberdeen MRC medical sociology unit.
- Bill Bytheway, statistical expert in the Aberdeen MRC unit.

- Dr Barbara Thomson, author of many research reports, and supervisor of the precious and inexorably enlarging data bank.
- Dr K John Dennis, who was said to have had an advisory interest in the 1967 Abortion Act brought to Parliament by David Steele MP (later Lord Steele), and with expertise in iso-immunisation (at this time exchange transfusions were senior obstetric staff responsibilities in decision and practice). Dr Dennis had exceptional teaching and communication skills and brought to the national television screens the popular and unique 'Living and Growing' series before proceeding to take up the inaugural chair at Southampton University Medical School.

These individuals, amongst others, created a stimulating intellectual and high-quality clinical environment which allowed Aberdeen's obstetrics department to grow in a visionary and progressive manner, ahead of many larger academic units elsewhere in the UK.

This environment was also supported by many who would subsequently make important contributions to obstetrics in centres throughout the United Kingdom and provided an opportunity for a significant number of young doctors to engage in research study, thus creating several potential advantages for the young aspiring obstetricians in early training. There was the satisfaction of adding new knowledge, gaining a forum to express their own ideas, perhaps even develop new practical approaches and have the opportunity to expose those to interdisciplinary criticism, (perhaps even internationally), not to mention the lasting benefit for their own professional development in the ever increasingly competitive world.

New concepts emerged from this intellectually rich network – a particularly significant one being pre-pregnancy counselling and care (PPCC) that spawned important medical texts (Perspectives in Pre-pregnancy Counselling and Care, editors HW Sutherland and NC Smith). This critical composite reviewed eating and diet preparation for pregnancy, as well as dealing with the needs for genetic counselling, early pregnancy loss, the immunology of pregnancy, and domestic hazards such as smoking, drinking and non-prescription drug use and other influential issues. Undoubtedly, other factors will be identified to help women to make the best health and lifestyle choices to favourably affect the outcome for planned conception and carefully managed pregnancy.

Such important developments, modifications and innovations constitute a paradigm shift in the delivery of maternity services to the benefit of women and crucially the offspring of these women not only in Aberdeen but also internationally.

8

Antenatal Care

Norman C Smith and Pat Smith

DURING THE 18TH and 19th centuries antenatal care was non-existent as an entity. There was no pregnancy test and most doctors agreed that the diagnosis could not be made until halfway through the pregnancy, after 20 weeks when foetal movements were felt. In any case, if clinical problems arose, there was little that could be done to treat them. Adjustments to diet and lifestyle were advised and laxatives were popular. The main clinical intervention was venesection (bloodletting), and women might be bled several times for the treatment of a range of symptoms including vomiting, palpations and headaches.

We know that a West Wing extension at Woolmanhill was built in 1762 under the guidance of Dr David Skene for 'poor distressed lying-in women' and in the 1800s there were various Dispensaries and Lying- in Institutions at locations near Upper Kirkgate. These were amalgamated and by 1892 there was an 'Aberdeen Dispensary, Vaccine and Lying-in Institution' to which six midwives were attached. Most of their work would have focused on the labour, delivery, and aftercare in the postpartum period. The term 'lying-in' relates to the postpartum period when the traditional practice was to have a long period of bed rest after delivery. In those days, there would have been prolonged and difficult labours for women to endure and, if they survived, a period of recovery was inevitable and justified. Although the term 'dispensary' is associated with the preparation and distribution of medicines, it also has an older meaning – a place where patients are treated, especially one run by charity.

Edinburgh has been given the credit for starting the first outpatient antenatal clinic in Britain. The history behind this is of interest. In 1899, the Lauriston Prematernity Home was opened next to Edinburgh Royal Infirmary. It accommodated unmarried, often destitute pregnant women. Dr Haig Ferguson looked after these poor women – we still use forceps named after him. He undertook regular ward rounds and realised the benefit of antenatal care. He petitioned hospital management for an antenatal department for all patients so that they could have the same benefits as the 'more limited clientele'. Eventually, in 1915, an outpatient antenatal clinic was opened. In Aberdeen, the Bank of Scotland building in Castle Street was purchased and converted to Aberdeen Maternity Hospital in 1900. Since all medical care had to be paid for, most women received no antenatal care at that time. The Maternity and Welfare Act of 1918 enabled local government to make arrangements for the care of expectant mothers (and children under five). Clinics were set up and staffed by local government employees. 'Prenatal clinics' were first recorded in 1918 and an antenatal annex was opened in 1919 at Castle Terrace.

Between 1920 and 1930 there was a substantial expansion in maternity care, and by 1930 the principles of antenatal care were firmly established with attendances at just over 50 per cent of notified births. The introduction of antenatal clinics was attributed to Dr Janet Campbell (1877–1954), who was a surgeon in London and a Senior Medical Officer for Maternity and Child Health to the Ministry of Health. Her father was a Scottish banker working in Brighton. She was concerned about the deaths due to eclamptic seizures and foresaw that pre-eclampsia could be detected in antenatal clinics by checking the blood pressure and the urine for protein. With her input, the Ministry of Health published a Memorandum on Antenatal Clinics in 1930 and specified the following required visits:

> The first visit should normally take place at 16 weeks, then 24 and 28 weeks, and fortnightly to 36 weeks, and weekly thereafter. The pregnant woman should be seen at the first, thirty-second and thirty-sixth week visits by the medical officer and the rest by midwives.

How these time intervals were chosen is unknown, but, remarkably, they remained unchallenged for half a century until the 1980s when Professor Marion Hall, a consultant obstetrician, and her team in Aberdeen published work questioning the need for all these visits, particularly in low-risk women.

The purpose of antenatal care was to reduce maternal mortality and an in-depth national enquiry into 5,805 maternal deaths in the years 1930 and 1932 revealed that there were avoidable factors in 34 per cent and one-in-five of these had inadequate antenatal care. Perhaps more importantly, and less easy to solve politically, was the social deprivation and poor housing of many. In the 1930s, specific antenatal clinics were established by local authorities who employed medical officers for this purpose. General practitioners were not happy with the consequent loss of fees. There was disillusionment among the professions, as there was little change in maternal mortality over the decade. The problem was that those most in need of care did not attend. In addition, little could be done for the intrapartum and postpartum deaths due to haemorrhage and sepsis.

In the 1940s, there was a decline in the maternal and perinatal mortality rates. Baird was a pioneer in his time and oversaw these falling rates. He, along with his registrar Dr John Wyper, published in the Lancet in 1941 a means of classifying perinatal deaths according to the primary obstetric factor that led to the loss. This classification was used nationally, and epidemiological comparisons made. Some thought that better antenatal care was related to the declining rates and Baird was cited as wondering 'how a few hours spent waiting on a wooden bench to have a quick palpation from a clinic doctor could have such profound effects'. He knew that the improvement in the social and nutritional status of the population had a huge effect. The discovery of antibiotics and blood transfusion in the late '30s and '40s were also pivotal in reducing maternal deaths due to haemorrhage, puerperal fever, and septic illegal abortion. Baird's advocacy of the fifth freedom to allow women to have a healthier life by reducing the burden of unwanted pregnancy through contraception, sterilisation and abortion were effective in reducing maternal and perinatal deaths in Grampian and this example was followed in the rest of the country. There were, on average, 40 maternal deaths per 1,000 births from 1900 to 1935, and this fell to ten per 1,000 by 1950 and is now less than ten per 100,000 in the UK.

The establishment of the National Health Service in 1948 had a dramatic effect. For the first time, clinical care by a midwife or doctor was available free of charge. The rate of hospital deliveries compared to home deliveries rose from 35 per cent in 1937 to 65 per cent in 1957. This prompted a trend to hospital based antenatal care and fewer GP obstetricians. However, in 1960, Dugald Baird drew attention to the advantages of locally based clinics for normal low-risk patients. In Aberdeen, there were local authority antenatal clinics in Holburn, Northfield and Hilton until the late '70s. In Aberdeenshire, Moray and Banffshire, due to the geographical distribution of the population and distance for travel, the role of the general practitioner for antenatal care remained important, and local maternity hospitals were present in Peterhead, Fraserburgh, Inverurie, Huntly, Banff, Keith, Elgin, Buckie, Forres, Torphins and Aboyne. General practitioners, along with midwives, provided antenatal care and referred women with risk factors for review by the visiting consultant.

Professor Marion Hall undertook studies with her research team in the 1970s and 80s and concluded that routine antenatal care was poor at predicting and detecting obstetric disorders and that overdiagnosis was common. She concluded that the number of visits (in place since the 1930s) could be considerably reduced for women without special problems.

In the 1980s all pregnant women had to be seen at least once by a consultant. Further work by Marion Hall's team showed that this was a waste of resource. There was consumer dissatisfaction with the overcrowded clinics and measures to increase their efficiency were required. Changes to the pattern of antenatal care occurred in the 1990s, permitting community midwives to give most of the antenatal care with fewer visits and referral to the consultant for women with risk factors. The role of the general practitioner was diminished.

Until the 1940s, saving the mother was the priority, but with Dugald Baird's research into the causes of perinatal mortality, focus was placed on saving the unborn child. In the late 1960s, technological advances were making it possible to assess the development and wellbeing of the foetus by both biochemical and biophysical means. From 1970 to 1980, the perinatal mortality rate (stillbirths and first week deaths) fell from 25 per 1000 births to 13. This was due not only to obstetric interventions but also improved social conditions, smaller family size and improvements in neonatal care. It is now six in 1,000 births.

Professor Arnold Klopper and his research team evaluated biochemical tests on the placenta and foetus in the second half of pregnancy. These were superseded by antenatal cardiotocography that gave an instant printout of the foetal heart rate pattern which reflected foetal wellbeing. The diagnosis of congenital abnormalities became possible with tests on blood and amniotic fluid. The most significant development that made further evaluation of the foetus and placenta was ultrasound.

Around 1970, a single room in the antenatal ward at AMH was allocated for an ultrasound scan machine. The world's first obstetric ultrasound scanner had been developed in Glasgow by Ian Donald, Professor of Midwifery at the Queen Mother's Hospital and Tom Brown, an engineer and reported in the Lancet in 1958. Ultrasound was being used at that time to detect metal flaws in steel ships. The history of obstetric ultrasound is fascinating and extensive. It revolutionised care of the pregnant woman and her foetus and a new specialty called foetal medicine evolved.

The first static scanners were bulky – eight feet high with a gantry – and images were created by rocking a transducer over the abdomen. The equipment needed dedicated physicists and the Aberdeen Department of Medical Physics under the direction of Professor Mallard set it up and maintained it. Dr Valerie Farr, who had trained as a paediatrician at the Royal Aberdeen Children's Hospital, was appointed as the first sonographer and ran the department until the late 1980s. By then there had been huge advances in the technology of the equipment and 'real time' images were now obtainable on small moveable machines. The foetal heart could be visualised as a moving structure and early viability of a pregnancy confirmed. Foetal measurement tables were devised that could be used to establish gestational age and growth of the foetus. Screening of the pregnant population was feasible and, with this need in mind, a new department was opened beneath the antenatal clinic in 1988. The single room in the antenatal ward was replaced by a department with four scanning rooms and a day ward for outpatients. By 1990, further advances in the resolution of the images meant that invasive procedures requiring continual visualisation of needles could be undertaken, making possible the prenatal diagnosis of chromosomal and genetic conditions and the assessment of Rhesus disease and other blood disorders.

By the turn of the century, every pregnant woman was having a booking scan in the first 12 weeks of pregnancy and a detailed scan at 20 weeks. Midwives, radiographers, and obstetricians were trained to an appropriate standard. As a profession caring for the pregnant woman and her unborn child, we had come a long way from the beginning of the century when the diagnosis of pregnancy was considered only reliable in the second half of pregnancy.

Indeed, the latter years of the 20th century saw a new dimension being introduced into antenatal care, which was one of antenatal intervention, including surgery on the unborn child. Most of these interventions included placement of catheters into various body cavities, including the bladder, and, in the early 21st century, plugging of the foetal trachea to stimulate lung growth in congenital diaphragmatic hernia.

Interventions were mostly carried out in very few specialist centres, given their rarity and the need for concentrating experience in the hands of a few. In Aberdeen, apart from diagnostic biopsy procedures on the placenta, all cases requiring foetal surgery or foetal interventional radiology were referred to London – an example of providing patients with the best possible care irrespective of location of their domicile.

9

Family Planning

Alison McCall

Birth Control and Abortion in Aberdeen until 1984

A DESIRE TO control fertility and limit family size dates back centuries. In the absence of effective means to prevent pregnancy, women used a range of methods to end an unwanted pregnancy. *Aberdeen's Journal* advertised abortifacients, couched in coded language, from the mid-18th century onwards. These Included: 'Dr Hooper's Female Pills', which promised to 'cause a free circulation in the blood and remove all obstructions'; 'Higson's Female Pills', 'safely removing obstructions'; 'Towle's Pennyroyal and Steel Pills' to 'quickly cure all irregularities'; and possibly 'Kersley's Female Pills', 'the leading remedy for all complaints to which females are liable'. Some of these pills may have worked, but at a cost to the health of the woman. Medical students at the University of Aberdeen were told about the dangers of such pills:

Rue, pennyroyal, etc – the dose must be large and may prove fatal to the person without abortion taking place.

Medical students were also lectured by Matthew Hay on the dangers of backstreet abortions:

Cases of abortion usually fall into the hands of untutored abortionists who have gained some sort of reputation for doing this sort of thing.

Students were advised that abortion was permissible in certain circumstances but warned:

> if you have to bring about an abortion, do not do it on your own
> responsibility, as you may get into trouble. Consult another medical
> man first.

Aberdeen's Journal also carried regular reports of foundling deaths. In the
1850s, for example, there were seven reports of the bodies of babies being
found, and many others were never known about or found: female, 1851,
Donmouth; premature baby, 1852, Broomhill; male 1854 Union Grove; female,
1854, Elmhill; male, 1856, Countesswells; female, 1857, Peacock's Close;
female 1858, Bon Accord Lane.

Towards the end of the 19th century, family size amongst middle class
professionals began to drop, although it is difficult to say whether this was
caused by the use of artificial means of prevention or through abstinence. The
birth rate reached a new low in 1890 and from then on the decreasing birth
rate was regularly referred to in Aberdeen's newspapers. In 1911 the birth rate
in Scotland was the lowest since records began in 1855, although the birth rate
in England and Wales was lower still. In an article in the Buchan Observer, in
1904, it was stated that it was 'almost safe to affirm' that the poor were entirely
guiltless of using artificial restrictions to limit family size. 'But if we take the
higher middle and upper classes it is by no means so easy to feel confident.'

It was against this background of an already declining birth-rate that Edinburgh-
born Marie Stopes founded Britain's first family planning clinic and published her book
Married Love, which described birth control in 1918. The book was controversial,
and an article on the controversy appeared in the *Press & Journal* in 1921.

Fenella Paton was the daughter of Kincardineshire MP John Crombie. She
spent much of her early life in London, where she supported Liberal causes. She
married John Paton of Grandhome in 1923. Fenella became an active member
of the Women's Liberal Association. Having been aware of family planning
clinics in London, she sought to introduce one in Aberdeen. In 1926, amid a
storm of controversy, she opened a clinic at 4 Gerrard Street.

The letters page of the *Press & Journal* gives a flavour of the public reaction
to the clinic. One James Hay of Bon Accord Square said that he was surprised
that Aberdeen was taking such an initiative, which he felt would afford 'a very
obvious encouragement to immorality'.

Social worker, Mary A Henderson, responded that she was

> thankful for that light of knowledge which has slowly filtered through
> walls of selfishness and prejudice from the exclusive grip of the well-to-

do and come at last to meet the need of the poor.

This was the second clinic in Scotland, following Glasgow by only a few weeks. Edinburgh did not have a clinic until 1933 and Dundee and Stirling until 1937. By contrast, England had 118 clinics by 1936. The value of the clinic was recognised by many of Aberdeen's doctors. Dr Bell, the tuberculosis officer for the region, referred his patients, as pregnancy was especially risky for women suffering from tuberculosis. Sufferers of epilepsy were also encouraged to attend.

The clinic provided advice only to married women, who were fitted with a Dutch cap. It was staffed by a nurse, Mrs Rae, with some clinics attended by a GP, Dr Florence (Flossie) J Malcolm. She graduated from the University of Aberdeen in 1923 and worked in her father's medical practice in Kemnay. Working for a family practice gave her more freedom than most other young GPs and enabled her to work for the birth control clinic without fear of adversely affecting her career. Florence Horsburgh, MP imagined the early days of the clinic when she wrote that it was not hard to

visualise the news of the clinic's existence spreading by word of mouth along the tenement stairs and the poorer cobbled streets and women drawing their shawls around their shoulders and taking their courage in both hands to make their hesitant way to the clinic.

Horsburgh felt that the clinic spelled an end to the 'domestic darkness of so many women condemned to the domestic drudgery and declining health that came with multiple and unending pregnancies'. Recognising that many of the women who might benefit the clinic had small children, childcare was provided to facilitate their visits.

Later, Dr Kathleen Fraser assisted, having heard a talk by Marie Stopes in Aberdeen in 1933. From 1938 on, Dr Mary Esslemont also worked some shifts.

Fenella Paton supported the clinic from her personal funds, with the support of her mother, Minna Crombie. Although Paton was in regular correspondence with Marie Stopes, the clinic remained independent of Stopes' organisation. However, Stopes did visit in 1934. Funding the clinic became increasingly onerous on Paton, and, in 1935, Aberdeen Council started to partially fund the clinic. Fenella Paton died of cancer in 1949, leaving a widower and six children.

In 1948, the clinic was taken over by the Aberdeen Corporation. Dr May Baird was head of the Public Health Committee and was a strong supporter of family planning. Thus, Aberdeen became the first local authority in the country to run a family planning clinic, before becoming part of the NHS. The Gerrard Street clinic was closed, and a new clinic was opened in Castle Street. This clinic served the women of Aberdeen and a Women's Advisory Clinic was opened two days a week at Woolmanhill to support women in the Shire. This was run by Dr Margaret McGregor who, from 1951 on, focused her career on family planning.

Having been at the forefront of birth control in Scotland for a decade, Aberdeen then took a further stride forward, thanks to one inspirational doctor – Dr Dugald Baird. Whilst working in Glasgow in 1934 Dr Baird had carried out a survey of 1,000 maternal deaths and found that one third were women who had six or more children. He had met Fenella Paton prior to coming to Aberdeen and knew of Aberdeen's position as one of the foremost places in Scotland in terms of birth control. This encouraged him to take up the position of Regius Professor of Midwifery at Aberdeen in 1936.

At that time, the law on abortion was unclear. In Scotland, a doctor could terminate a pregnancy if he believed the mother's health to be at risk. Provided the doctor acted 'in good faith', the termination was legal. However, many doctors interpreted 'in good faith' more conservatively than Baird, who terminated 200 pregnancies on therapeutic grounds between 1937 and 1947. He also offered voluntary sterilisation to women with large families.

Aberdeen's position as a world leader in contraception was cemented when in 1961 Dugald Baird published *A Fifth Freedom?*:

You will recollect that Franklin Roosevelt in a speech on 6 January 1941 said:
In the future days, which we seek to make secure, we look forward to a world founded upon four essential freedoms.
The first is freedom of speech and expression.
The second is freedom of every person to worship God in his own way.
The third is freedom from want.
The fourth is freedom from fear.
And I would suggest that it is time to consider a fifth freedom – freedom from the tyranny of excessive fertility.

This declaration became known around the world.

Family planning services focused on married women, and in particular women who had already had several children. Life for a single mother who did not have the support of her family was almost impossible and young women often travelled to give birth elsewhere and have their baby adopted. Likewise, some young women travelled to Aberdeen, some from the south of England, to give birth and place their child for adoption. Families would explain a daughter's absence by claiming that she was caring for a sick relative. Aberdeen newspapers carried small ads advising of babies available for adoption.

HIS MAJESTY'S THEATRE

THIS WEEK — CONTINUOUS DAILY FROM 1.40 P.M.
■ ON THE SCREEN ■
A FILM OF UNVARNISHED TRUTH ON THE
DANGERS OF IGNORANCE!

'UNMARRIED MOTHERS'
(Cert. X)

Showing : 1.40 — 4.10 — 6.40 and 9.10.
A powerful human drama on one of to-day's greatest social
problems !

✦ ADULTS ONLY ✦

An advert appearing in the *Evening Express*, 9 December 1955, page 2, highlighting a controversial showing of a film about single mothers.

(Reproduced courtesy of Aberdeen Journals)

In 1955, His Majesty's Theatre showed the film *Unmarried Mothers*, showing the attitudes then prevalent.

In the 1960s, attitudes towards unmarried women gradually changed. At the start of the decade, all those who attended the birth control clinic were married. Numbers had climbed from 479 new attendees in 1960 to 653 in 1966, and then jumped to 1,013 new attendees in 1967. In 1970 there were 1,457 new attenders. Between 1964 and 1966 only 12 unmarried women attended, ten of whom were engaged and had arranged their weddings. From 1967, the numbers increased: 74 unmarried women in 1969, only 33 of whom were about to be married. From 1971, when women were able to self-refer to the clinic, the numbers jumped again, to 148 in 1971 and 239 in 1972, of whom 33 in 1971 and 48 in 1972 were about to marry. The majority of the single women were students, followed by nurses, teachers and white-collar workers.

In May 1964, 'the Pill' became available in Aberdeen, which further increased the numbers of those attending the clinic. Dugald Baird described this as a

Great advance on any of the previous methods available and, if its freedom from long term toxic effects could be assured, should greatly decrease the need for the clumsy and unattractive mechanical methods now in use.

There was a further large increase in the number of women accessing the family planning clinic when it became free in 1967. Aberdeen was the first place in the UK to remove all charges for advice and contraception – a move which was described as 'sex on the rates' by the *Evening Express*. The newspaper admitted there were sound economic reasons for providing free contraception, asking 'how much longer can we afford the cost of taking unwanted children into care?' However, they argued that 'birth control issues cannot be judged purely in financial terms, particularly where the unmarried are involved' citing unnamed 'doctors in Aberdeen' warning about a rise in promiscuity and the spread of venereal disease.

Regardless of these fears, free contraception provided tangible benefits for Aberdeen. In 1969, the Annual report of City Medical Officer of Health, Dr MacQueen stated that the Pill and a unique free family planning service have contributed to Aberdeen having the lowest birth rate in Britain. The free family planning service and the earliest family planning clinic provided by a local authority in Britain were described by Dr MacQueen as 'one of the jewels in Aberdeen's health crown'. Between 1961 and 1972, the birth rate in Aberdeen had dropped from 17.6 to 13.2, but the percentage of higher-risk pregnancies had dropped further. By 1970, the percentage of births to women who already had three or more children had dropped from 13.3 per cent in 1960, to 7.6 per cent. Smaller families meant that women were completing their families at an earlier age – the percentage of births to women over 35 dropped from 9.3 per cent in 1961 to 5.5 per cent in 1971.

Dr Margaret McGregor retired as medical officer in charge of family planning in 1969, having become a national leader in the field. Her contribution further enhanced Aberdeen's reputation as a progressive centre of excellence.

During the 1960s, abortion was increasingly contentious, as moves were made to clarify the legal position. Dugald Baird saw himself as making an important contribution to the debate:

> What I have done is to act as a spearhead for those who are not so strongly placed. A Scottish professor has considerable status and the security which that brings... One hears talk about modernising the abortion laws. Certainly, the law should be clarified and spelt out in words of one syllable. But the work has been done for 20 years, it has all been documented, and I haven't gone outside the law.

In this he was backed by the police. As Chief Constable William Smith of the Aberdeen City Police explained:

> What we are concerned about is the procuring of abortion with criminal intention. We have no connection with what the doctors do in the hospitals.

In Aberdeen, prior to 1967 the abortions that were done were usually performed on married women with existing children, many of whom were sterilised at the same time. The combination of access to contraception, and termination of high-risk pregnancies resulted in low stillbirth and perinatal mortality rates. It also meant that unregulated and dangerous back street abortions became increasingly rare. The police were unaware of there having been any such abortions in Aberdeen after 1962.

Dugald Baird retired in 1965 and his work was continued by his successor, Professor Ian McGillivray. As a member of the advisory committee of the

Abortion Law Reform Association, he recommended Aberdeen's approach as a good model for future laws. Numbers rose in Aberdeen from 90 in 1960 to 198 in 1966. In addition, up to 300 women a year from outside the area applied to Aberdeen but were rejected. McGillivray stated that a trial of a new antibiotic drug could not be carried out because the number of criminal septic abortions was so small that there were not enough cases of septicaemia. In 1967, the Abortion Act was passed.

Aberdeen entered the 1970s proudly declaring that it 'enjoys what are widely considered to be the most comprehensive birth control and sterilisation facilities in the country'. This did not come cheap. The cost of running the clinic had risen from £3,000 a year in 1960 to £31,000 in 1972. However, the drop in the birth rate had many benefits. Between 1967 and 1972, health visitor and health assistant visits to babies dropped from 21,811 to 18,889 annually, freeing staff up to increase the number of home visits to the elderly from 23,486 to 37,112 annually. At the same time, the pupil teacher ratio in Aberdeen's primary schools fell from 23.6 to 21.2.

Statistics were gathered which showed other benefits of reduced family size. A comparison between the heights of first-born and fourth-born girls in Aberdeen in 1970 revealed that the first-born girls were 0.51 inches taller when they started school and 0.62 inches taller when they left school. There was a more marked difference between the heights of girls from social class I and social class V, which varied by 2.2 inches at school leaving age. From this, was extrapolated that girls from social class V who were also the youngest in a large family would experience a significant adverse impact on their health.

The service also played a role in education. The Family Planning Association and Marriage Guidance both produced leaflets which were distributed by the clinic. One leaflet, 'Sex Difficulties in the Wife', noted:

It is pathetic that women should spoil their marriages because of ignorance about Family Planning. Many a marriage has made a completely new start after the wife has visited a specialist in contraception and been set free at last from the haunting fear of unwanted pregnancy.

Another marriage guidance leaflet, 'Sex in Marriage', reflected:

It is a good thing that couples should aim at having three or four children or even more, but there should in most cases be at least two years between the births.

In 1970, family planning services suffered what Dr Ian MacQueen described as a 'major catastrophe' when a wall collapsed at Castle Street, forcing the clinic to close. Contraception was available at Airyhall Clinic in Springfield Road, but Dr MacQueen said that women found it difficult to attend. As a result of this, new city centre premises were found and in 1972 the clinic moved to 2 West Craibstone Street.

A survey of pregnant women in 1972 showed that only 66 per cent of women with unplanned pregnancies were pleased to be pregnant, showing that there was still work to be done to make it possible for women to avoid being unhappily pregnant.

Keeping the public informed was an ongoing task. Small advertisements appeared in the *Press & Journal*, but in 1976 the *Evening Express* reported that many women in Aberdeen still did not know how to access contraception. Dr Marjory Hamilton said that although the clinics were advertised in doctors' surgeries and libraries there were no adverts in more 'public' public places. She stated:

FAMILY PLANNING

Family Planning advice and pregnancy testing available for Aberdeen Residents.

2 West Craibstone Street,

Tel. 56368,

for Information.

Advert in the *Press & Journal*, 27 March 1974.
(Reproduced courtesy Aberdeen Journals)

We want every woman in Aberdeen – married or unmarried – to know that we are here to help her avoid unwanted pregnancy. And we don't care tuppence about her marital status.

The clinic moved to Golden Square on 1 May 1984. Sexual Health is currently delivered at the Health and Social Care Village at Frederick Street.

Although not based in Aberdeen, the Bairds' son, Professor DT Baird, carried on his parents pioneering work. His research helped the 'morning after pill' RU-486 gain approval for use in the UK in 1991.

Family planning in Aberdeen has transformed in less than a century, from a clinic which offered one form of contraception, the Dutch cap, to married women only, to a service which provides a range of options to all the women of Aberdeen. As a result, Aberdeen, as elsewhere, has been transformed, with smaller family sizes helping reduce poverty, overcrowding and ill health. Contraception enables women to delay starting a family, to space out children, and to limit family size, giving them control over their lives. For this we owe a debt of gratitude to Aberdeen's pioneering doctors and campaigners.

Further Reading

Elliott, Kirsten, 'Birth Control Clinics in Scotland 1926–c1939', *JSHS* Vol 34, Issue 2

Debenham, Clare, *Birth Control and the Rights of Women*, EB Taurus 2014

Family Planning and marriage guidance pamphlets, University of Aberdeen MS 3179 / 8 /5

Family planning services in Aberdeen archive, University of Aberdeen MS 3179

Aitken-Swan, Jean, *Fertility Control and the Medical Profession*, Croom Helm 1977

Horsburgh, Florence, 'The back street beginnings of birth control' *Press & Journal* 4 December 1972

Lecture notes on medical jurisprudence and on public health by Matthew Hay and taken down by John Stuart 28 April 1896–14 October 1899. University of Aberdeen MS 3128 /2

10

A Short History of Nursing Homes, Mother and Baby Homes and Maternity Homes in Aberdeen

Fiona Rennie and Lesley Dunbar

THIS CHAPTER DESCRIBES how some maternity services evolved during the late 19th and 20th centuries for women in the city – not only for better-off women who had their babies in private or independent nursing homes, but also for young, disadvantaged women, often initially from the east end of Aberdeen, who were seen as particularly vulnerable and needed support and health and welfare services for themselves and their babies. Fortunately, a small group of formidable local women influenced and campaigned on their behalf to ensure these services were provided. The section has four parts: nursing homes; mother and baby homes; maternity homes; regulatory framework.

Also outlined is how some of these private nursing homes evolved into publicly owned and run maternity homes. Although many of these homes have now closed, with the last to go just over 30 years ago, some older readers today are familiar with and may still have fond memories of them – Fonthill, Summerfield and Queen's Cross Maternity Homes.

The information that follows has, in the main, been gathered from Aberdeen journals and affiliated publications and represents women's history in the making.

Nursing homes

During the late 19th century and the first half of the 20th century, nursing homes were entirely different. They were private hospitals providing medical care with dedicated maternity beds. They were usually owned and run by women, some remarkable and dedicated women. At this time, few unmarried women owned property, let alone owned and ran businesses.

In this section, the many private nursing homes in Aberdeen which also provided maternity facilities, and the women who owned and ran them, are briefly outlined. These include:

Armstrong Nursing Home 1905–50, became the St John Nursing Home
Northern Nursing Home 1894–48 , later Watson and Fraser Nursing Home
Mrs Rose's Nursing Home 1900–22, also known as the Richmondhill
Nursing Home
Central Nursing Home, renamed Carden Terrace Nursing Home,1926, then becoming Rubislaw Nursing Home in 1934
St Swithin's Street Nursing Home 1925–37
Hamilton Place Maternity Home 1925–27
Bonnymuir Nursing Home 1926–41
Osborne Nursing Home 1930–40
Forest Avenue Nursing Home 1932–40
Cuparstone Nursing Home 1934–49
Kings Gate Nursing Home 1935–45
Ferryhill Nursing Home 1935–44
Fonthill Nursing Home 1923 – became the Fonthill Maternity Home in 1948

Armstrong Nursing Home

The Queen's Jubilee Institute of Nursing was founded in 1887 to celebrate Queen Victoria's Golden Jubilee. From then until the 1960s, these institutes across the UK trained district nurses and Miss Isabella Armstrong was the first Queen's Nurse in Aberdeen to be appointed to this small and select group (1892). She left Aberdeen in 1898 for Liverpool to take up the post of Inspector of Nurses for the north of England. She returned to Aberdeen and in 1902 was registered as a daily visiting trained nurse or district nurse at. In 1905, she established Miss Armstrong Nursing Institute, a nursing home at 15 North Silver Street (her sister Jean, was the matron at Morningfield Hospital from 1895–1908) which moved to 21 Albyn Place, Aberdeen in 1908.

In 1919 Miss Armstrong gave up the ownership of her nursing home and died a year later. Miss Christina Deichen Ross, at the age of 36, took it over and renamed it the Armstrong Nursing Home. Miss Ross was a very experienced nurse who had worked in the Citadel in Cairo from 1915–1917 and at the 36th

Station Hospital in Palestine 1917–19.

Miss Ross made the Armstrong Nursing Home a Limited Company in 1936, naming the senior nurse Miss Bannie Mackie and herself as its subscribers.

In the late 1930s, Miss Ross showed an exhibition of films of her tour from New York across the Rockies to Vancouver then to New Zealand, Australia and then Cape Hope and Johannesburg in South Africa, raising money for local groups, including the Mother and Baby Homes. Miss Ross enjoyed a long retirement but died in 1972, aged 89.

St John Nursing Home

In 1950, the Armstrong Nursing Home was bought by the Order of St John and renamed the St John Nursing Home. Miss Bannie Mackie succeeded Miss Ross as matron and retired herself in 1970. She died four months later. The nursing home later became St John Hospital, and subsequently, as it is now, the Albyn Hospital – currently a private hospital in Aberdeen.

Northern Nursing Home

In 1894, Miss Alice Horsenail from Braintree, Essex arrived in Aberdeen. Previously she had worked at St Bartholomew's Hospital in London. Miss Horsenail was well qualified and had wide nursing experience. This helped her to establish a nursing home with Miss Mary Gavin Barber – the Northern Nursing Home which was initially at 2 Bon Accord Square, with Miss Horsenail as the superintendent. It moved to 3 Carden Terrace in 1897. Thereafter, Miss Horsenail's Northern Nursing Home moved to 5 Albyn Place (1904).

In 1914, Miss Alice Horsenail retired from the Northern Nursing Home due to ill health and moved to Surrey dying two years later. Miss Agnes Abel and Miss Riach became the principals of the Northern Nursing Home where they had worked for 13 years.

In 1928, Miss Agnes Abel and Miss Riach retired from the Northern Nursing Home and the new principals then became Miss Anne Primrose Douglas and Miss Bell. The Matron of the Northern Nursing Home, Miss Anne Primrose Douglas, retired in 1948. During World War 1 she had been a member of the Territorial Force Nursing Service and worked on a hospital ship in the North Sea. Her nursing services earned her the Royal Red Cross medal. This award was established in 1883 by Queen Victoria with Florence Nightingale being its first recipient. It was awarded to women who had shown devotion while nursing the sick and wounded of the British army and navy. Miss Douglas would enjoy a long retirement, dying in 1967, aged 87.

Watson Fraser Nursing Home

In 1948 the Northern Nursing Home at 5 Albyn Place became the Watson Fraser Nursing Home after it was acquired with a bequest of £30,000 from Miss Anne Mary Fraser. The Watson name was from Miss Fraser's mother's maiden name. Miss Fraser had left a bequest in 1926 to set up a nursing home in Aberdeen:

> The charges should be kept sufficiently moderate to be within families means and the nursing home should not compete in anyway with the excellent nursing homes in the city.

The Watson Fraser Nursing Home trustees had held lengthy negotiations with the Aberdeen Royal Infirmary Directors. Plans for a nursing home had been included in the original 1929 plans for the Infirmary site at Foresterhill. However, by 1938 the trustees were still in negotiation with the directors of Aberdeen Royal Infirmary. The directors had suggested having paid maternity beds for the Infirmary included in the home. The trustees consulted with the Council and found this did not agree with what the bequest had stated. The Infirmary needed private maternity beds onsite and did not consider the site was complete as long as it remained without a pay bed section.

In 1939, the trustees finally agreed that if residents required specialist medical treatment that was not available in private nursing homes and could afford to pay adequately in full, then treatment could be offered at the hospital. However, this was all postponed due to World War II. In 1948, the Directors of the Infirmary bought the Northern Nursing Home, and renamed it the Watson Fraser Nursing Home and it became the Infirmary's paying bed section. It closed in 1969. The buildings have subsequently become commercial premises.

Mrs Rose's Nursing Home (Richmondhill Nursing Home)

In 1900, Mrs Margaret Rose first opened Mrs Rose's Nursing Home at 58 Carden Place but thereafter opened a superior nursing home at 52 Kings Gate in 1902 which was well equipped with the latest x-ray machines and a surgical theatre. With this newly refurbished nursing home, she converted the original premises at 58 Carden Place to a nurses' residence.

In the Aberdeen Post Office directories, 52 Kings Gate was listed as Mrs Rose's Nursing Home but it was also known as Richmondhill Nursing Home.

During World War 1, Mrs Rose had been a member of the Territorial Force Nursing Service working with wounded soldiers at the Oldmill Military Hospital (at Woodend Poorhouse, now Woodend Hospital), as a theatre sister and assistant matron. She earned the highest Red Cross honour – the Associate Royal Red Cross medal for this work (the honour had been introduced during World War 1, in 1915, to be awarded to fully trained nurses of an officially recognised nursing service, who had shown exceptional devotion and competence in nursing).

Mrs Margaret Rose retired in 1922. Her daughter qualified as a midwife that same year. Mrs Rose died in 1932. The Morningfield Hospital bought the Richmondhill Nursing Home as a nurses' residence.

Central Nursing Home

Miss Kate Leslie Scott opened the Central Nursing Home at 15 Carden Place, Aberdeen in 1906 and by 1915, three of these private nursing homes (Central, Armstrong, Northern) were working in conjunction with the Maternity Hospital facilities at Castle Terrace.

In 1916, the Central Nursing Home had acquired another property at the other side of the road at 1 Carden Terrace, naming it the Carden Terrace Nursing Home.

Miss Scott put the Central Nursing Home at 15 Carden Place up for sale in 1926. She had owned it for 20 years. She continued working at Carden Terrace Nursing Home and renamed it the Central Nursing Home.

In 1933, Miss Scott died in service which led to the Central Nursing Home being put up for sale. Miss Scott had been the Chair of the Council of Scottish Midwives Association and had also been heavily involved in planning and setting up the new Maternity Hospital site at Foresterhill.

Rubislaw Nursing Home

The Central Nursing Home was taken over by a group of local businessmen from the city and in 1934 they made it a limited company, renaming it the Rubislaw Nursing Home. The Rubislaw Nursing Home moved to 55 Queens Road in 1940, as the premises at Carden Terrace had proved to be inadequate and needed to be refurbished.

In 1958 the Rubislaw Nursing Home, the last remaining private maternity home, closed at Queens Road and Aberdeen Maternity Hospital began to accommodate private patients at what was now known as the Rubislaw Wing which opened on the 16 April 1958 and had 15 beds. The Rubislaw Wing at the Aberdeen Maternity Hospital reduced the number of private maternity beds from 15 to ten in 1966, and two years later in 1968 they were further reduced to six beds. A single fee-paying maternity bed at the City Hospital was also discontinued. 55 Queens Road was incorporated into the Hamilton School, which has itself subsequently been integrated into the Chester Hotel.

St Swithin Street Nursing Home and Hamilton Place Nursing Home

56 ST SWITHIN STREET.
THE above PROPERTY is for Sale or to Let. Suitable for private dwelling-house or nursing home. Accommodation—3 public rooms, 5 bedrooms, kitchen and scullery etc. Electric light and part heating. There is an up-to-date operating theatre and plant. Assessed Rental, £60; Feu-duty; £4 15 11. For further particulars apply to Messrs WILSONE & DUFFUS, Advocates, 7 Golden Square, Aberdeen.

Advert in the *Evening Express* (11 April 1940) notifying readers that the St Swithin Street Nursing Home was for sale as either a dwellinghouse or a nursing home.

At 56 ST SWITHIN STREET, THURSDAY FIRST, at 2.30 p.m. SALE OF SURPLUS HOUSEHOLD EFFECTS AND SURGICAL APPLIANCES. Including: — 3-piece Hide Suite with Velvet Cushions, 5-piece Oak Bedroom Suite, 2 Dressing Tables, 4 Kitchen Chairs, Arm Chair, Large Table, Small Tables, Kitchen Clock, Sun Ray Lamp, Surgical Drums, Surgical Pivot Chair, 5 Beds (2 Hospital), Wash Hand Basins, Theatre Chair, Mattresses, 2 Cradles (bed), Bed Rest, Gramophone Records, Dog's Basket and Cover, 9 Vols. International University Course (new), quantity Bed and Table Linen, Culinary Utensils, Pots and Pans, etc., Hose Pipe, Carpet Sweeper, etc., etc. On view morning of sale.

An advert in the *Press & Journal* (15 May 1937) detailing items for sale from the Swithin Street Nursing Home.

In 1925, a further two nursing homes opened. Firstly, St Swithin Street Nursing Home at 56 St Swithin Street and secondly a Maternity Home at 20 Hamilton Place, which only remained open for two years. In 1937, St Swithin Street Nursing Home closed.

Bonnymuir Nursing Home

In 1926 Mrs Collins opened Bonnymuir Nursing Home at 92 Bonnymuir Place. The home closed after 15 years in 1941.

Osborne Nursing Home

Mrs Fred Morrison was a registered midwife who had qualified with the Central Midwives Board. In 1930, she opened Osborne Nursing Home at 60 Osborne Place. In 1932, the Osborne Nursing Home moved to 32 Carden Place and closed in 1946.

Forest Avenue Nursing Home

Also in 1930, Miss Christina Catherine Ross had been a midwife for a year and had opened a private maternity home at 135 Union Grove. In 1932 she moved to 83 Forest Avenue and named it Forest Avenue Nursing Home. She advertised under the lodgings column in the local press offering 'accouchements' (meaning the act of giving birth to a baby).

However, in 1940, Forest Avenue Nursing Home was closed and put up for sale due to the proprietor Miss Christina Catherine Ross being charged and put on trial at Aberdeen High Court for conducting illegal operations there and at other private residences across the city. Her co-accused was Mrs Mary Rennie Patton. Mrs Patton already had a conviction. In 1927, she had been charged with culpable homicide after an illegal operation and had been sentenced to three years penal servitude. She had subsequently also lost her Central Midwives Board Certification.

Cuparstone Nursing Home

In 1934, Cuparstone Nursing Home opened at Cuparstone House, 34 Great Western Road and was managed by Miss M Stewart. It closed in 1949.

Kings Gate Nursing Home and Ferryhill Nursing Home

In 1935 Kings Gate Nursing Home opened at 50 Morningfield Road. Also opened was Ferryhill Nursing Home at 14 Ferryhill Place run by Nurse Miss Madge Taylor.

In 1944 Ferryhill Nursing Home moved to Eldersie House at 332 Broomhill Road and became Broomhill Nursing Home and ended its maternity provision.

All these private nursing homes had offered midwifery services and constituted a significant part of the provision of maternity facilities for childbirth in the city at that time in the pre-NHS 20th century.

Mother and baby homes

In 1915 a women's conference took place in Aberdeen and a delegation of formidable women formed a group which included Dr Agnes Thomson, Anaesthetist at the Aberdeen Children's Hospital, Clementina Esslemont, founder of the Mother and Baby Child Welfare Association and Miss Margaret

Macdougall, Matron at the Aberdeen Maternity Hospital.

The delegation met with the Finance and Public Health Committee in the Town Council to seek funding to support a new maternity home for the city. There was also an urgent need for a maternity home for 'khaki babies' who were 'illegitimate' babies – but more than that. Their name derived from the fact that many of these babies were fathered by men who could not marry the mother because they were fighting at the front; some of these men had been killed before the baby was born. The babies were termed 'khaki' because their fathers' army uniforms were that colour.

The previous year, in 1914, there were 148 births in the Aberdeen Maternity Hospital, with 96 being illegitimate, and 16 births in the poorhouse, with 14 being illegitimate. Although the Finance and Public Health Committee had sympathy with the delegation, they felt they could not justify recommending a grant from the Common Good Fund to the Council. In England, state aid to establish maternity homes was provided by the UK Government to English local authorities. There was no similar legislation to provide funding to Scottish local authorities for maternity homes in Scotland.

The Finance and Public Health Committee also had before them a letter from the National Association for the Prevention of Infant Mortality and the Welfare of Infancy. The letter outlined a resolution adopted by their executive committee, requesting that the UK Government offer funds to establish local authority-run infant and maternity centres in Scotland and suggesting that the Aberdeen Town Council should pass a similar resolution:

> Because of the need for an increase in the number and activities of infant welfare and maternity centres in Scotland, the council are of the opinion that it is most desirable that state aid in the form of financial grants on the same basis as those now afforded to similar centres in England and Wales should be made by the government at as early a date as possible. In the event of this recommendation being adopted, the Finance and Public Health Committee suggests copies of the resolution should be forwarded to the Chancellor of the Exchequer and the Secretary of State for Scotland.

At the Committee meeting, it was recommended that the Council send a copy of the resolution to the Chancellor of the Exchequer at 11 Downing Street.

The establishment of a Mother and Baby Home in Aberdeen was thus the outcome of the work of the Mother and Child Welfare Association whose members had included Agnes Thomson and Clementina Esslemont. Twenty other local women's organisations helped support vulnerable unmarried mothers in the city. Several mother and baby homes were set up for disadvantaged, poor, vulnerable and unmarried women from 1919 and run as publicly owned health services until 1948 with the establishment of the National Health Service.

In order for the Mother and Baby Home to be financially secure, the local authorities, where the women came from, provided financial support to the Home for the upkeep of the young women and their babies. This incurred considerable administrative work for a voluntary group as some young women were coming from England, becoming a burden for this voluntary organisation. A solution was found in 1948 with the Mother and Baby Home's Board asking the Aberdeen Association for Voluntary Services to take over the administrative duties of the Mother and Baby Home Board's Treasurer and Secretary. At this time, it was common for the Association to take on secretarial work to support independent voluntary organisations. The Mother and Baby Home General Committee continued to make its own decisions on its governance.

Aberdeen's mother and baby homes included:

Burnside Mother and Baby Home 1919–32
Loch Street Mother and Baby Home 1919–39
Thorngrove 1933–54
Aberdeen Mother and Baby Home 1942–72 (later Richmondhill House).

Burnside and Loch Street mother and baby homes

In 1919 the Aberdeen Mother and Child Welfare Association worked along with the Town Council with funding provided by the Scottish Board of Health for the Association to open two mother and baby homes – Burnside at Westburn Road which was for convalescing mothers and babies, and the Loch Street Mother and

Baby Home for unmarried mothers having their first baby. This was at 41 Loch Street, next door to the Aberdeen Soup Kitchen. These newly opened homes were stocked from across the city, and included cash and donations as well as items from other nursing homes.

In 1935, Loch Street Mother and Baby Home had capacity for six mothers and ten infants. It ran for 20 years until it closed in 1939.

Burnside House was converted from an 18th-century mansion to a mother and baby home for convalescing mothers by the Aberdeen Mother and Child Welfare Association.

Burnside House gave its name to Burnside House, now part of the Aberdeen Royal Infirmary site, Cornhill Road, a clinic providing dermatology services.

Thorngrove Home for Mothers and Babies

In 1933, Thorngrove Home for Mothers and Babies opened at Thorngrove House, 500 Great Western Road, Mannofield. It was initially used as a maternity home for unmarried mothers having their first pregnancy. In 1935, the accommodation provided for six mothers, as well as 50 babies who were awaiting adoption. It closed in 1954 and is now residential accommodation.

Aberdeen Mother and Baby Home (Richmondhill House)

In 1942, the Aberdeen Mother and Baby Home opened in the city at 25 Westfield Terrace. Aberdeen was the last city in Scotland to open a home for unmarried mothers and their babies. Previously mothers and babies were separated, living in different homes from each other with mothers going to the Central School which was a Public Assistance Institution and Hospital during World War II and with babies going to Thorngrove House.

The founder was Dr Agnes Thomson. The mothers stayed for a month to six weeks before birth and for six weeks to two months after confinement.

In 1948, the Aberdeen Mother and Baby Home moved to Richmondhill House, 22 Kings Gate. In 1951, 44 babies were born at the Mother and Baby Home at Richmondhill House as well as, unexpectedly, two lambs. The lambs' mothers were employed to keep the rough grass down in the grounds of the house.

By the start of the 1970s, half the mother and baby homes in Scotland had closed and in 1974 the Aberdeen Mother and Baby Home amalgamated with the Aberdeen Association of Social Services. The Mother and Baby Home would continue to fundraise and do so publicly.

It would remain an independent entity called the Friends of Richmondhill. The Home's Executive Committee became a standing committee of the Association and was named the Richmondhill Committee. The Aberdeen Mother and Baby Home became known as Richmondhill House and was converted into six bedsits for unsupported mothers and children on the top floor. Sessions on practical skills, childcare skills and social skills were run for the young mother residents.

The Home was taken over by the Aberdeen Association of Social Services (now Voluntary Services Aberdeen, Aberdeen's oldest charity) in 1970. It had changed its remit from offering short term support before and after birth and now helped unsupported mothers with residential and day care.

In 1982, Richmondhill House was no longer solely for mothers and babies but also helped vulnerable women. In 1995, the Maisie Munro Children's Centre was established. Today, it is also the base for Richmondhill House Family and Children Services, run by Voluntary Services Aberdeen and includes the VSA Toy Library.

Maternity homes

With maternity services having previously been part of nursing homes provision, privately owned maternity homes (Fonthill and Queens Cross) and Summerfield Hospital were acquired by the corporation before becoming part of the NHS in 1948:

Fonthill Maternity Home 1946–1990
Summerfield Maternity Home 1948–1991
Queen's Cross Maternity Home 1945–1975

Fonthill Nursing Home (later Fonthill Maternity Home)

In 1923, the Corporation of Aberdeen held a public 'roup' (auction) at the Townhouse to sell the house at 62 Fonthill Road. Mrs Mary Rae bought it and the Fonthill Nursing Home opened the following year. Fonthill Nursing Home was purchased by the Aberdeen Corporation and became Fonthill Maternity Home in 1945.

In 1946, Fonthill Maternity Home re-opened after refurbishment. There were 18 beds with five wards, three with four beds and two with three beds. The home was staffed and run by Aberdeen Maternity Hospital.

In 1973 Queens Cross and Fonthill Maternity Homes were closed for a month due to ancillary workers being on strike.

In 1988, it was decided all NHS maternity

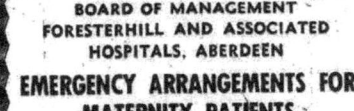

BOARD OF MANAGEMENT
FORESTERHILL AND ASSOCIATED
HOSPITALS, ABERDEEN

**EMERGENCY ARRANGEMENTS FOR
MATERNITY PATIENTS**

Mothers in labour who have been booked for
delivery at

**FONTHILL and QUEEN'S CROSS
MATERNITY HOMES**

should Telephone Aberdeen Maternity Hospital,
Forestrehill — Tel. 23423, Ext. 2069.

Most mothers and babies will be discharged the
day after delivery and should be collected by a
relative or friend. Mothers should bring where
possible: baby clothes, disposable nappies, bath
towels, sheets and pillowcases.

On 3 March 1973, the Board of Management of Foresterhill published interim emergency arrangements for maternity patients who had been booked for delivery at Fonthill and Queens Cross Maternity Homes to organise alternative provision of service whilst ancillary workers were on strike.

(Courtesy of Aberdeen Journals)

homes were to be closed and all maternity services were to be based at Aberdeen Maternity Hospital at Foresterhill. The savings from the closures of the Fonthill Summerfield and Queen's Cross maternity homes were to contribute towards meeting costs for older people's care.

On Friday 16 March 1990, Fonthill Maternity Home was finally closed. Its name lives on in the Fonthill Ward at the Aberdeen Maternity Hospital. The former Fonthill Maternity

Fonthill Maternity Home used for deliveries from 1945 to 1990. Initially a nursing home in Aberdeen, it subsequently expanded into maternity care.

Home building was later converted into flats in an exclusive west end property development.

Summerfield Hospital and Woodend Hospital

In 1935, Woodend Hospital became an annex for the overcrowded Aberdeen Maternity Hospital with 16 maternity beds. Summerfield Hospital became a maternity annex alongside Woodend. Summerfield Hospital had also converted an existing chronic sick ward of 16 beds to maternity beds in 1939.

Until 1946, Woodend Hospital and Summerfield Hospital had acted as annexes for the Aberdeen Maternity Hospital but in 1948 Summerfield Hospital became a maternity home and was renamed Summerfield Maternity Hospital. The annex at Woodend Hospital was no longer required for maternity beds.

In 1961, Summerfield Hospital had 23 beds, 10 for confinement and 13 for long term antenatal patients, increasing to 30 beds by 1970 when there was a shortage of staff.

On 21 December 1991, Summerfield Maternity Hospital closed. Its name was given to a ward in Aberdeen Maternity Hospital and the site was converted to a new administration building for 200 staff of NHS Grampian.

Queen's Cross Nursing and Maternity Home

Aberdeen City Council acquired King's Gate Nursing Home in 70 Carden Place and changed the name to Queen's Cross Maternity Home. Queen's Cross had four wards containing 14 beds, two with ground level front rooms, each of which had four patients, and two rooms upstairs with three to a room.

Councillor May Baird, Public Health Convener, referring to Summerfield Hospital and Queen's Cross, said:

> The addition of these two homes is very welcome. The Maternity Hospital has double the cases it should be handling, and some mothers were having to travel as far as Huntly to have babies.

After it closed as a maternity unit in 1989, having seen the delivery of much of the city's current older generation, Queen's Cross Nursing Home was subsequently converted into a bar and restaurant, but was devastated by fire on 23 December 2019.

Regulation of nursing homes

Some key legislation which sought to improve maternity services and reduce maternal and babies deaths in nursing and maternity homes in Scotland is also included in this section.

Midwives and Maternity Homes (Scotland) Act 1927

In 1927, the Midwives and Maternity Homes (Scotland) Act became law. It aimed to reduce the number of unqualified midwives in Scotland and sought to lower the maternal death rate in Scotland, which was deemed too high. The registration of Maternity Homes became compulsory as from January 1928. After registration, the home received a certificate to display in the building. If maternity homes did

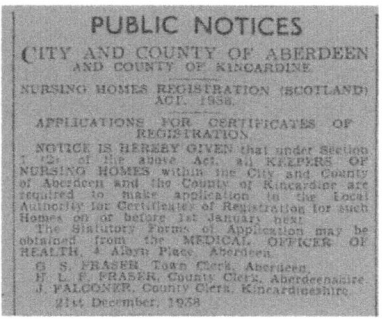

Nursing home registration. Public notice published in the *Press & Journal*, December 1938, detailing the requirement to apply for a Certificate of Registration by all keepers of nursing homes within the city of Aberdeen, Aberdeenshire and Kincardine.

(Courtesy of Aberdeen Journals)

not adhere to the regulations, owners were fined no more than £50 the first time. Subsequently their owners faced imprisonment not exceeding three months.

In March 1928, the Public Health Committee of Aberdeen Town Council recommended that all eight maternity homes in the city be registered with the local authority. In 1939, all nursing homes had to register with the Town Council.

Maternity Services Bill (Scotland) 1937

In November 1942, the Maternity Services Bill (Scotland) 1937 was finally enacted in Aberdeen. It had been delayed due to the war and left up to local authorities to decide when to introduce the changes. It contained improvements in the standard of midwifery with home births, the provision of more adequate nursing to stop unqualified midwives and the provision of medical services for all maternity services in Scotland.

And so ended an era...

Although in the early decades of the 20th century nursing homes that offered maternity beds were popular for women who were 'well-heeled' they had long had their day. As the decades progressed, maternity services further evolved with mother and baby homes being provided for disadvantaged young women who, along with their children, were stigmatised for being unmarried.

Some of the privately owned nursing homes evolved into publicly run maternity homes with the introduction of the National Health Service. Anyone having their second child was given the opportunity of being in a nursing or maternity home, away from clinical hospital surroundings and with a more homely feel. Maternity homes no longer exist in the city. Everything today is offered inclusively on-site at AMH. Stays in hospital are shorter and there is more provision for aftercare at home. Moreover, private maternity beds will no longer be an option at the new Baird Family Hospital, with the ethos being to provide an inclusive service that responds to patients needs as opposed to the ability to pay.

11

Neonatal and Perinatal Medicine

George Youngson, Mike Munro and David Lloyd

SURVIVAL OF INFANTS (0–1 year) in Scotland prior and up to the 1950s was poor but had improved significantly in the latter part of the 20th century. The dramatic fall in infant mortality was due to improvements in public health and the standards of medical care, including provision of antibiotics. Similarly, mortality in premature and small neonates under 2,000 grams in birth weight continued to improve in the UK from the 1950s onwards due to the medical advances in neonatal care. Specialised neonatal care had not really developed in the UK until the late 1960s when the intensive care, including ventilation of newborn and particularly premature babies, began to happen across the country.

Local, Scottish and UK neonatal mortality rate and infant mortality were on average 30 to 40 deaths per 1,000 live births each year (which had declined dramatically by over 85 per cent to 5 per 1,000 per year by 2003).

A graph outlining the impact of improved public health measures on infant mortality and the death during the 20th century.

(Courtesy of National Records of Scotland)

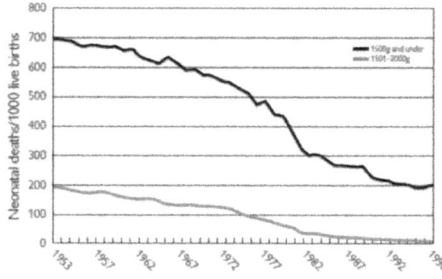

Neonatal mortality rate per 1,000 live births under 2,000 g. England and Wales, 1953–96.

(Taken from Macfarlane A and Mugford M: *Birth Counts 1984 and 2000*. London: the Stationery Office showing a substantial reduction in neonatal deaths.)

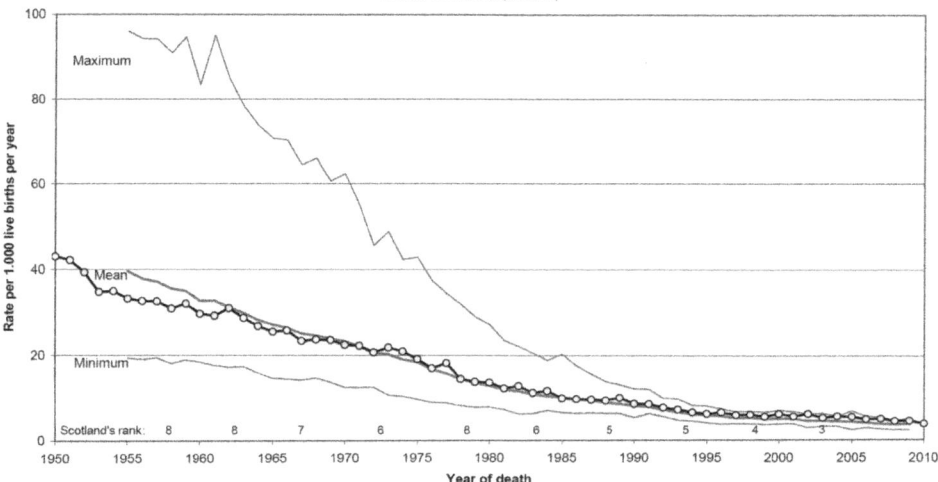

Infant mortality rates among males
Scotland in context of maximum, minimum, and mean rates for 16 Western European countries
Source: WHOSIS (April 2012)

Graph showing substantial reduction in male infant mortality rate between 1950 and 2010 and where Scotland ranks among 16 Western European countries

(Data obtained from the World Health Organisation Statistical Information System)

Much of that early improvement in the 1940s and 1950s was due to a better understanding of the importance of nutrition, early detection of infection and early preventative use of antibiotics as well as an improved understanding of the importance of the health of the mother during pregnancy and prior to delivery. Additionally, the value of breast milk for the sick neonate was readily appreciated and early attempts were made to establish a milk bank.

During the 1960s, Sir Dugald Baird had worked with Professor Ross Mitchell, who was Professor of Child Health at the University of Aberdeen and Royal Aberdeen Children's Hospital, to plan and build the first 30-cot neonatal unit in Aberdeen Maternity Hospital which opened in 1963. The driving force for the development of the neonatal unit was Ross Mitchell and he, along with Dr Mike Tunstall, obstetric anaesthetist, planned the details of the first neonatal unit with intensive care facilities in Aberdeen. Indeed, this unit, along with the neonatal unit in Hospital for Sick Children in Toronto, was amongst the first to start ventilating newborn and premature babies.

A handwritten record of the volume of pooled breast milk used in the Special Nursery during the year 1952. A total of 18,852 fluid ounces were used to assist babies feeding.

(Courtesy of NHS Grampian)

It was soon joined by Dundee's neonatal unit, to become the first purpose-built large intensive care units for the newborn in Scotland and certainly amongst the first in the UK. They represented a major advance because, for the first time, they provided the space for all the new equipment required to support premature babies. They also provided, again for the first time, dedicated medical and nursing staff who were trained in neonatal medicine. And they provided a dedicated and purpose-built environment to meet the specific needs for the care of newborn babies. Furthermore, being identifiable hospital units, they commanded their own resources, which was a considerable advantage in 1963 in Aberdeen.

Ventilatory care of newborn babies was particularly challenging by dint of the mismatch between the size of the patients involved and the dimensions of existing equipment which had been designed for adults and children. Dr Mike Tunstall along with Dr George Russell, a paediatrician from the Royal Aberdeen Children's Hospital, worked to devise several creative ways to provide that respiratory support. Much of that involved modifying existing equipment but some innovative technology was required.

Additionally, other specialist treatments such as phototherapy (light treatment) for babies with jaundice was soon to be developed as were other ways of providing breathing support without the need for ventilation.

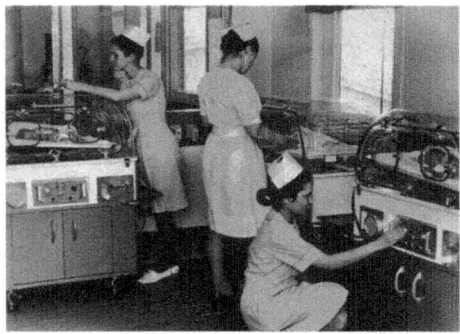

The busy and overcrowded 30-cot neonatal unit housing many incubators which was developed in the Rubislaw Wing of Aberdeen Maternity Hospital in the early 1960s.

(Courtesy of NHS Grampian)

In Aberdeen, the opportunity had been taken in the 1970s to convert one of the clinical rooms in the floor above the labour suite in the maternity hospital (the Rubislaw Wing) to be a 'special nursery'. This had the distinct advantage that, unlike many other units throughout the United Kingdom, where the neonatal unit was built into the children's hospital, which could be distant from the associated maternity hospitals, these two units in Aberdeen – the labour suite and the neonatal unit – were collocated. The major disadvantage, however, was the lack of space for equipment and staff that was becoming increasingly essential for provision of care, particularly for premature infants, and the work environment became increasingly hectic and congested with the real potential for cross infection between babies. Professor Ross Mitchell had moved to Dundee and was replaced by Professor Alec Campbell in 1972 who similarly had been extremely supportive, enthusiastic, and contributed much to neonatal care and its future development. Neonatal staffing had initially been inconsistent, but Dr David Lloyd who had been appointed 1973 as a lecturer-registrar in adult medicine and paediatrics underwent further specialty training in neonatology and perinatal medicine in Halifax, Nova Scotia and returned to the neonatal unit in Aberdeen as a single-handed consultant in 1978.

The original neonatal unit in the Rubislaw wing of the maternity hospital, which at the time of opening had been felt to be overly lavish, was by the late 1970s proving inadequate for the task. This was due to the increase in multiple births and the increasing survival rate of very low birthweight infants. The unit had been designed to have a maximum of ten ventilated babies but had at one time over 50 babies within it.

Infection of the type which had been documented by Alexander Gordon almost 200 years previously, puerperal sepsis, continued to be problematic.

A study by Dr Tom Reid, who was a bacteriologist in the University of Aberdeen laboratories, examined 369 random deliveries in Aberdeen Maternity Hospital in 1975 and showed a group B Streptococcal vaginal carriage rate in newly delivered mothers of 49 per 1,000; a neonatal colonisation rate of 19 per 1,000; maternal and neonatal morbidity rates of 16 and two to seven per 1,000, respectively; and an overall neonatal mortality of one per 1,000 live births. These were rates higher than previously had been appreciated and raised concerns about potential for cross-infection.

This location also had several other associated problems, not least of which was the extremely poor air conditioning, such that in warm summer weather the unit became unbearably hot for the staff, but in cold weather, the unit was cold which was a problem for the babies as well as the staff. Its other main problem was the lack of storage for the various items of equipment required for neonatal care which were accumulating, due to the continually evolving needs between 1960 and 1980.

There was general agreement that a new, dedicated facility was required for neonatal care, but the necessary capital funding was not available to the health board. Accordingly, plans were eventually put in place to call upon the generosity of the people of North East Scotland, so often mischaracterised for their frugal traits, to fund-raise through charitable donations for the building of a new neonatal unit – the 'special nursery'.

A charity was created – Friends of the Special Nursery – whose patrons were Lady Astor of Hever and Sir Harry Secombe, a beloved British singer, actor and comedian. Lord Astor (husband of Lady Astor) had bequeathed £75,000 in his estate to help with the building of a new neonatal unit in Aberdeen with the money only to be made available if the health board agreed to take on the running costs of the unit and the upkeep.

Planning was started in 1981 and by February 1983 the charity was able to hold its inaugural meeting. Caroline Henderson, Fiona Burnett of Leys and Tricia Lively spearheaded the drive to establish the charity for fundraising purposes and to create an environment that was appropriate for the mothers and babies of that time. The previous unit had catered poorly for maternal support. This new facility contained rooms for mothers to live in, a quiet room for sensitive consultations, a restroom for staff as well as pre-discharge to allow mothers the opportunity to accommodate the needs of their baby in the transition to home, as well as special care and intensive care facilities, all designed within a 40-bed complex.

This new identity and presence of a dedicated unit promoted the place of neonatal and perinatal medicine within the health services offered to North East Scotland, but additionally helped attract new staff and enhance training opportunities for medical and nursing staff to allow development of new services.

Through the characteristic generosity of the community of North East Scotland and the development of the charity, the new 'special nursery' opened in 1988, staffed by two specialist neonatologists (Dr David Lloyd, and Dr Paul Duffty), who were subsequently joined in 1992 by a third neonatologist – Dr Phil Booth. From this new neonatal unit located adjacent to Aberdeen's Maternity Hospital, Aberdeen's neonatal services flourished and became the tertiary neonatal referral service for the north of Scotland. Over the next 30 years, neonatal demand continued to increase, partly due to increasingly immature babies' surviving and with improvements in antenatal care and the survival chances of babies with multiple correctable anomalies. Neonatal equipment continued to evolve and multiply and once again, as in the 1980s, expansion of storage, clinical and family space had been required.

With specialist equipment, specialist environment and most importantly a specialist neonatal nursing workforce, this unit has made a major impact on the survival and quality of care of premature and newborn babies.

The design of the unit was more than simple attention to the aesthetics and a suitable environment for babies, parents and staff; it also provided for separation of babies accommodating their care dependency needs. Crucially, it provided a degree of protection against cross-infection – lessons learned from the early history of midwifery in Aberdeen as highlighted by Dr Alexander Gordon.

Alongside the developments in neonatal medicine, the unit also allowed the development of neonatal surgery without the need to transfer babies to other surgical centres in the United Kingdom as appropriate to the baby's condition. It facilitated the close collaboration and cross-specialty working between the neonatal surgeons and the neonatologists who jointly could contribute their expertise to the care of babies with surgical conditions. This joint care model was slow to be adopted elsewhere in the United Kingdom but is now accepted as the best provision of skills, expertise, and facilities for neonatal surgical care.

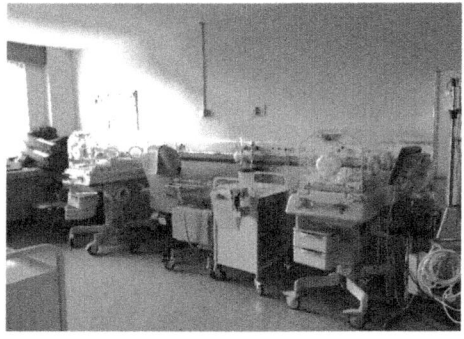

The Special Care Area, Neonatal Unit, 2020, highlighting the lack of space between incubators and cots.
(Courtesy of NHS Grampian)

Once again in the early 21st century, however, societal expectation, along with the more intensive and acute medical care being offered to newborn and premature babies, the 'special nursery' had reached the end of its useful life. A lack of space, alongside a lack of privacy for families, demonstrated the inadequacies of the current facility.

An unmet need for end-of-life care as well as many other specific care measures along with much needed expansion of space, is all planned for the new Aberdeen Neonatal Unit to be integrated into the Baird Family Hospital. The lessons learned from the many years of delivering neonatal services in Aberdeen Maternity Hospital will culminate in the building of the Baird Family Hospital and its new Neonatal Unit.

The construction of the Baird Family Hospital, just as the name implies, will allow family integrated care to develop. Family integrated care (FICare) is a model that places families as partners in the neonatal care team and provides a structure that supports the implementation of family-centred care. The Baird will also promote neonatal transitional care. Transitional care indicates that a baby, requiring neonatal care, is never separated from parents and family. In transitional care, parents can stay with their babies, in fully contained living spaces, for as long as they need to. To aid this, there will be ten transitional care rooms adjacent to the new neonatal unit. A fully integrated transitional care area of this scale will be a first for Scotland.

Neonatology has raised its awareness to the needs of the family beyond the medical needs of the baby and this has been reflected in the planning and design of the Baird Family Hospital.

12

Surgical Care of Babies and Infants

THE SURGICAL CARE of babies and infants, along with older children, had been provided at the end of the 19th century in the Royal Aberdeen Hospital for Sick Children (as it was then) which had opened in 1877 at Castlehill. And by the turn of the 20th century, it was now collocated with the new Aberdeen Maternity Hospital in Castle Terrace (whether the collocation was by chance or by design is not clear from the records of the day).

The relocation of both hospitals to the Foresterhill site occurred in two stages, the Children's Hospital in 1927 and Aberdeen Maternity Hospital in 1937, no longer collocated but both built close together.

Drawing of the Royal Aberdeen Hospital for Sick Children on the Castlehill site.
(From *A Short History of the Royal Aberdeen Children's Hospital* by Prof John Craig. University Press, Aberdeen)

The 'Old RACH' (1927–2004)

The care of babies, infants and children continued to be delivered from the Royal Aberdeen Children's Hospital. The care of babies and infants in particular (up to their first year of age) required a separate ward in RACH where cross-infection could be reduced by nursing these babies in single cubicles. But a need to also keep mothers and babies together whenever possible was recognised as

A picture of the 'old' Royal Aberdeen Children's Hospital 'lightly built' in 1927 as the first hospital on the Foresterhill site, ultimately closing in 2004 when the current hospital, adjacent and connected to Aberdeen Royal Infirmary, replaced it.

an important principle of care and a separate unit was created adjacent to the infants ward – the Craig Unit (named after Professor John Craig – Professor of Child Health at the University of Aberdeen). This comprised single rooms to which 12 mothers and their babies could be admitted. The Craig Unit accommodated babies with a full range of clinical conditions, providing the babies were well enough to not require constant nursing supervision. Amongst other functions, the unit was intended to support and promote breast feeding by mothers. This unit was opened in 1953 but post-operative surgical care was accommodated, in the main, in the adjacent infants' ward.

All neonatal surgery and the surgery of infants was carried out in the operating theatres of Royal Aberdeen Children's Hospital (RACH), requiring transfer of babies from the neonatal unit to theatres by ambulance, returning to the neonatal unit post-surgery. But if babies had been discharged from the neonatal unit prior to their need for surgery the policy was for them to be admitted to the infant ward of RACH (rather than the neonatal unit again) for fear of cross-infection when returning a baby who had been discharged from the neonatal unit back into that environment.

This remained the established practice for the next 40 to 50 years, but by the end of the 1980s RACH was continuing to degrade badly in its fabric. It had been 'lightly built to last 30 years' in 1927 but it was apparent to all by the end of the 1980s – if not before – that its replacement was significantly overdue. There were numerous false starts but ultimately by the end of the decade of the 1990s, permission was given to start planning for a new hospital and in 2004, the new RACH was officially opened by Her Majesty, Queen Elizabeth II.

The 'New RACH', 2004–present

The current Royal Aberdeen Children's Hospital opened by Her Majesty Queen Elizabeth in 2004.

The problems and challenges of transferring sick newborn babies from the neonatal unit to operating theatres at RACH, often with urgent conditions, made for an unstable patient transfer and a hazardous ambulance journey, the location of the new Children's Hospital remaining geographically distant from the neonatal unit. Proposals to build a bridge between Aberdeen Maternity Hospital and Neonatal Unit, with the east block of Aberdeen Royal Infirmary to allow trolley transfer without the need for ambulance transfer of neonates and critically ill pregnant women, failed to materialise. This unsatisfactory transport arrangement continues to the present time, ultimately to be resolved by the creation of the Baird Family Hospital and its physical linkage with RACH.

Trend towards specialisation in surgery and its implications for Aberdeen

Of all surgical subspecialties, paediatric surgery is amongst the most recent to have been developed as a separate, distinct entity. And within its scope of practice, neonatal surgery is amongst the most technically challenging and demanding aspect within its sphere of clinical responsibility. It was and continues to be, in large measure, an emergency service with the clinical presentation of surgical conditions influenced in many instances by the timing of the delivery of the baby. Accordingly, elective planning of surgery is the exception, and most operations are undertaken on an unscheduled basis soon after the birth of the baby. This branch of surgery is restricted to specialist centres throughout the United Kingdom and North America with such units typically being developed in regional children's centres with associated medical schools.

Neonatal surgery emerged as fledgling subspecialty across North America and Europe in the 1940s. The 1950s saw survival for the first time of newborns with complex congenital anomalies (such as oesophageal atresia and tracheo-oesophageal fistula) as a possibility, but survival prospects were still remote. In 1950, there were fewer than 10 neonatal surgeons in the UK, but this expanded to more than 40 by the mid-1970s.

Scotland developed its own cadre of paediatric surgeons from the mid-1940s onwards but the practice in Aberdeen for several decades was for the most recently appointed adult general surgeon to join his two predecessors in having clinical responsibilities for Royal Aberdeen Children's Hospital – irrespective of having had prior training in children's surgery or not – and with that role be responsible for newborn surgery contained within paediatric surgical practice. Whilst this model was satisfactory from some points of view, it was unsatisfactory from many other aspects, failing to provide a durable and consistent consultant presence, instead producing surgeons who had cross-site working with both adults and children within their portfolio of responsibilities and varying levels of preparatory experience with neonates for this increasingly demanding surgical specialty.

Aberdeen, nonetheless, produced international leaders in the field of paediatric surgery, such as Professor Andrew Wilkinson, who initially practised in Aberdeen as a senior lecturer in adult general surgery but who went on to develop a career in paediatric surgery, becoming the Professor of Paediatric Surgery at the Hospital for Sick Children on Great Ormond Street in London. As previously noted, his contributions to the field of clinical biochemistry and fluid and electrolyte management of patients provided surgical sciences with the fundaments of clinical practice.

Another important contributor to paediatric and neonatal surgery over a 30-year period from the 1960s in Aberdeen was Professor Peter F Jones, who made many clinical and academic contributions to the general surgery of children and neonates and who had a reputation for surgical skill which was celebrated internationally.

Several adult general surgeons, including Mr Stanley Miller, had undergone additional subspecialty training at Great Ormond Street in paediatric surgery and along with the trend of increasing anaesthetic sub-specialisation, these clinicians ensured the quality of surgical care to be on a par with the remainder of Scotland. However, from the 1950s and '60s onwards, paediatric, and neonatal surgery in both the children's hospitals of Edinburgh and Glasgow had been delivered by full-time paediatric surgeons, rather than adult surgeons with an interest in surgery of childhood as was happening in Aberdeen. The emergence of paediatric surgery as a specialty which was distinct from adult general surgical practice provided opportunities for training and rationalising the staffing of surgical services in the North East of Scotland. The need for a dedicated paediatric surgical service became evident.

George Youngson, who had been appointed as a consultant surgeon in 1984 with responsibilities in both paediatric surgery and adult general surgery, transferred all his clinical responsibilities to the Children's Hospital and became the first full-time paediatric surgeon for Aberdeen in 1988. He had been a single-handed surgeon in the early 1990s but was soon joined by other dedicated paediatric surgical consultants (G Ninan, A Mahomed and C Driver) and a cohort of four (soon to be five) surgeons now provide neonatal and paediatric surgical services for Aberdeen, North East Scotland and specialist services for the Grampian and Highland regions, as well as the islands of Orkney and Shetland.

Expansion also occurred in other surgical specialties including orthopaedics, plastic surgery, ear nose and throat surgery, and others, all of which included surgeons who had been specifically trained in the care of newborns, infants and children. Surgical staff included many notable individuals such as Ian FK Muir, an internationally renowned plastic surgeon who devised the formula used all over the world (called the Muir and Barclay formula) for fluid resuscitation in burns. Paediatric orthopaedic surgeons (Alec Adam and Tom Scotland) provided a round-the-clock quality of trauma and orthopaedic surgical care for babies and children which was second to none.

Coincident with the development and surgical services was a need for expansion in paediatric anaesthesia and this increasingly emerged as a distinct subspecialty within the field of anaesthetics. The previously mentioned Dr Tunstall and Dr Edith Beveridge along with Dr Robertson and Dr Parry were replaced on retiral by specifically trained anaesthetic colleagues (Johnston, Byers, Sheikh, Campbell, Wilson and others) who provided an around-the-clock anaesthetic service for neonates, babies and children.

The service had therefore changed from a programme of care that was dependent upon adult-based providers to one that was specifically dedicated to and focused on the needs of neonates, infants and children.

Paediatric medicine had for some time already sub-specialised in areas of gastroenterology, neurology, nephrology, child protection, community paediatrics and children's cancer services – paediatric oncology, which for 20

The entrance to the new Royal Aberdeen Children's Hospital. Artwork in the hospital was funded, created, and provided by the Archie Foundation.
(Courtesy of NHS Grampian)

years was delivered by a single-handed doctor – Dr Derek King.

With the relocation from the old Children's Hospital to a new Children's Hospital, a new configuration of wards took place with an increased provision for children and parents to stay together in single rooms. This accommodated the need of babies and their parents in a way that meant a specific ward for babies and infants was no longer required.

Moreover, if parents could not or did not wish to reside along with their children in the ward, a new facility was provided: the Children's Hospital family unit which was purpose-built to offer parental accommodation containing lounge facilities and kitchen and sitting room. This provided superb facilities – particularly for those parents requiring long-term stay with their children and those from rural and distant locations, especially in the Highlands and Islands. The funding and running of this unit was provided by the Archie Foundation – the children's hospital charity which is also responsible for funding new equipment and other facilities in the neonatal unit of the Baird Family Hospital.

The new hospital provided superior facilities, including education and play facilities and as with the medical specialties, increased specialisation occurred within nursing with pain nursing, nursing leads in gastroenterology, cystic fibrosis, neurology, gastroenterology all taking place with care also being supported by teams of therapists including speech and language, occupational, physiotherapy, dietetics and clinical psychology. This expanded team, along with clinical scientists such as audiologists, optometrists and others provide high quality specialist services for infants babies and children across north and North East Scotland.

In Aberdeen, newborn babies requiring surgical intervention continue to be transferred from the Maternity Hospital Neonatal Unit to the operating theatre at Royal Aberdeen Children's Hospital and the geographic separation of these two hospitals poses substantial logistic challenges for the clinicians involved in the care of these babies as well as clinical challenges for the babies themselves. It is testament to the collaboration and skill of surgical, anaesthetic, nursing and neonatal staff, that the quality of care offered to premature infants with congenital anomalies and other surgical conditions secured such optimal surgical outcomes.

Whilst the trend elsewhere has been for all surgical neonates to be housed within surgical units in Children's Hospital, Aberdeen has adopted a shared-care model with close liaison between neonatal surgeons, neonatologists and anaesthetists, ensuring high-quality perioperative care with the surgical babies being cared for adjacent to other neonates within Aberdeen's Neonatal Unit. This has increasingly become the model adopted elsewhere in the UK and is being used across Europe and North America.

With the opening of the Baird Family Hospital, Aberdeen's neonatal services will again move to a new state-of-the-art facility. This time there will be geographic links between the neonatal unit and the diagnostic and operating theatre facilities of Royal Aberdeen Children's Hospital as well as state-of-the-art operating facilities within the Baird Family Hospital, should it be necessary for a neonate to be operated upon in situ. This will allow seamless care as required from the neonatal period through infancy into childhood and adolescence.

Child health in the broadest sense has been delivered for the region from the central hub of Royal Aberdeen Children's Hospital, soon-to-be complemented by neonatal medicine delivered in the adjacent Baird Family Hospital with benefits to babies and children from the synergies involved in the collocated architecture.

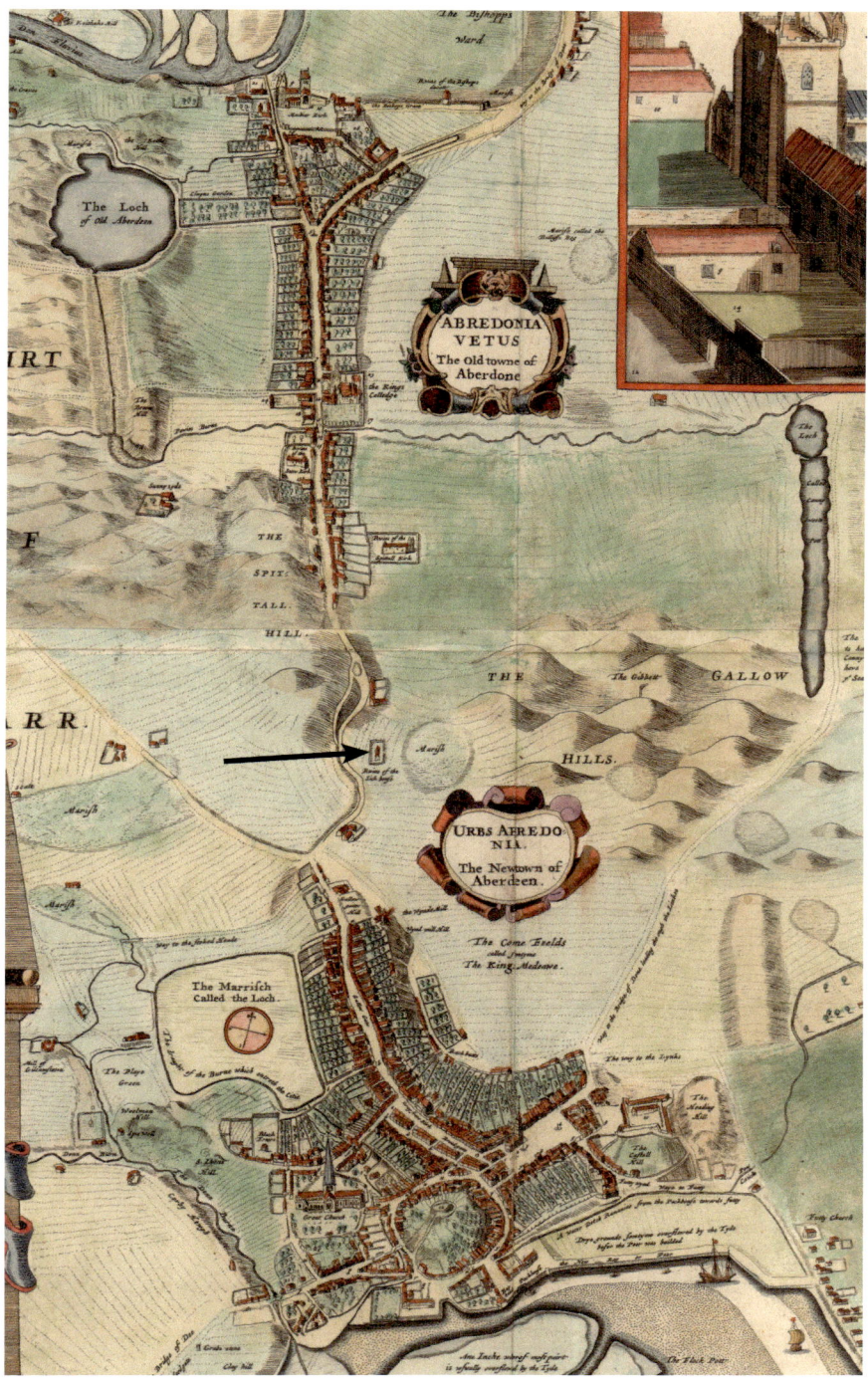

Parson James Gordon of Rothiemay's map (1661). The arrow points to the location of the Lepers' Hospital in Spittalhill in Aberdeen, midway between the Burgh of Old Aberdeen and the New Town of Aberdeen.

(Reproduced courtesy of the National Library of Scotland)

Agnes Sutherland (1850–1933) midwife in
Aberdeen for over 20 years, in midwife uniform.
(Photograph by permission of Lizanne Peace Blake,
her great, great granddaughter)

Rachel Lumsden, Lady Superintendent of the
Royal Aberdeen Hospital for Sick Children
at Castle Terrace. She was additionally Lady
Superintendent, Head Nurse, and Matron at
Aberdeen Royal Infirmary at Woolmanhill.
(Picture on display at Royal Aberdeen Children's
Hospital and reproduced courtesy of NHS Grampian)

Nurse Lindsay, newly qualified midwife,
Aberdeen Maternity Hospital.
(Reproduced by kind permission of University of
Aberdeen George Washington Wilson Collection
MS3792/F5746)

From a mural In St Nicholas Lane, Aberdeen,
celebrating women of the city, this detail
illustrates the tuition of midwives.

1869 map of the city centre of Aberdeen, including the Upperkirkgate, Broad Street and St Nicholas St; prior to the 20th century, Guestrow, Barnett's Close (parallel to Upperkirkgate), was the site of the city's most prominent Dispensary and Lying-in Clinic.

(Reproduced courtesy of the National Library of Scotland)

Thorngrove House (Great Western Road), converted into a home for mothers and babies in 1933.

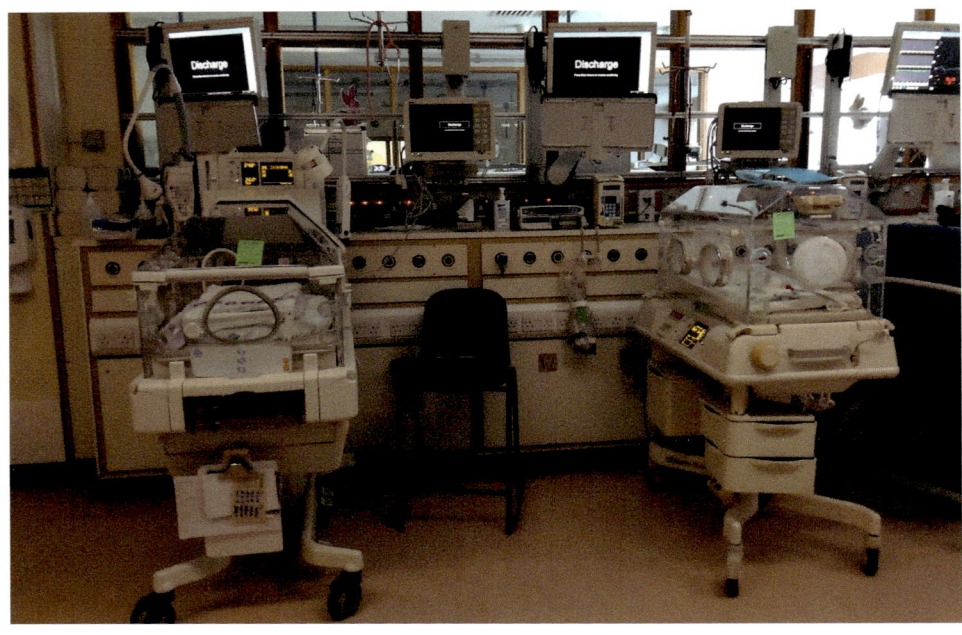

Photograph taken in 2020 of the intensive care beds in the current neonatal unit in Aberdeen Maternity Hospital which opened originally in 1988.

(Picture courtesy of NHS Grampian)

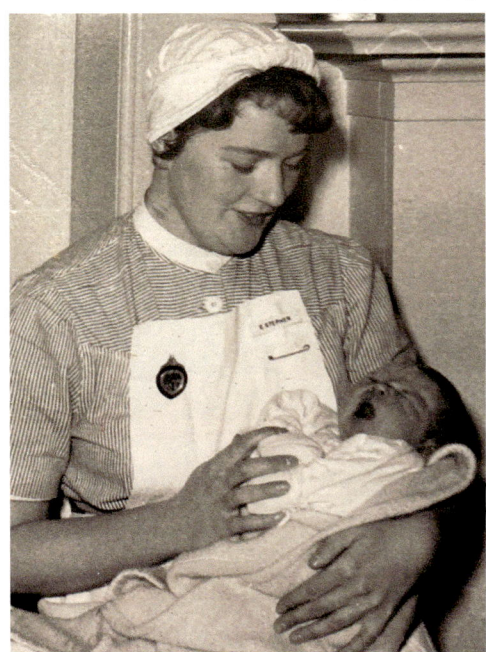

Aberdeen midwife Emma Clark, pictured in the 1960s having recently delivered this baby.

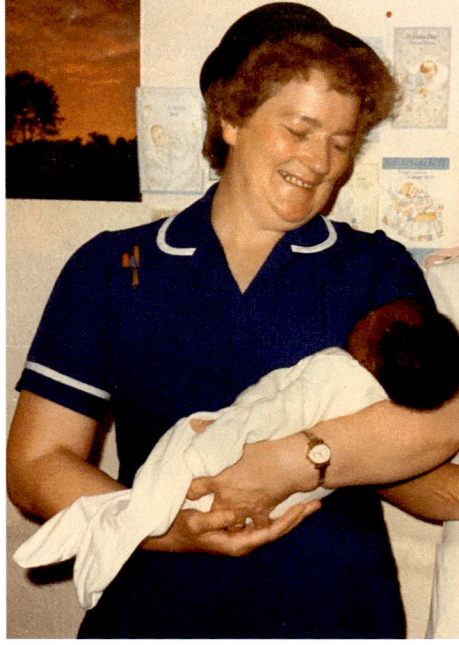

Emma Clark with newborn baby, pictured in the 1970s.

(Photograph courtesy of Emma Clark)

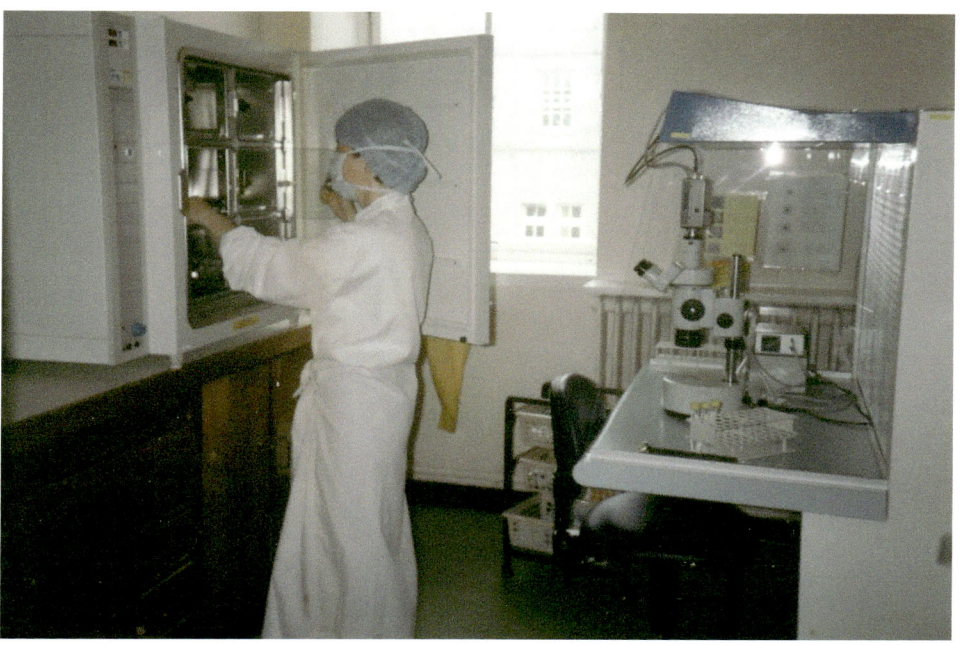

In vitro fertilisation being processed in 1989 in a laboratory created from a converted office in Aberdeen Maternity Hospital.

(Picture courtesy of NHS Grampian)

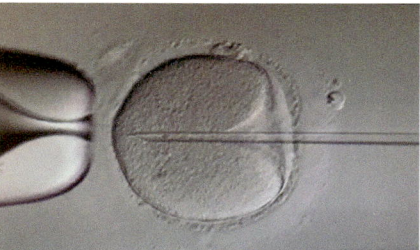

Image obtained through a microscope of intracytoplasmic sperm injection (ICSI).

(Image courtesy of Dr Liz Ferguson, Laboratory Manager)

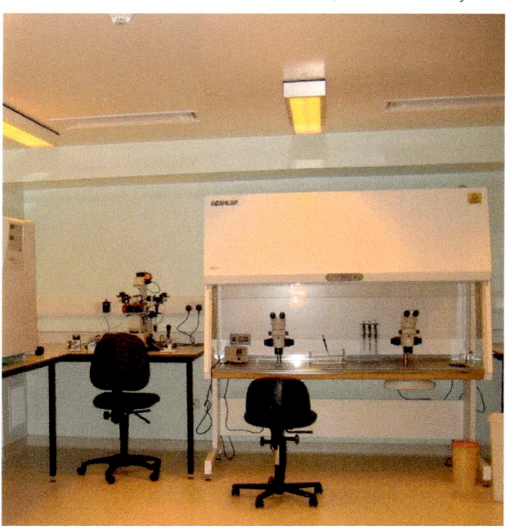

The state-of-the-art laboratory in the unit pictured in 2007.

(Photograph courtesy of Dr Mark Hamilton)

Images of the Nobel Prize Gold Medal awarded to JJR Macleod in recognition of his contribution to the discovery of insulin while working with Dr Frederick Banting in Toronto in 1921.

(Photographs courtesy of Prof Donald Pearson)

Left: Portrait by the artist Alberto Morocco of Lady May Baird CBE who along with her husband Professor Sir Dugald Baird made major contributions to women's health, notably in cervical screening and family planning. Right: Portrait of Sir Dugald Baird CBE KVO, Regius Professor of Midwifery in the University of Aberdeen 1937–65. He was a staunch advocate for women's health during pregnancy and supporter of fertility control and reproductive rights for women.

(Portrait of Lady Mary Baird by permission of NHS Grampian;
Portrait of Sir Dugald Baird by permission of Aberdeen Medico-Chirurgical Society)

L–R: John Randall, Alan Templeton and Mark Hamilton on the tenth birthday of Aberdeen Reproduction Unit in 2009.

(Photograph courtesy of Dr Mark Hamilton)

Class photograph of the first-year midwifery students at Robert Gordon's University in 2019.

(Photograph courtesy of Fiona Gibb)

Fig 34: The stained glass window inside the existing chapel of Aberdeen Maternity Hospital.
(Courtesy of NHS Grampian)

'Cutting the turf' for the Baird Family Hospital in December 2018.
(Courtesy of NHS Grampian)

13

Research in Women's Health

Maggie Cruickshank, Doris Campbell and Sohinee Bhattacharya

FROM THE EARLIEST days, research into women's health and wellbeing was an integral part of the clinical service in Aberdeen, such that it is difficult to disentangle the intertwined threads of research driven by clinical need from research-informed service delivery. Both health service delivery and academic research were led by polymaths who were doctors, midwives, scientists, and epidemiologists all rolled into one – the complete package. It is impossible to tell where audit ended, and research began. Unsurprisingly, a large part of the research throughout the years focused on maternity care.

Early research

One of the earliest records of audit and research coming out of Aberdeen was Alexander Gordon's treatise on puerperal fever. In his publication entitled 'A treatise on childbed fever', Gordon described for the first time a condition that had reached epidemic proportions in Aberdeen between 1789 and 1792, killing hundreds of women after childbirth and affecting many more. Alexander Gordon had been appointed the attending physician to the infirmary when he described this infection of the lining of the womb following delivery. Using meticulously collected records of women who delivered at the lying-in hospital, he was able to demonstrate the infectious nature of puerperal fever by demonstrating its association with outbreaks of erysipelas and the second wave of infection following the initial outbreak. His treatise, which highlighted the transmission of infection by medical and midwifery staff and the importance of hygiene to prevent this 'hospital acquired infection', was not only ground-breaking but also preceded the more accepted work of Semmelweis from Vienna by some 50 years. This implication of clinical staff in the outbreak caused an uproar and Gordon was forced to leave Aberdeen and resume his career as a naval surgeon. This piece of research started out as an audit into why so many mothers were dying soon after giving birth and paved the way for reviewing all maternal deaths and the idea for confidential enquiries into maternal deaths was born.

Perhaps even earlier than Sir Alexander Gordon, or at least his contemporary, Dr David Skene was the person credited with establishing midwifery training in Aberdeen. He was trained in London by Professor Smellie and brought some of his ground-breaking ideas to Aberdeen. Amongst them were the use of special forceps to deliver the baby, a special manoeuvre to deliver the aftercoming head of a breech baby and vaccinating the infant against smallpox and measles. Through the years, Aberdeen has kept up this tradition of training midwives, giving them equal status with physicians and led the trial which culminated in shared antenatal care and the midwives' unit in the labour ward complex.

Confidential Enquiry into Maternal Deaths

Fast forward to the 20th century and we see a huge range of research initiatives in midwifery beginning to be put in place.

The Confidential Enquiry into Maternal Deaths (CEMD) is a national audit programme in the UK investigating all deaths occurring in women during pregnancy, childbirth or within six weeks of delivery of a baby. Although the current system of national confidential enquiries started in 1952, four years after the inception of the NHS, maternal death reviews were conducted locally and one of the first known reviews in the UK was started in Aberdeen by Professor Matthew Hay in 1917. Starting from the premise that childbirth was a natural process, and every maternal death was unnecessary, all maternal deaths occurring in maternity units in Aberdeen were investigated. This was a huge shift in the paradigm of health care for women, as before this women's lives were thought to be dispensable. What started off as a local hospital-based audit in Aberdeen was adopted by the whole nation as part of the newly started National Health Service. The main aim of the CEMD was to assess the avoidable causes of maternal deaths and thereby reduce maternal morbidity and mortality by recommending improvements in clinical care. The CEMD also identified gaps in knowledge and recommended areas for future research and audit. Before 1952, maternal deaths were reported to the Ministry of Health on an ad hoc basis. The first consolidated report of the CEMD was published in

1955 and covered 1952–54. As maternal deaths reduced in number and each enquiry became more complex, a single report was published triennially for the whole of the United Kingdom. As time went on, maternal morbidity (severe complications during pregnancy or childbirth) and more recently stillbirth and neonatal deaths, were added to the remit of the confidential enquiries. This evolved role is reflected in MBRRACE (Mothers and Babies: Reducing Risk through Audits and Confidential Enquiries) who are currently responsible for carrying out the work of CEMD in the UK.

Throughout the evolution of the national confidential enquiries, Aberdeen continued to play a crucial role, providing panel members and until recently co-hosting the Scottish Programme for Clinical Effectiveness in Reproductive Health (SPCERH) which was responsible for carrying out all audits in Scotland. The national system of confidential enquiry in the UK remains to this day the gold standard for all such audits and has now been adopted in many countries worldwide.

Classification of the causes of stillbirth

Sir Dugald Baird arrived as the new Regius Professor of Midwifery in Aberdeen from Glasgow in 1937. As an extension of the confidential enquiries into maternal deaths, he saw that the next targets for improvement in the quality of maternity care were to be stillbirths and neonatal deaths. Stillbirths first became notifiable in Scotland in 1940 but the audit was limited in its scope as there was no agreed way to group the causes of stillbirth. Most classification systems depended on the pathological findings post-mortem and, therefore, had limited use in improving clinical care. The classification system for causes of stillbirth developed by Sir Dugald Baird and a young registrar, Dr John Wyper, in Aberdeen for the purpose of audit and surveillance was published first in 1941. This classification system, known as the Aberdeen Classification System, based on clinical findings rather than pathology, was further elaborated in 1954 and is used to this day in some centres in its amended or revised form.

Programmed from birth

Sir Dugald was a visionary and is credited with starting the Aberdeen Maternity and Neonatal Databank, among other things, with an eye to future research. To this day, this unique database records and stores all obstetric and fertility related events occurring in women living in Aberdeen City. Initially, the data was held on punched cards, but by 1986 it was redeveloped onto an electronic database. This database now holds data for all Aberdeen City births from 1950 to the present day and most of the pregnancies occurring in the Grampian region of Scotland from 1976 onwards. This database now includes data from four generations of the same families. In 1950, when the database was started, there were no computers. At first the data was collected in Cope-Chat cards – punched cards with complete notches for those with specific complications and holes for those without. These were sorted using knitting needles so that the cards with complete notches would fall out of the pack when the knitting needle was passed through a hole. The data was computerised into tapes in the mid-1970s and then into a relational database in 1986. The computerisation helped easy retrieval of data, not only from each pregnancy, but also from subsequent pregnancies belonging to the same mother. This was possible by linking pregnancy records using a unique number given to women when they attended the Aberdeen Maternity Hospital. Later, this became the Community Health Index, or CHI, number used throughout Scotland in primary and secondary health care. Thus, opportunities to study the health of the mother and her baby became obvious, giving rise to a whole body or programme of research which can be classified as:

1. Effect of events occurring early in pregnancy on the birth of the baby. For example, by studying the pregnancy and birth records within the database we found that mothers who suffered bleeding during pregnancy were more likely to deliver premature babies.
2. How a previous pregnancy affects the subsequent pregnancy and delivery. For example, if a mother suffered from high blood pressure in a previous pregnancy, she was twice as likely to be hypertensive in her next pregnancy.
3. Following up the mothers to assess their health in later life. Mothers who suffered from pre-eclampsia or miscarried their pregnancy were more likely to develop cardiovascular disease in later life.
4. Following up the children. Aberdeen Children of the Nineteen Fifties are a cohort of children born between 1950 and 1956 who took part in a detailed survey when they were at school. The results from this reading survey were linked to the birth records of these children stored in the Aberdeen Maternity and Neonatal Databank. They were also invited as adults to take part in a questionnaire survey, and they were linked to records of any hospital admissions or death records held centrally in Scotland. As you can imagine, this gave us a very rich and comprehensive source of data on a group of people who are now 65 to 70 years of age.

Several research papers have resulted from the study of this cohort, but recently we found an excess risk of premature mortality in the offspring born to mothers who were either underweight or obese during pregnancy.

5. Intergenerational study. Because Aberdeen is such a wonderful city, Aberdonians have lived here for generations and grandmothers, mothers and daughters have all given birth in the 'Matty' and have consequently been immortalised in the database. Just to give an idea of numbers, the AMND currently has records of around 38,000 mother daughter pairs, around 7,000 grandmother-mother-daughter trios and 200 great-grandmothers. These intergenerational linkages enable us to study the effects of mothers' or grandmothers' pregnancy complications on the pregnancy and delivery in the next generation. For instance, we showed that women who were themselves born preterm were more likely to deliver premature babies.

From the late 1990s, Prof David Barker's hypothesis that human beings are programmed in their mother's womb to develop chronic diseases in later life, started gaining popularity. The databank set up by Sir Dugald Baird in Aberdeen offered a unique opportunity to test this hypothesis through several birth cohorts and record linkage.

Research into maternal nutrition

Even before scientific research suggested a strong connection between maternal nutrition and the outcomes of a successful pregnancy, our predecessors were conscious of the necessity to augment the mother's diet as she was 'eating for two'.

In Aberdeen, Sir Dugald Baird noticed better pregnancy outcomes in his private maternity patients who were taller and bigger built than those accessing public hospitals. Post war studies showed decreases in stillbirths and neonatal deaths which some attributed to improved diet due to rationing, but Sir Dugald commented that there were inconsistencies between social classes. For example, the upper classes – well fed before the war – had a similar decrease in baby deaths as the lower classes. Early research using data from the Aberdeen Maternity and Neonatal Databank confirmed the association between maternal stature and the birthweight of the offspring. This spawned both physiological and nutritional work from the early '50s in collaboration with the Rowett Research Institute which studied similar associations in farm animals. This also resulted in the setting up of a research unit within Aberdeen Maternity Hospital originally called the Obstetric Medicine Research Unit, then in 1965 with the coming of Professor Ian MacGillivray to Aberdeen the research unit changed its name to the Clinical Research Unit. Now it is the home of infertility research. In 1950–51, the first detailed study of dietary intake in pregnancy was undertaken in Aberdeen on just under 500 women.

In the '50s and early '60s, safe techniques for assessing maternal physiological adaptation to pregnancy were developed, leading to determining what weight gain during pregnancy could be considered 'normal' and the components of weight gain – the baby, placenta, maternal fat and tissue changes and water retention were described according to the weeks of pregnancy.

In order to evaluate how such changes affected pregnancy outcome, weight gain was categorised as low (poor), normal or high (excess). Both low and high gains were associated with stillbirths and early neonatal deaths. The former was attributed to nutritional problems, and the latter to the development of pregnancy hypertension (pre-eclampsia).

The end of the '60s and the beginning of the '70s brought research into how both weight gain and pregnancy outcome could be changed or improved by dietary manipulation. In the USA, restriction of dietary intake in women with excess weight gain was widespread with the intention of decreasing the incidence of pregnancy hypertensive disease and worldwide studies of dietary supplements were springing up with the particular aim of decreasing the rate of low birth weight. Aberdeen was no exception. Unfortunately, the trial of a balanced protein-energy supplement started in the last trimester in thin women with a low weight gain up to then resulted in statistically non-significant increases in birthweight (only 45 grams) and maternal weight gain. This finding was confirmed from other developed countries. In less well-developed areas, where women are undernourished before pregnancy, there was modest effect of diet supplementation on birth weight.

In a matched controlled study, energy restriction over the last ten weeks of pregnancy with the intention to decrease the rate of pre-eclampsia in women with a high weight gain also failed to show any difference in the rates of pre-eclampsia between those dieted and control subjects. However, birth weight was slightly reduced, and the offspring seen when aged 4–6 years were still shorter and lighter than controls. This finding has since been replicated in several countries.

By the early '80s, this left the question about energy limitation in obese women in pregnancy – would it have similar effects or would the obese have more than enough stored energy to compensate? Dietary restriction over the last ten weeks of pregnancy once again showed no change in pre-eclampsia but did still have an effect on baby weight, albeit less of a decrease. There was also a decrease in weight gain.

In all the previous studies detailed body composition was assessed to determine how changes in this during pregnancy might link to nutrition, and in this work in obese women, the late pregnancy decrease in weight gain was entirely attributable to less retention of water but no change in body fat.

Finally, a repeat of the '50s diet assessment by a 7-day weighed survey was carried out in 1984 with the following conclusion: daily intake of nutrients were less in 1984/85 than in 1950/51. Both surveys found that taller women ate more than shorter women and that birthweight was not associated with dietary intake during pregnancy.

All this confirmed Sir Dugald Baird's early assertion that, except in famines, childhood and early adulthood nutrition was more important than dietary intake during pregnancy in determining a successful pregnancy outcome.

More recently, the pendulum has perhaps swung too far in some parts of the world such that we are facing a crisis related to overweight and obesity in the population, including in pregnant women. A series of research articles from Aberdeen found strong associations between maternal overweight and obesity and increased risk of cardiovascular disease and mortality – not just in the women themselves but also in their adult offspring.

Nutrition research in the latter part of the 20th century and early in the 2000s turned to look at the role micronutrients might play. Both changes in trace elements and vitamins were examined throughout gestation. In conjunction with other worldwide studies the conclusion reached was that deficiencies of trace elements in the diet are unlikely in pregnancy.

A large-scale study of dietary vitamin intake in approximately 2000 pregnant women, known as the Seaton Cohort, was started to investigate maternal antioxidant intake during pregnancy and the risk of childhood asthma. The children were followed up at several ages: six, 12 and 24 months, five and ten years and the 15 year follow up is currently underway. This is the only study with both detailed maternal dietary intake, blood nutrient levels and foetal measurements. Thus, it is a particularly valuable resource to study the early origins of asthma, and also potentially other common chronic conditions such as hypertension, obesity and 'metabolic' abnormalities such as plasma uric acid.

Epigenetics (the way genes are expressed beyond the DNA sequence of the gene, by the effect of lifestyle or diet for example), has emerged recently as one of the most important biological mechanisms linking exposures across the course of life to long-term health. If genetics provide the blueprint for life, epigenetics is the way that blueprint is read or interpreted without actually changing the blueprint. It is influenced by genotype and genetic variation as well as by a range of environmental exposures, including diet and nutrition, social status and the early emotional environment. The Seaton Cohort has provided an excellent opportunity to study this in more detail.

During an earlier trial in 1967, based in Aberdeen Maternity Hospital with a view to preventing anaemia, pregnant women were given folic acid, a vitamin B supplement, either a small or large dose, and the outcomes of their pregnancy was compared with those who received a placebo. The rate of such anaemia was unchanged. Then it became routine during pregnancy for women to be asked to take folic acid supplements to prevent any congenital defect of the nervous system (spina bifida, for example) in the newborn. The question about possible long-term harm to either mother or baby was raised and the early trial participants were followed up after 20 years. There appeared to be a small increase in the risk of breast cancer in women who had received a very high dose of folic acid in pregnancy. Fortunately, this increase in risk was no longer evident in a further follow up study of the mothers.

This trial has also provided another excellent opportunity to improve our knowledge of the role of such a nutrient taken by mothers during pregnancy and epigenetic markers in later life. Forty-seven years after the trial, the children born to mothers participating in this trial were contacted using the Community Health Index register and were asked to fill out a questionnaire and provide a saliva sample. We analysed the saliva and found some regions of the genetic code where there were differences in levels of 'DNA methylation' (a type of epigenetic change) in the children who were given folic acid (when they were in the womb) compared with those who were not. The results of this study suggest that taking folic acid in pregnancy is associated with epigenetic changes that can be seen many years after it is taken with possible subsequent effects on general and cardiovascular health.

Pre-eclampsia research

Pre-eclampsia is a condition where women develop high blood pressure while pregnant associated with protein in urine and swelling of the legs and other parts of the body. This condition, if severe, can be life-threatening for both the mother and the baby, especially if it progresses to eclampsia with superadded convulsions. Professor Ian MacGillivray as the Head of Department of Obstetrics and Gynaecology in Aberdeen had a special interest in this condition and is credited with deriving a classification system for hypertensive disorders of pregnancy. This classification system differentiated between the relatively innocuous gestational hypertension (simply high blood-pressure in pregnancy) through the more dangerous pre-eclampsia and eclampsia with superadded proteinuria and convulsions, respectively. This classification system has been adopted by the International Society for the Study of Hypertension in Pregnancy (ISSHP) and is used to this day.

Pre-eclampsia was believed to be a condition that was restricted to pregnancy and the only form of treatment was to deliver the baby. In most cases of pre-eclampsia, women's blood pressure went back to normal once they had delivered their babies. In a study led by Aberdeen researchers, around 3000 women were followed up for an average of 20 years and found that women who had pre-eclampsia during their pregnancy had a higher risk of developing heart disease and stroke in later life.

Fertility control

When in 1965 Sir Dugald Baird published his famous speech on the fifth freedom – the freedom from the tyranny of excessive fertility – the only forms of birth control available to women were the Dutch cap, condoms or abortion. Although abortion or termination of an unwanted pregnancy only passed into law in the UK in 1967 through the Abortion Act, termination of pregnancy under certain medically approved circumstances had been previously carried out in Scotland. In Aberdeen, the successor to Sir Dugald, Professor Ian MacGillivray, saw the need to evaluate the methods of pregnancy termination and sterilisation and their effects on both physical and mental health, short and long term. Several studies were undertaken in collaboration with the MRC Medical Sociology Unit. As in other countries with liberal abortion laws, this produced a dramatic drop in the rates of unsafe abortion. Together with medical abortion, which was also later pioneered in Aberdeen, women were empowered to take further control of their fertility. This heralded an era where not just women's physical wellbeing but also that of their choice became an integral part of their clinical care.

At the other end of the spectrum, Aberdeen was also one of the first centres in the UK to start investigating and treating infertility. Much of the research carried out by this Assisted Reproduction Unit is covered in a later section, but one aspect deserves particular mention.

The unit's work led to the recommendation that women should not receive multiple embryos when undergoing IVF treatment. Previously, several embryos were transferred in order to maximise the chances of success. However, this led to multiple pregnancies and serious risks to the mother and children. Aberdeen research showed that the chances of success were not reduced when only one embryo was transferred. This is now accepted practice worldwide.

IMMPACT (Initiative for Maternal Mortality Programme Assessment)

Carrying on in the long Aberdeen tradition of investigating maternal health, IMMPACT was a global health research initiative aiming to improve the health of mothers in low- and middle-income countries where maternal mortality remained unacceptably high. Supported by the Bill and Melinda Gates Foundation and led by Professor Wendy Graham of the University of Aberdeen, IMMPACT's focus countries were Ghana, Burkina Faso and Indonesia. The main output from this research initiative was an innovative toolkit for measuring maternal mortality and assessing the effectiveness of complex interventions to reduce maternal deaths in challenging circumstances.

As the University of Aberdeen celebrates its 525th anniversary, the NHS and Aberdeen Maternity and Neonatal Databank their 70+ birthdays and two and a half centuries after the discovery of childbed fever, Aberdeen continues to fly the flag of research into women's health, following in the footsteps of trailblazers like Sir Alexander Gordon and Sir Dugald Baird but also carving their own niche and always punching above their weight.

14

Reproductive Medicine in the Maternity Hospital

Mark Hamilton

THOSE OF US lucky enough to have worked in Obstetrics and Gynaecology over the last three decades or so have had the privilege of being party to a transformation in practice, arguably greater than has occurred in any other sphere of medicine. The impact of the astonishing advances in reproductive and genetic science on our professional lives has been far beyond anything we might have imagined at the start of our careers.

It is easy to be complacent as much as it is hard to imagine life before we had access to endoscopic examination of the reproductive organs; before ultrasound provided us with the opportunity to evaluate in real-time the dynamics of ovarian function; before targeted pharmacological therapy was available to manipulate egg production; before gamete manipulation, in vitro fertilisation, and the science of cryobiology were available to us; before pre-implantation assessment of the embryo and the avoidance of the transmission of genetic disease were possible; before mitochondrial replacement therapy and the concept of gene therapy could be considered real possibilities.

Diagnostic approaches to assessment to infertility at the time of the post-war baby boom were relatively crude and largely focused on assessment on anatomical structure and organ specific pathology. Therapeutic options were limited to surgical treatment of tubal disease, the use of novel agents to promote ovulation in women with infrequent periods and donor insemination in the presence of abnormal sperm counts. Infertility as an issue was dealt with in the rough and tumble of the general gynaecology clinic and interventions, with the best intentions, were largely ineffectual and sometimes hazardous.

Early days

In the 1960s Arnold Klopper, a young academic attracted to the stellar environment of the Obstetric Medical Research Unit in Aberdeen established by Sir Dugald Baird, was involved in early work to establish an understanding of steroid biochemistry relevant to ovarian function. His influential studies over the next 20 years on the development of measurement of placental steroids in urine provided clinicians with useful, albeit indirect information, on the health of babies. The names of his collaborators within Aberdeen at that time are a catalogue of individuals who made significant contributions in their own right in the years to follow – Alec Turnbull, John Dennis, Ian McGillivray, Ian Cooke, Callum McNaughton, Frank Hytten, John Stowers and later Allan

Photograph of Prof Arnold Klopper, Professor of Reproductive Endocrinology at Aberdeen University who was involved in exploring the relevant steroid biochemistry for understanding ovarian function.

(Reproduced from *British Medical Journal*, 2015; 350: p367 with permission from BMJ Publishing Group Limited)

Templeton, amongst others. Assays of ovarian steroids provided data that led to a clearer understanding of the dynamics of follicular development and corpus luteum function. Around the same time, Professor Ian Donald and colleagues in Glasgow introduced the application of ultrasound in the assessment of foetal growth and development. Together with urinary oestriol and pregnanediol hormone measurements, we attempted to reassure ourselves and our patients with regard to foetal health.

Evaluation of urinary oestrogen and progestogen profiles in relation to menstrual rhythm followed. This facilitated increased understanding of disturbances in the processes of ovulation and, with the use of anti-oestrogens which emerged in the late 1960s, Klopper researched their effects on hormone profiles and menstrual pattern and established targeted treatment for the many women with associated infertility. Pituitary derived gonadotrophins were also emerging and with their more powerful effects on the ovary the dangers of creating multiple pregnancy soon became apparent despite steroid monitoring. Urinary oestrogen levels reflected ovarian function 24–48 hours previously, and even the development of assays in plasma, more proximate in terms of interpretation to follicular activity, did not provide the precision needed to assess the quantity of follicular response to treatment. Klopper, by now a Professor of Reproductive Endocrinology in the University, wrote in a 1976 review in the *British Medical Journal*:

> Unfortunately even a slight overdose of FSH will cause numerous follicles to develop and all will be ovulated by the human chorionic gonadotrophin. The litters that may result from such an unhappy therapeutic accident have been one of medicine's less fortunate contributions to the lay press. It was not until the late 1970s that follicle development was reliably documented on ultrasound, with the first papers on the technique emerging from Glasgow. Initial imaging techniques using static B-mode scanners were cumbersome and expensive.

The author's own research at that time utilised such equipment in the Queen Mother's Hospital in Glasgow. The convenience, economy and precision of real- time ultrasound emerged in the early 1980s and this provided accurate and immediately relevant data to assist in ovulation induction programmes and complemented the emergence of in-vitro fertilisation (IVF) as an option for care.

The arrival of IVF: research and clinical service expansion

It is interesting to recall that Patrick Steptoe, who with Robert Edwards carried out the pioneering work leading to the birth of the first test-tube baby in 1978, was a champion of the use of laparoscopy as an investigative tool, and indeed his early papers on his surgical experience were received by the establishment with no small degree of scepticism. It was of course his laparoscopic skills which enabled the collection of oocytes from mature follicles and led ultimately to the first IVF pregnancy reported in the *Lancet* in 1976. This, unfortunately, evolved into an ectopic gestation necessitating its surgical removal. Edwards and Steptoe's tenacious and exhaustive work overcame many disappointments on the way to an eventual intra-uterine pregnancy and the successful delivery of Louise Brown. While the announcement of her birth in 1978 had a profound influence on clinical practice, the impact of the arrival of assisted reproductive treatment on wider society was and remains immense.

Allan Templeton, returning to his alma mater, took up the University of Aberdeen's Regius Chair of Obstetrics and Gynaecology in 1985. The pedigree of local excellence in clinical care and enthusiasm for research was consolidated with his arrival and the establishment of a team of nurses and clinicians dedicated to the delivery of a comprehensive fertility service followed. The setting up of an infertility clinic, and with it an Aberdeen IVF service, was an immediate priority. The first patients took part in a research programme led by Templeton, fellow clinician Ioannis Messinis and scientist Paul Fowler. They were interested in the subtleties of the endocrine control of ovulation and used granulosa cell culture and biochemical studies on follicular fluid in their studies. It seemed opportune to combine this research work with attempts at IVF itself. At that time, follicular fluid aspirations and egg retrieval were carried out laparoscopically in the gynaecology theatres in Aberdeen Royal Infirmary. This presented significant logistical challenges, and a fair degree of goodwill and collaboration, in adding these critically timed procedures, at relatively short notice, to routine theatre lists. The team were significantly reinforced by the theatre input of Tahir Mahmood who was carrying out early research work on the pathogenesis of endometriosis at this time. Laboratory support for the programme was dispersed between the Klopper laboratory adjacent to the gynaecology wards in ARI and the research laboratories in the University Department in the Maternity Hospital. Although only a small number of patients were involved in the programme at this time, a pregnancy resulted and the first IVF baby in Aberdeen was delivered in 1990, a moment of great pride for all involved. The success of these initial experiments led to the decision to initiate a clinical IVF programme wholly based in the Maternity Hospital.

The advent of vaginal ultrasound scanning simplified IVF treatment considerably. Follicle tracking no longer required the patient to have a full bladder and, under sedation, egg recovery was rendered a minor operative procedure capable of being carried out without the resources of an operating theatre. The top floor of the Maternity Hospital, adjacent to the University Offices and research laboratories was adapted to include a scanning and egg recovery room, an embryology laboratory and an administrative and nursing office. This core facility generated a remarkable *esprit de corps* amongst those who worked there. The thrill of pioneering a new clinical service generating hope for so many who had struggled with the deep pain of infertility was intoxicating. John Randall, research fellow at the time, was the first IVF dedicated clinician. Lorna Bell in the laboratory, prepared gametes, carried out in vitro fertilisation and embryo culture preparatory to transfer to the uterus. Alison McTavish was recruited as nurse co-ordinator and Elaine Stirton was the administrator-secretary.

The numbers of cycles carried out in the first year of the service was small. The author joined the team as a Consultant and Senior Lecturer in 1990, having trained in Glasgow and Singapore. This brought a wealth of experience in the use of ultrasound in follicular monitoring and oocyte retrieval and allowed for expansion of the clinical service.

In parallel with the development of IVF, the infertility clinic service which offered assessment, diagnostic services and first line treatment, including ultrasound-monitored ovulation induction and donor insemination, was growing. An office adjacent to the antenatal clinic was adapted for dedicated use while consultations took place in the clinic rooms. The infertility clinic kept its notes separate from ARI files in the office which was a significant step forward administratively. Sandra Cant led the nursing team, Alyson Rayner and others carried out follicle scanning, and Margaret Carmichael was the clinic secretary. Together they provided a first-class patient centred service.

Innovation

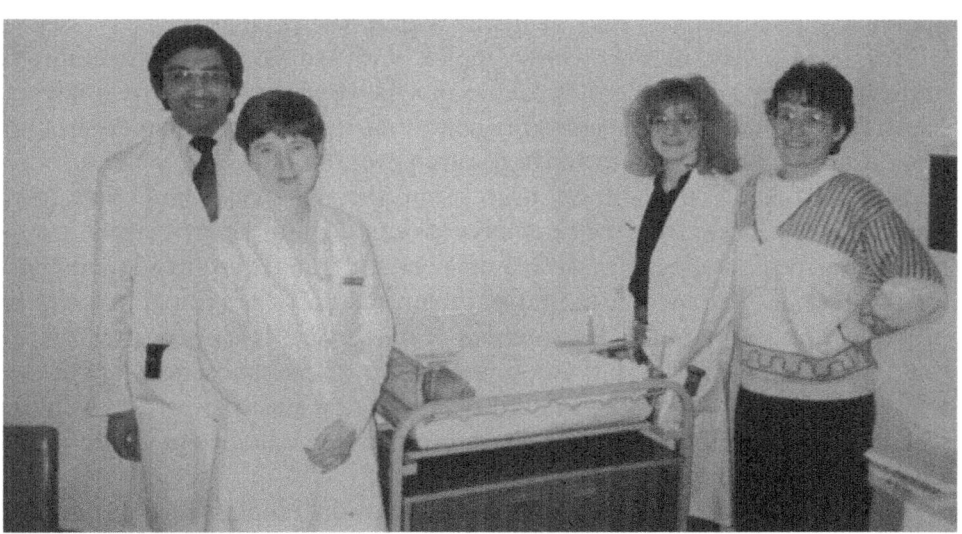

Members of the Aberdeen Reproduction Unit (ARU) photographed in 1998.
(Photograph courtesy of Dr Mark Hamilton)

A signature feature of the Aberdeen approach was the fact that nursing staff underpinned the front-line delivery of high quality, empathic care. The notion of delegating clinical management, including the administration of ovulation inducing drugs, protocol-driven decision making and monitoring with ultrasound was a significant departure from the previous dogma of such work only being possible with the hands-on input of medical staff. This enhanced role of the midwife-nurse, as first promoted in AMH, became an example of good unit practice for centres throughout the UK and many visitors were accommodated within the Infertility Clinic and the newly named Assisted Reproduction Unit (ARU) to observe this in practice.

Eventually the negative connotation of the name 'Infertility Clinic' was changed to that of the more positive 'Fertility Clinic' – and a logo emerged!

As with many other services within the Maternity Hospital, the fertility and reproductive endocrine clinics served as both the secondary and tertiary referral centre for the entire region. An internal referral system from gynaecological colleagues in Aberdeen, as well as referrals from Moray (Elgin)

The logo of the Assisted Reproduction Unit (ARU) in Aberdeen Maternity Hospital. (Photograph courtesy of Dr Mark Hamilton)

and Highland (Inverness) was established. Outside referrals, from the Central Belt to the Western Isles, were frequently received as the reputation of the quality and breadth of services available within Aberdeen grew.

Administratively, matters were complex, with the ARU under the umbrella of the University and the Fertility Clinic an NHS based service. Sperm analyses, sperm freezing, and donor sperm storage were carried out in the NHS Andrology laboratory in parallel with an active research programme led by Stewart Irvine (University Lecturer). The funding to set up the IVF service had come from research funds. These were the early days of campaigning for an increase in NHS funding for IVF, but the reality of that time was that many resourced treatments for themselves. The income from treatment, paid for the critical investment in staff, equipment and the development of the service. It is interesting to note that many of the clinical staff employed over the years subsequently became senior members of staff in the Maternity Hospital, while many others went on to establish themselves in careers in reproductive medicine elsewhere in the United Kingdom and beyond.

The regulation of the sector was delegated to the Human Fertilisation and Embryology Authority by an Act of Parliament in 1990 and the Centre received its first licence shortly after. Professor Alan Templeton served on the Authority for several years in the early 2000s and was instrumental in the promotion of database research using the national registry established by the Authority. The Clinic also set up an in-house clinical and demographic database relevant to every patient attending the clinic. This was modelled on the Aberdeen Maternity and Neonatal Databank, so successfully introduced by Sir Dugald Baird, and has since provided valuable data for many influential linkage studies.

The amalgam of safe and effective patient-centred clinical care allied to high impact research cemented Aberdeen's burgeoning national reputation as a centre of excellence. Through the '90s and '00s new options in Assisted Reproduction emerged at a bewilderingly fast rate and all who worked within the Centre felt themselves to be at the cutting edge of innovation in laboratory and clinical science. Aberdeen's approach was always to embrace the new technologies with vigour and as a consequence the history of the service closely followed that of the history of the specialty.

Breakthroughs

Male infertility had for so many years been an area of desolation within clinical practice. Little had been able to be offered to men with low or absent sperm counts. Donor insemination was a disappointing compromise for some, while for many their infertility remained unresolved. The development in Belgium of intra-cytoplasmic sperm injection (ICSI) as a laboratory technique was a major advance offering hope for men with even the lowest of sperm counts. One of the scientific team, Dr Srikantharajah, visited Brussels and thereafter initiated ICSI within AMH, resulting in the first baby born in Scotland using micro-assisted fertilisation in 1995.

Dr Asaratnam Srikantharajah was one of the scientific team who after visiting Europe, initiated ICSI within the Assisted Reproduction Unit in Aberdeen, resulting in the first baby born in Scotland using micro-assisted fertilisation in 1995.

(Photograph courtesy of Dr Mark Hamilton)

In men with azoospermia (absence of sperm in seminal fluid) techniques to retrieve sperm directly from the epididymis using micro-surgery were also first introduced to Scotland in Aberdeen. Many referrals from elsewhere in the country came to the Centre in these distressing cases. Improved laboratory space and equipment was required and in 1993 the laboratories moved from a single room to an expanded suite of rooms on the former research ward on the Maternity Top floor. This allowed the installation of a dedicated ICSI laboratory in what had been a sluice area in the ward.

Cryobiology, or the freezing of sperm, eggs and embryos was a significant adjunct to routine treatment. Aberdeen generated the first babies in Scotland from cryopreserved embryos. Pioneering work within the unit on oocyte freezing and subsequent options to fertilise the thawed egg were tested and provided the first evidence to recommend ICSI as the insemination technique of choice. The science of screening embryos for genetic abnormality before implantation within the uterus was in its infancy and the research programme within the centre carried out several influential studies in this emerging field. A philosophy of attracting talented clinicians and scientists to Aberdeen to train in the practice of advanced reproductive medicine and learn and carry out research was established.

Regulation

A heavily regulated area of medical practice was always subject to intense scrutiny and perforce the Centre had to respond to the demands of externally determined standards. Not least was the introduction of the European Union Tissues and Cells Directive (EUTCD) in 2004 when we were required to set up a Quality Management (QM) system. This had a massive effect on the sector throughout the country and units were required to radically upgrade administrative processes relevant to document control, validation of procedures, audit and quality outcomes, patient information, staff appraisal and many others. The impact this had cannot be underestimated and the demands on QM naive staff were enormous. Aberdeen Fertility Centre went about this with vigour and were the first unit in Scotland, and only the second in the UK, to obtain ISO 9001 certification in 2007. Clinical and administrative excellence led to a continuous stream of visitors to the Unit from many parts of the UK and Europe to learn from our experiences.

Beyond managerial change, the EUTCD also demanded a radical re-appraisal of the working environment, both in clinical and theatre areas. The need to upgrade air quality within the laboratory in accordance with Good Medical Practice Guidelines became a legal necessity. Crammed into the rooms of what had at one time been a postnatal maternity ward on the top floor of the hospital was never going to meet the standards and major investment was required or the unit would be faced with the threat of closure. An agreement between NHS Grampian and the University led to a major refurbishment of the laboratory and theatre space within the Centre costing some £1 million. The transformation was remarkable, and the laboratories were kitted out with state-of-the-art equipment. Allied to the capital investment by the NHS was a commitment by the university-run service to bring down the then-lengthy waiting times for NHS funded treatment to less than one year.

National leadership

The national picture with respect to the funding and organisation of clinical services in infertility has transformed in the last 20 years. The hugely influential Expert Advisory Group on Infertility Services in Scotland (EAGISS) report in 1999 initiated a progressive improvement in Health Board investment available to deliver on unmet need. Further impetus in improving access to treatment has been maintained through the continued work of the National Fertility Group and many in Aberdeen have been significant contributors to this effort. It is fair to say that in Scotland the national approach to establishing equity in access to care has been a model of good commissioning practice and without question we enjoy the most favourable funding profile within the whole United Kingdom. More than 70 per cent of the cycles carried out in the unit are now funded by the NHS. Furthermore, the eligibility criteria for NHS funding and the number of cycles available per couple is uniform throughout the country. The postcode lottery of unfairness, which pervades commissioning elsewhere in the UK, does not apply in Scotland, a matter of which we can be proud.

Commissioning healthcare has the capability of influencing clinical practice for the better. Allan Templeton, in his role as President of the Royal College of Obstetricians and Gynaecologists, and myself, in my role as Chair of the British Fertility Society, contributed significantly to the promotion of single-embryo transfer as the norm. National procurement in Scotland, predicated on the principle of achieving health gain with minimal risk for patients, for the most part, explicitly requires single embryo transfer, thereby reducing the risk of generating multiple pregnancies. Forty years or so after Klopper's initial observations on the impact of multiple birth perhaps we can be assured that his concerns have, in general, been addressed.

Training

The comprehensive nature of reproductive medicine care requires the establishment of collaborative clinical practice across a range of disciplines. Nationally, RCOG approved subspecialty training programmes were established across the country from the mid-1980s.

Templeton was a strong advocate for this level of training in the several subspecialist areas of Obstetrics and Gynaecology. Recognition as a training centre in Feto-Maternal Medicine was achieved in the late 1980s and Reproductive Medicine followed in 1991. I assumed Directorship of the programme and Dr Umesh Acharya successfully completed his programme in 1994. Notably, Aberdeen was the first centre in the country to establish training in four subspecialty areas at the same time with additional programmes active in Gynae-oncology and Sexual and Reproductive Health, a remarkable achievement for the time.

In Reproductive Medicine, links with colleagues across a great number of specialties throughout the Foresterhill Campus were established. Combined clinics were delivered in Urology (by Sam McClinton), General endocrinology (John Bevan), Paediatric endocrinology (Amalia Mayo) and many others. Reproductive Surgery, and in particular laparoscopic management of endometriosis, required high level input and Dr Peter Fisher, and subsequently Dr Kevin Cooper, contributed notably in this regard. Genetics and the associated new technologies were increasingly relevant to clinical practice, and Professor Neva Haites, Dr John Dean and Professor Zosia Miedzybrodska from the Genetics Department, were willing and enthusiastic colleagues. Collaboration with the Neonatal Unit was often required, particularly when dealing with the obstetric challenges in complex cases, sometimes associated with multiple pregnancy.

Our subspecialty training programme has been immensely successful and following Dr Acharya a succession of outstanding trainees emerged equipped to lead clinical services in many parts of the UK and beyond, as well as in several instances locally in Aberdeen.

The scale of operations compared to the pioneering days has increased markedly. Each year in Aberdeen over 700 new couples are now referred with infertility. A steady referral rate in Gynaecological Endocrinology currently exists, approximately 70 cases per year. Once a month there is a combined Andrology Clinic served by a consultant urologist and a combined Reproductive Endocrinology Clinic shared with a consultant physician. Donor insemination, ovulation induction with gonadotrophins and microsurgery are carried out exclusively under the auspices of the Fertility-Endocrine Clinic. A dedicated Recurrent Miscarriage Clinic takes place once a month and counselling and support for these patients are provided through the Fertility Clinic. Collaboration with Paediatric Endocrine and SARH colleagues facilitate the delivery of paediatric gynaecology services. The Scottish Genital Anomaly Network is a valued collaborator. The Assisted Reproduction Unit (ARU) carries out more than 500 fresh cycles of IVF & ICSI per year with a further 120 cryopreserved embryo transfer cycles in addition. Many referrals from outside the region are direct to the unit, bypassing the more common channel of referral via the Infertility Clinic. An active oocyte donation programme exists. Fertility preservation for those facing potentially sterilising treatment for cancer and other conditions is a significant advance. Surrogacy services are available. Multidisciplinary team meetings regularly occur to agree clinical care for those with complex medical, genetic and surgical problems.

Research

Research is integral to the function of the Neonatal Unit and a broad portfolio of interests is maintained. These have included the Chief Scientists Office (CSO), Wellcome Trust and the National Institute of Health Research (NIHR) funded work in several key areas encompassing systematic reviews of interventions in infertility, studies on the epidemiology of reproductive failure and clinical trials. A worldwide network of collaboration evolved with internationally based research colleagues in Auckland, London, Athens, Nottingham, Sao Paolo, Egypt, USA, Hong Kong, Australia, Denmark and the Netherlands. Under the leadership of Professors Siladitya Bhattacharya and Abha Maheshwari, Aberdeen Reproductive Medicine continues to lead international opinion in clinically relevant spheres.

The distress and pain of unwanted childlessness presents a severe burden on as many as one in six couples of reproductive age. Aberdeen has a proud record stretching back many decades in innovation and excellence in the delivery of care. Many individuals who have contributed to Aberdeen's history in reproductive medicine are reluctantly and with apologies are not mentioned here. However, any and all who worked in the fertility centre held and continue to hold it in deep affection and take pride in their association with the service. The opening of the Baird Family Hospital will be yet another exciting chapter in the story of how we deal with the broad range of problems, uncertainties, options and challenges faced in this most fascinating of clinical subjects.

15

Midwife Education

Fiona Gibb

MIDWIFERY IS ONE of the world's oldest occupations with many references in ancient Greek and Roman texts and was even mentioned in the Old Testament. The word midwife is from old English, meaning 'with woman', referring to the individual who is with the mother at childbirth. Before the 17th century, midwives were usually women without formal education or qualification and had various degrees of experience of pregnancy and childbirth. Midwifery knowledge would have been shared verbally or practically, through apprenticeships or working with lay midwives. Established midwives were known to their local communities and were called to help based on their reputation. Often, being a grandmother was the only credential a midwife had or needed and to this day the word for midwife is the same as grandmother in many languages. In Scotland, midwives were known as 'howdies' or, in the North East of Scotland, 'howdie wifies'.

As medical education became more developed from the mid-18th century, it became more common for male practitioners, or 'accoucheurs', to attend births and consequently medical men came to dominate midwifery education. Formal midwifery education training courses were established in Edinburgh by Professor of Midwifery Joseph Gibson in 1726, which was the first in the UK. Pupil midwives would attend lectures, or a medical professional led course, or would work in one of the few maternity hospitals. In Aberdeen, the earliest record of systematic midwifery education was in 1758 when Dr David Skene established midwifery lectures with Dr John Gregory. The 'Aberdeen Dispensary, Vaccine and Lying-in Institution' was something of a misnomer since it was not until 1892 that six midwives were attached to the dispensary. In these times, 95 per cent of women were delivered at home with a 'howdie' who learned by apprenticeship but with no structured training or registration.

These visiting midwives, who will have had local training of some sort, quickly found that home conditions were very bad with serious overcrowding, and it was evident that a central maternity hospital was essential. In the beginning there was difficulty in getting people interested in the project, but the managers of the new dispensary had decided to rent a house in Barnett's Close for the lying-in department where 'patients whose houses are too wretched for them to receive proper attention could be placed under thoroughly trained nurses and receive some comfort at a most critical and trying period'. (Dr David Skene)

In the 19th century, each of the four main maternity hospitals in Scotland – Aberdeen, Dundee, Glasgow and Edinburgh – worked separately, and certificates were awarded to midwives who trained there. The Aberdeen Medico-Chirurgical Society, however, had already started their register of midwives which enhanced the practice of midwifery in the city and anticipated the future registration of midwives by almost a century. The society established a Midwives Board in 1827 and no member of the society would recognise a midwife unless she was registered.

Although there were efforts to formalise education and regulation of midwives prior to the 20th century, it was the Midwives Act in England and Wales (1902), Scotland (1915) and Ireland (1918) which outlined the framework for training, registration, and regulation of midwives, and protected the legal

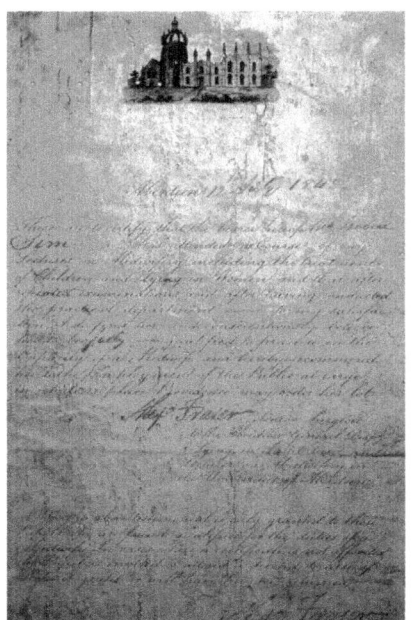

Left: Handwritten Midwifery Course Certificate issued 1842. The text reds:

These are to certify that the bearer thereof Mrs Isobel Sim ____ has attended one course of my Lectures on Midwifery including the treatment of Children and Lying-in Women, and that after repeated examinations, and after having conducted the practical deportment ____ to my satisfaction, I do find her and conscientiously believe her to be fully____ qualified to practice in the capacity of a Midwife, and hereby recommend her to the Employment of the Public at large in whatever place Providence may order her to do.

Alex. Fraser, Senior Surgeon

To the Aberdeen General Dispry. & Lying-in Institution and Lecturer in Midwifery in the Universities of Aberdeen.

N.B. The above testimonial is only granted to those Pupils who are found qualified for the duties of a Midwife. In cases when a certificate is not afforded the Pupil is invited to attend a Second Course of Lectures gratis or will have her fee returned.

Alexr. Fraser

(Reproduced by permission of Aberdeen Medico-Chirurgical Society)

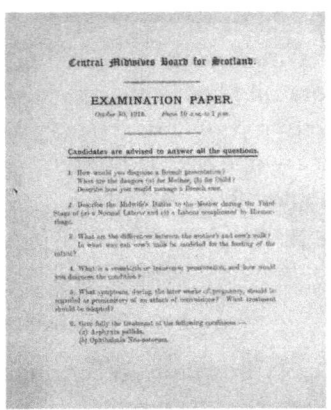

CMB Examination Paper, 1916.
(Courtesy of National Records of Scotland, CMB 4/5/1)

professional status of the midwifery title. Up until 1915, any person in Scotland could call themselves a midwife and could practice. However, this became illegal following the implementation of the Act.

Consequently, the Central Midwives Board (CMB) was established to promote consistency in the education and regulation of midwives across Scotland and the rest of the UK. The CMB was responsible for approving training institutions, reviewing curriculum for student midwives and validating who could teach and examine students' competence prior to sitting the CMB examination. The first course was three months and midwives kept case books of all births attended. The first exams were held on 11 February 1915 and on 30 October 1916. Aberdeen Maternity Hospital was unconditionally approved for midwifery training by the CMB institution in 1916. Those who taught were either lecturers who were medical practitioners with relevant experience or teachers who were experienced midwives, both of which had to be approved by the board.

The early training of nurses in Aberdeen at the Aberdeen Royal Infirmary in 1875, the trustees of the late Robert Donaldson 'offered to grant a sum of money yearly to approved applicants who might... desire and agree to qualify themselves as Nurses'. This became known as the Donaldson Scheme, under which women undertook 12 months of training on the wards. Preference was given to applicants 'willing to receive a portion of their time in the Fever Wards'. At the end of the 12-month period, eligible nurses received a Certificate of Efficiency and a monetary payment, 'the whole amount, including Dress, Lodging and Gratuity, not to exceed Fifteen Pounds to each Person'. The hospital's administrators reported that the services of the trained nurses 'are much valued and eagerly sought by professional men and private families'.

The first national nurse training scheme was introduced in 1885 with Scottish Poor Law legislation. By 1886, Rachel Frances Lumsden, the matron or Lady Superintendent at the Aberdeen Royal Infirmary, who had given her services voluntarily, had initiated a system of nurse training which included three courses of lectures – general nursing, elementary anatomy and surgical nursing, and elementary physiology and medical nursing. Five years later a three-year training programme was introduced. By 1901 the average hospital nurse

received 17 pounds annually plus maintenance for a 70-hour week... and could be hired out for private nursing by her hospital to boost fee income.

This hiring out of nurses was an important source of extra income for the hospital as trained nurses were much in demand by the upper and middle classes.

Midwifery training and education expanded radically between 1916 and 1983. The course was six months for those who were nurses, and 12 months for those who were not (known as direct entry midwifery). An option existed in the late 1950s to train for six months in Aberdeen and six months outside the city. Lectures were increased in number and provided a wider range of maternity care knowledge with inclusion of wider antenatal care principles. It was mandatory for students to witness ten births before they could attend a birth themselves. Thereafter they had to provide care for at least 20 women within an approved training institution with at least five cases within womens' homes.

As the CMB revised their rules over the years, there was progression from midwifery 'on the job training' to more formal 'education' with recognised academic achievement. There were many prolific midwives who were at the forefront of developing the profession through publication and education, including Sheila Kitzinger (1929–2015), Mary Cronk (1932–2018) and Ina May Gaskin (1940). In 1954, (the year of her retiral), a seminal education textbook, *Myles Textbook for Midwives* by Aberdeen Midwife Maggie Myles (1892–1988), was published. Maggie travelled the world promoting the formal education of midwives and as a result became a revered international midwifery educator. Ten different editions of the textbook were released in her lifetime with the 17th edition published in 2020 still on the essential reading list for student midwives today. Maggie edited nine of the first ten editions herself.

Education for midwives and nurses in Aberdeen was further developed when the Foresterhill College of Nursing opened in May 1967 with an initial complement of 850 students. The CMB agreed the college could provide the theoretical element of student midwife teaching, however, due to the fact the Principal was not a midwife, Aberdeen Maternity Hospital became the approved institution with the matron in charge of recruiting and supervising students who had received the theoretical education in the college. Midwifery education did not physically move into the college until 1988.

One major modification to midwifery education at this time was the cessation of direct entry midwifery courses in 1968 across the UK, meaning that all midwives had to be registered nurses before they could undertake education as midwives. This controversial decision continued to be debated until the 1980s with some arguing that a nursing background was essential to practice safely as a midwife and others who argued that this further contributed to a medical model of childbirth. The publication of the Peel Report (Maternity and Midwifery Advisory Committee, 1970) named after John Peel, a consultant obstetrician, recommended 100 per cent hospital birth, which led to an increased use in medical technology and the dramatic move from away from birth at home which had been the most common place of birth till this time.

In 1972, the UK joined the European Economic Community and consequently the first EEC Midwifery Directives were implemented in the UK in 1980. These directives presented two ways that a person could become a midwife: either after three years of direct-entry midwifery training or two years midwifery training for those who were already nurses. The CMB agreed on 18 months of education for registered nurses. However, they could not agree on direct entry midwifery in Scotland, despite the availability of courses across European countries. It was nearly ten years later in 1990s before direct entry midwifery courses were re-introduced in Scotland. This coincided with a significant change in policy rhetoric to promote choice of maternity care and place of birth at the turn of the 21st century.

In 1983, following changes to legislation and organisation of healthcare, the CMB was disbanded and the United Kingdom Central Council for Nurses, Midwives and Health Visitors (UKCC) was set up, which eventually evolved into the Nursing and Midwifery Council (NMC) in 2002. The NMC continue to set the educational standards and approve midwifery programmes in universities to this day. Education transferred from the NHS to the university sector in the mid-1990s with the aim of raising the societal profile of midwives and the profession and widening access to a range of educational and research resources.

Nursing and Midwifery education in Aberdeen transferred from Foresterhill College to Robert Gordon University (RGU) in 1996 and became the School of Nursing and Midwifery. Direct-entry midwifery returned to Aberdeen in 2001. The design of midwifery education continued to evolve and since 2009 midwifery has been an all-graduate degree profession and the majority of courses across the UK are now direct entry. RGU continues to be one of only three approved educational institutions in Scotland providing pre-registration midwifery and students undertake placements across six NHS boards in the north of Scotland, including NHS Grampian.

In 2020, the school was renamed the School of Nursing, Midwifery and Paramedic Practice to reflect the portfolio of healthcare education. Student midwives complete 4,600 hours of education divided between an equal balance of theory in university and clinical practice over a minimum of three years full time (NMC 2019). Despite the UK leaving the EU, courses continue to comply with the EU Directives for the recognition of professional qualification which includes that student midwives must provide care to at least 100 women antenatally and 100 women and their babies postnatally as well as support at least 40 women to give birth. Midwifery practice itself is changing and promotes the Scottish Government (2017) 'Best Start' recommendations for maternity care which emphasises that all women, babies and families receive equitable, high quality, safe and compassionate care. The NHS is usually the first employing organisation for midwives at the start of their career and the strong partnerships between the university and the NHS prepare midwives not just for registration but ongoing continuing professional development to deliver evidence-based care.

Over a century on since the Midwives Act in Scotland, careers in midwifery have expanded much further than previous generations with a variety of roles across management, leadership, education and research. As the needs of women and families change over time and maternity care advances, there are many career pathways for midwives covering diverse roles, be that a Specialist Midwife, Consultant, Lecturer or Researcher. Midwifery education continues to be at the forefront, not only so that midwives fulfil their potential but also to push forward maternity care for women and their families and the future development of the profession.

16

Pregnancy and Diabetes

Donald WM Pearson and Hamish W Sutherland

1882 Puerperal diabetes – the first case series

THE STREETS OF London were busy when James Matthews Duncan left the Obstetric Society after his presidential lecture. He had attended school and university in Aberdeen where he had graduated MA in 1843 and MD in 1846. Throughout his distinguished career, he published extensively on many aspects of obstetric practice; he coined the term 'missed abortion' and described the mechanism of placental separation. However, he had chosen the topic 'Puerperal Diabetes' for his lecture to the Obstetric Society in London in 1882. His subsequent publication in the Obstetric Society of London's Transactions is considered the first clinical series addressing the problems associated with diabetes and pregnancy.

In the 19th century, girls and young women had a very poor outlook if they developed diabetes mellitus. Those with 'severe' diabetes were often infertile and underweight, and most young people with this type of diabetes did not survive till adulthood. Matthews Duncan commented that 'the notices of any special influence of diabetes on the female function are very scanty and of very little value'.

From his own experience and in review of the literature published before 1882, he identified 22 pregnancies in 15 women aged between 21 and 38 years who had a range of clinical situations. Some women had established diabetes before pregnancy and others developed diabetes of varying severity during pregnancy. The foetus died in 13 out of the 19 recorded pregnancies; the mother died during pregnancy or within a year in nine of the cases.

If he had been able to look into the future, Matthews Duncan would have been intrigued to learn that many clinical and scientific advances in the field of diabetes and pregnancy were introduced by people trained in Aberdeen working elsewhere or by university and hospital staff working in the North East of Scotland. Advances would include crucial developments such as the discovery of insulin, the promotion of self-management, hosting key international meetings to share knowledge and the development of national and international guidelines. The clinical services for women with diabetes in the North East of Scotland developed in parallel with scientific advances. This chapter will consider how services for women with established Diabetes Mellitus (mainly type-1 DM) and for women with Gestational Diabetes (GDM) evolved in the Aberdeen Maternity Hospital.

Seeking solutions 1900–30

Local initiatives to treat diabetes

When our physiological knowledge is somewhat further advanced, and when skilled observers have occupied the field, all diseases… will have their puerperal variations well defined, and suitable therapies adjusted to them.
—James Matthews Duncan, 1882

Thomas Fraser and John James Rickard Macleod graduated MB ChB at the University of Aberdeen in 1898. Fraser spent his career in the North East of Scotland where he held the position of Obstetric Physician as well as a range of other clinical roles before he became a General Practitioner in the city. Most of Macleod's research was undertaken in North America, though he returned to Aberdeen as Regius Professor of Physiology for the last few years of his academic career.

Between 1880 and 1920, scientists around the world were investigating the pancreas and attempting to isolate the pancreatic substance which had the key role in regulating blood sugar levels. The islets of Langerhans were considered as the pancreatic source of the glucose lowering factor, but it proved very difficult to separate the active component of the islets from the digestive 'exocrine' cells of the pancreas. Both young Aberdeen graduates of 1898 became involved in the search for an effective cure.

In 1901, the Aberdeen zoologist Dr John Rennie found that the 'principal islet' of monkfish could represent a more accessible source of the active substance for the treatment of diabetes. Between 1901 and 1907 Rennie and his physician-accoucheur colleague Dr Thomas Fraser carried out a series of experiments on patients with diabetes in Aberdeen Royal Infirmary at Woolmanhill. At this time 'severe' diabetes had a very poor prognosis with no effective treatment available. Attempts at treatment using the fish extract given by mouth or, on occasion, by injection over periods of a few weeks produced disappointing results but an effect was recorded in some. The extract had minimal effect if boiled and given by mouth and caused a local reaction when given by injection. However, one patient showed a significant improvement with a fall in urine glucose excretion and some weight gain. Unfortunately, the patient died eight days after the supply of islets ran out. However, groups throughout the world struggled to find an effective treatment during the early years of the 20th century – no treatment was available for children and young women with diabetes. Life expectancy was short, infertility was common, and pregnancy was extremely dangerous. The prognosis for young women with diabetes would remain perilous until the breakthrough was made 3,000 miles away by a team led by the other eminent Aberdeen graduate.

A major breakthrough – the discovery of insulin

On 31 May 1931, the Regius Professor of Physiology at the University of Aberdeen left his office in Marischal College and turned left towards King Street rather than turning right to go home to Bieldside. Professor John James Rickard Macleod was back in the city where he had graduated in 1898, having returned as Regius Professor of Physiology in 1928. He had had a very distinguished undergraduate career with numerous prizes including the Matthews Duncan medal in Obstetrics. After graduating in Aberdeen, he had been awarded the Anderson Scholarship which funded distinguished graduates to pursue research for up to two years. He studied physiological chemistry in Leipzig. His research continued in London and in 1903, aged 27, he was invited to apply for the Chair of Physiology at Western Reserve University in Cleveland, USA. He became an international authority on carbohydrate metabolism; he published on a range of topics and lectured extensively. In 1918 he moved to the University of Toronto where the facilities and support for scientists were excellent.

That evening in Aberdeen, in 1931, he was to address the Aberdeen Medico-Chirurgical Society on the subject 'Some problems in Diabetes'. Carbohydrate metabolism had always been fascinating for Macleod. His textbook *Physiology and Biochemistry in Modern Medicine* had run to several editions and his research had a focus on metabolism. Around ten years earlier in the University of Toronto a young surgeon named Frederick Banting had approached him seeking lab space and animals to investigate an idea.

Banting wanted to investigate a potential way of isolating the internal secretion of the pancreas. Macleod agreed to provide laboratory facilities for Banting, showed him how to perform some of the procedures on the dogs, helped design the experiments and allocated a medical student, Charles Best, to help Banting with laboratory analysis such as blood glucose measurement. After some promising early results, the biological chemist James Collip joined the group. In a short space of time the group developed a method of extracting a purer form of the active substance which Macleod named insulin.

Insulin was effective when given subcutaneously but care was required to avoid excessive doses. The group expended great effort, energy and thought to prove the importance of their discovery and that the extract corrected the metabolic abnormalities in diabetes. On 11 January 1922, after a remarkably short period of intense research and multiple experiments on animals, insulin was used in clinical practice to treat a young man with 'severe' diabetes. The patient thrived on insulin injections; the Toronto group had made one of the most important discoveries of the 20th century. Banting and Macleod were awarded the Nobel Prize in 1923. Banting shared his prize with Best, and Macleod shared his with Collip.

Perhaps some of Matthews Duncan's concerns about 'Puerperal diabetes' could now be addressed. With insulin treatment, women with diabetes survived, regained weight and saw their fertility returned. Maternal mortality associated with pregnancy reduced dramatically but the perinatal mortality rate remained very high. New approaches would be required.

How would this new treatment be introduced across the globe? In Aberdeen the challenge of initiating insulin would be taken up by a young man who graduated around the time of the discovery and another Aberdeen graduate played the leading role in developing diabetes care across Great Britain.

Early diabetes clinical services – 1920s to 1950s

Introducing Insulin to the North East of Scotland

Alexander 'Sandy' Lyall was severely injured at the Battle of Ypres in 1917, but after a year in hospital he returned to Aberdeen to graduate MA in 1920 and MB ChB with Honours in 1923. As the most distinguished graduate of his year, he gained a scholarship from 1924 to 1926 to work in St Thomas' Hospital in London where another Aberdonian, Professor Hugh MacLean, held the Chair of Medicine.

MacLean had turned his attention, and that of his department, to the study of diabetes and Lyall had the opportunity to experience one of the first diabetic clinics in Britain.

Sandy Lyall returned to Aberdeen to take up his appointment as Consultant Physician in Metabolic Diseases and Consultant in charge of one of the first Departments of Clinical Chemistry in the UK.

His laboratory was in the Outpatients Department, Aberdeen Royal Infirmary, Woolmanhill. A follow-up system for people with diabetes was established and by 1927 there was 'an embryo of a diabetic clinic'. Lyall reports:

Care of the diabetic mothers formed a separate study and complete cooperation was established with the Physicians and Obstetricians of the Old Maternity Hospital at Castlehill and the Maternity Hospital at Foresterhill.

Women with diabetes were visited in the wards by Sandy Lyall or his colleague Peter Mitchell and seen as out-patients in the diabetic clinic. The practice of medicine in the 1920s was very different from the 2020s. Few effective drugs were available, and insulin was totally different from anything that had preceded it. It had to be given by injection subcutaneously with glass syringes and was very effective but also dangerous if too much was administered. Monitoring with urinalysis was time consuming and results did not reflect current blood glucose levels. In pregnancy, urinalysis could be misleading. Education of people diagnosed with diabetes was essential to ensure insulin would be used effectively and appropriately. Another Aberdeen graduate was sharing his personal and professional experience of diabetes to improve diabetes management across Britain and beyond.

Initial experience with insulin in pregnancy – 1930s to 1950s

I've got some insulin. Come back quick it works.
—1923 telegram for RD Lawrence

Aberdeen medical graduate Robert 'Robin' Daniel Lawrence received this telegram from a colleague with whom he had worked in King's College Hospital in London. The young Aberdonian had developed diabetes mellitus in November 1920 and had followed the very strict diet which was the only treatment option for people with his type of diabetes. The 'starvation' diet meant food was withheld till ketonuria resolved. Food was gradually introduced till ketones reappeared. Lawrence's health deteriorated despite adhering to the diet and he moved his medical practice to Florence since he had been advised that the climate may help his condition. But his urine was full of sugar and acetone, and he was losing weight. He was sceptical about any possible treatment for his condition. However, he decided to return to London. He started subcutaneous insulin and made a remarkable recovery. Lawrence recognised the complexities of insulin treatment and the importance of education to facilitate self-management. People with diabetes needed careful instruction and education on insulin administration, diet, exercise, monitoring and indeed all aspects of life.

In 1925 Lawrence published the first edition of *The Diabetic ABC* for patients and *The Diabetic Life* for professionals. These publications provided simple instructions on how someone with diabetes could cope with the challenges of diabetes in everyday life. Over the next 30 years Lawrence became the dominant figure in British diabetes.

He built up the diabetic service in King's College Hospital and, with the author HG Wells, set up the joint patient–professional organisation, the British Diabetic Association (now Diabetes UK). In addition to his instruction manuals, he published academic articles on clinical and scientific diabetes topics. Lawrence's extensive clinical practice and personal experience of diabetes gave him considerable scope to develop the field of clinical diabetes.

Lawrence's opinions on marriage and pregnancy in diabetes changed considerably during his lifetime. During the first decade after the discovery of insulin, Lawrence wrote that pregnancy in women with diabetes was uncommon and the benefit of insulin was almost exclusively on maternal mortality. In the 1920s, his advice was dominated by considerations regarding the inheritance of diabetes and the risks of pregnancy to the mother. In earlier editions of *The Diabetic Life* he wrote:

> Marriage is not dangerous to men... women must be cautioned of the danger to themselves as well as to their offspring. The balance of opinion is that, while marriage cannot justly be forbidden, pregnancy is highly inadvisable in all but the exceptional case.

Until the mid-1930s this was the standard approach. Indeed, I met a co-helper at a Diabetes UK Children's Camp in the 1980s and she had been advised against marriage only a few decades before. By 1937, Lawrence took a much more positive approach: 'many cases have been successfully conducted through pregnancy by the use of insulin and usually a normal child is born'.

He had a longstanding interest in diabetes and pregnancy and reported that he had followed 200 cases before 1941, and 141 cases between 1941 and 1948. This was a much greater experience than most clinicians could expect, even in heavily populated cities. Most centres had a few pregnancies each year and it was difficult to draw conclusions about optimal management.

In his 1942 paper he reported on 54 pregnancies with an overall foetal loss of 33 per cent. He noted that foetal loss was reduced to 23 per cent with 'optimal care' but was 70 per cent without optimal care. Results in the UK remained poor until the 1950s when clinicians decided to admit all pregnant women at 32 weeks and deliver them at 36 weeks. The original reason for admission, during which the woman was in bed for 20 hours a day, was 'to improve blood flow to the uterus'. However, this also meant the diabetes could be better monitored and controlled. Results improved on this regimen and foetal mortality fell from 25 per cent to 13 per cent. These findings had a major influence on clinical practice across the UK during the 20th century but changes were happening towards the middle of the century as new approaches were appearing across the globe.

Developing the service

The evidence of physiology makes it certain that pregnancy brings about important changes in the quantity or constituents of the blood.
—James Matthews Duncan

Clinical practice for women with diabetes in Aberdeen Maternity Hospital changed with the appointment of Dr (later Professor) John Marcus Stowers. He had an interesting background. He was born in Nagpar, India on 3 March 1919. After completing his undergraduate and post graduate training in London at University College Hospital (UCH) and Harvard University he was appointed to the post of Senior Lecturer in Medicine and Consultant in the Professorial Unit in Dundee. In 1961 he moved from Dundee to Aberdeen to the post of Consultant Physician with a special interest in metabolic diseases. John Stowers had developed type-1 diabetes when he was a young man. He believed that people with diabetes should lead a full and active life and keep blood glucose levels as near to the normal range as possible. This was challenging in the 1960s since diabetes was self-monitored by urinalysis which was time consuming and of varying reliability. Urinalysis was particularly unreliable in pregnancy.

Stowers felt that the prolonged inpatient model of pregnancy care was unsuitable for women in the North East of Scotland, where half of the population lived outside the city of Aberdeen. He followed European thinking on pregnancy management whereby women had frequent and systematic clinic review during pregnancy but no routine admissions unless necessary.

The combined service

A weekly, joint antenatal clinic started in Aberdeen Maternity Hospital in 1962. Women with diabetes had a joint consultation with a midwife, diabetologist and obstetrician in the same clinic room. On site access to laboratory staff, dieticians (since 1977), social work and diabetes specialist nurses developed over the years. Staff often referred to it as the 'combined clinic' since it represented a combination of several health professional disciplines. The main aim was to admit women to hospital as infrequently as possible and arrange discharge from hospital as quickly as possible. This approach was different from the model followed by some UK centres, as mentioned above, in the 1960s. Hamish Sutherland was appointed Senior Lecturer and Consultant in Obstetrics in 1970. Over the next 20 years Stowers and Sutherland and others from different disciplines developed a clinical service and research team which gained an international reputation. Over the course of pregnancy, women with diabetes interacted with a whole range of professionals at the combined clinic. The clinic midwife could involve the diabetes specialist nurse or dietitian for a particular issue before directing the patient to the consulting room with the physician and obstetrician. The consultation was usually a combination of interactions between the woman, midwife, obstetrician and the physician. As pregnancy progressed, the balance shifted from mainly diabetes issues to mainly obstetric issues. Increasing numbers of patients over the decades meant that two teams of obstetricians and physicians were needed to see all the patients, and although the aim was to support women as much as possible in the community by regular review admission to the Ashgrove antenatal ward was a regular occurrence.

Effective in-patient services for women with diabetes were crucial to ensure optimal blood glucose control accompanied high quality midwifery care. Lesley Mowat, the midwifery sister, had special training in diabetes. She herself trained many junior (and senior) doctors, midwives and, most importantly, pregnant women on the practical ways to manage their diabetes effectively. Outside the combined clinic, the antenatal ward became the focal point for the combined team. In-patients were seen on the daily ward round and reviewed at some point by a visiting diabetologist. Lesley trained a cohort of midwives on the practicalities of diabetes management. Dieticians visited Ashgrove Ward and the post-natal wards regularly. The principles of management in the combined clinic, the antenatal ward, the labour suite and neonatal care all developed in parallel with research and educational initiatives across all the relevant specialties.

The Pre-pregnancy Clinic (PPC)

In Grampian, all healthcare professionals in contact with women who had established diabetes were made aware of the importance of planning pregnancy and the local arrangements for care of pregnant women. When young girls were transferred from RACH to the adult diabetes clinic at age 14, mothers of the children were often surprised that contraception, the PPC and pregnancy services were included when the various clinical support services were explained to their daughters. During the 1970s, Dr Anne Brunt, clinical specialist at the Diabetic Clinic at Woolmanhill, worked in liaison with the Royal Aberdeen Children's Hospital clinic and had an outpatient list at Woolmanhill which accommodated young women in their reproductive years. Contraception and family planning could be discussed with this group.

In Aberdeen, the PPC was initially integrated into the Tuesday afternoon combined clinic but in the 2000s it was set up as a standalone clinic at the JJR Macleod Centre for Diabetes, Endocrinology and Metabolism at Foresterhill.

Studies published from Aberdeen reported the significant benefits from pre-pregnancy care. The comprehensive pre-pregnancy programme was set up to optimise glycemic control prior to conception, review all medications, assess fitness for pregnancy (screening and managing complications), check rubella status and other blood tests, like renal function, thyroid function, and encourage a healthy lifestyle, like stopping smoking. Folic acid is routinely taken when contraception is discontinued.

The pre-pregnancy clinic was an opportunity to introduce an intensive insulin regimen if required. Over the decades, women moved from twice daily premixed insulin to four or five injections a day to continuous subcutaneous insulin infusion (CSII) via an insulin pump. Self-monitoring by urinalysis was superseded by blood glucose monitoring in the 1970s. Glycosylated haemoglobin (HbA1c) is a blood test which reflects blood glucose control over the previous 12 weeks approximately. It was very useful pre-pregnancy to decide when it would be advisable to discontinue contraception. The nearer the HbA1c to the normal range the less risk of congenital abnormality in the offspring. In later pregnancy, HbA1c values need to be interpreted in the context of pregnancy but it can provide a useful guide if control is deteriorating. At the PPC, previous obstetric and gynaecological issues are identified and infertility is managed if there is a delay in conception. Contraception is discontinued when blood glucose control is optimal.

Optimising blood glucose control

Blood glucose control was assessed by a combination of home blood monitoring results and HBA1C, which as noted above reflects longer term blood glucose control. The PPC was often the first opportunity for women and their partners to meet Sister Lesley Mowat and the midwife team. She reinforced their skills in blood glucose monitoring, management of diabetes during intercurrent illness and management of hypoglycaemia. She would support them through pregnancy and kept in touch with many families long after delivery.

Around 50 per cent of women attended for formal pre-pregnancy care with the other 50 per cent attending for care already pregnant. Although some had not attended for formal pre-pregnancy care, most women knew of the service and had been made aware of the importance of good control in early pregnancy, so they made an appointment whenever they suspected they were pregnant. Women who had attended for formal pre-pregnancy care were invited to an appointment for the combined clinic as soon as a period was missed.

Management of type-1 diabetes in early pregnancy

Maintaining optimal blood glucose control during early pregnancy can be very challenging. Insulin requirements are variable. Appetite is changing and morning sickness occasionally evolves to hyperemesis gravidarum (excessive vomiting associated with pregnancy). Thankfully, this is an unusual complication in women with diabetes.

Women with type-1 DM (Diabetes Mellitus) who had attended the PPC usually did not require admission to the antenatal ward, but others sometimes needed a short admission in early pregnancy for intensive education and optimisation of blood glucose control.

Glucose monitoring technical ability was assessed and glucose meters were updated by the nursing team. Stowers noted in 1983:

> The advent of the era of patients monitoring their own blood glucose
> level has been attended by a progressive reduction of the time spent in
> hospital... they are admitted urgently if the control is bad or, of course,
> if the urine passed in the non-fasting state contains more than a trace of
> ketones to Acetest or ketostix.

At the first combined clinic visit after conception, the joint consultation would ensure all relevant obstetric and medical data were recorded, and a standard programme of review was followed for the rest of the pregnancy. Up till 28 weeks' gestation most women were seen at a minimum of monthly intervals, then two weekly intervals until 36 weeks and weekly (at least) until delivery. This was modified for women from the more distant regions of Grampian or the Islands so that some routine follow visits ups were done in places like Elgin, Fraserburgh or Lerwick.

During the 1970s and 1980s, in the general diabetes clinic population beyond pregnancy, many people in Grampian used a 'sliding scale' of twice-daily premixed insulin with 'reverse testing' (a guideline developed by Stowers whereby the morning test result was used to decide the evening dose and the previous dinner test was used to decide the breakfast dose). Prior to or during pregnancy this regimen was changed to a much more intensive one. The number of injections a day increased significantly with short acting insulin injected before meals and twice-daily basal (background) insulin before breakfast and before bed. Insulin pump therapy was used on an experimental basis in some centres in the 1980s, but, for most, use of pumps in pregnancy was put on hold for a couple of decades until the technology improved after the millennium. Insulin requirements sometimes drop towards the end of the first trimester but thereafter insulin requirements usually increase significantly. For some women, this proved very challenging and hypoglycaemia was an important consideration.

Hypoglycaemia unawareness is more common in pregnancy, and this can have implications for day- to-day living. A husband working away from home (perhaps offshore) may lead to a request for another family member or friend to spend the night with the insulin-injecting woman. Driving was not advised if hypoglycaemic awareness was lost during pregnancy. One of Lesley Mowat and her team's important tasks was to ensure partners knew how to recognise and manage hypoglycaemia. Glucagon injections (which reverses hypoglycaemia) were demonstrated so that severe episodes could be managed at home. High blood glucose levels also had to be avoided. Pregnancy is recognised as a condition of 'accelerated starvation'. This may have advantages in evolutionary terms since it means that the foetus has access to nutrition even if the mother has limited food supplies. However, this process depends on a careful balance between the various hormones, including insulin, that control lipid breakdown. During pregnancy, adequate insulin reserves can be depleted with the potential for the development of diabetic ketoacidosis (DKA). This is a very serious condition and was probably one of the causes of the very high maternal mortality described by Matthews Duncan in the pre-insulin era.

Managing the Problems

Foetal growth and macrosomia (large for dates babies)

The foetus is sometimes described as enormous, or its weight is extraordinary.—James Matthews Duncan, 1882

During the first International Colloquium on Carbohydrate Metabolism in Pregnancy and the Newborn held in Aberdeen in July 1973, there was discussion on the issue of foetal macrosomia (large for dates babies).

'Such infants present a striking almost pathognomonic picture. Most conspicuous is obesity, the round cherub's cheeks, buried eyes and short neck. Many infants have a plethoric appearance, reddened skin and an abundance of head hair'. The audience was reminded that:

Infants of diabetic mothers constitute a special population because they have been exposed to an abnormal intrauterine environment, and besides the surviving infants, form a new population being practically unknown 30 years ago.

Investigations carried out in Denmark had shown that, in comparison to control infants, newborn infants of diabetic mothers (IDM) weighed on average 550 grams more and were 1.5 cm longer than control infants of similar gestation and that the increased growth was due to over nutrition and that increased fat was the main difference in body composition. The audience was reminded that there was a tendency to a reduction in birth weight for mothers who had longer term diabetes with evidence of complications. The resulting Pedersen hypothesis proposed

A growth impulse act through the fetal glucose-insulin system. This growth present in all infants, if not caused by, is then intimately related to the maternal blood sugar level during pregnancy.

This reinforced the need to optimise blood glucose control of mothers with diabetes. Monitoring foetal growth during pregnancy was challenging and depended on the combination of clinical assessment and regular ultrasound.

Other conditions in mothers

Blood pressure control was important and managing hypertension during pregnancy could be challenging. Although the absolute numbers of women with diabetic kidney disease is small the individuals were very well known to the service. Women with established nephropathy had very frequent admissions to the antenatal ward to assess foetal growth and maternal blood pressure. Careful monitoring of renal function with involvement of colleagues from the Hypertension service and the Renal Team was often needed, and such pregnancies rarely progressed till term.

Retinopathy in the eye is another diabetes complication which can deteriorate both in association with the strict onset of glycaemic control for pregnancy and due to the biochemical and hormonal changes of pregnancy; thus, the fundi were checked at pre-pregnancy assessment, at booking and during each trimester.

Timing of delivery

Pregnancy is very liable to be interrupted in its course, and probably always by death of the foetus.—James Matthews Duncan 1882

During the 1970s and 1980s there was much debate about the optimal time for delivering a mother who had invested so much effort into adapting her lifestyle, optimising her blood glucose control and attending for very frequent appointments. The balance of risk between premature delivery of an infant who could develop respiratory problems was countered by the risk of unexplained stillbirth if the pregnancy carried on after 37 weeks. Clinical examination was undertaken at each visit and ultrasound scanning was performed regularly. An early scan for viability was followed by a gestational age scan between 11 and 13 weeks in association with biochemical screening and specific foetal measurement to risk assess for chromosomal abnormalities. A detailed anomaly scan including four chamber view of the heart and outflow tracts between 20–22 weeks was followed by regular growth scans in later pregnancy.

The improved glycemic control and careful foetal monitoring in the 1970s encouraged clinicians to extend the pregnancy and, if all was well, elective delivery could be arranged nearer to 39 weeks. As pregnancy progressed, an experienced obstetrician would be aware of the interplay of maternal metabolic control, foetal growth, diabetes complications and obstetric condition. Timing and mode of delivery were crucial decisions and depended on a host of interacting factors. At the 1978 colloquium in Aberdeen it was stated that

In diabetic pregnancy the length of gestation is of great significance for the perinatal mortality. Timing of delivery is probably of greater critical importance than any other decision.

Preterm birth

Birth before 37 weeks of pregnancy is one of the leading causes of perinatal and neonatal mortality and morbidity and, despite the improvements referred to above, preterm delivery is still more common for mothers with diabetes. Preterm infants are at increased risk of hyaline membrane disease and infants with breathing difficulties need particular support in the Neonatal Unit. In the 1970s, experimental work showed that antenatal corticosteroid treatment in the general pregnancy population could reduce the risk of respiratory problems related to prematurity. Corticosteroids were shown to decrease neonatal death rate, the incidence and severity of respiratory distress syndrome (RDS) in neonates and brain haemorrhage in preterm infants. When the evidence-base for this intervention became apparent, national guidelines recommended the routine use of corticosteroids to all women at risk of early delivery between around the 24- and 34-weeks' gestation. The protocol involved the intramuscular injection of a corticosteroid. The new protocol was introduced across AMH and had major implications for the care of women with diabetes.

Mode of delivery

As noted previously, perinatal mortality remained very high in diabetic pregnancy during the period after the discovery of insulin until the 1950s. In 1949, Peel and Oakley reported a perinatal mortality of 37 per cent in women with diabetes and in nearly 20 per cent of these cases intrauterine death occurred in the last four weeks of pregnancy and before the onset of labour while a further 10 per cent were intrapartum stillbirths. By 1973, caesarean section was the most often chosen method of delivery and the trend was especially marked in the delivery of patients having a first baby.

In Aberdeen, each pregnancy was considered given the available evidence. If optimal blood glucose control had been achieved with no findings of foetal macrosomia, vaginal delivery at 39 weeks would be the aim, recognising that labour would be continuously monitored and intervention by emergency caesarean section undertaken if indicated.

Management of diabetes during labour

Hyperglycaemia during labour may predispose to hypoglycaemia in the neonate so the aim in labour was to maintain the maternal blood glucose as close to the normal range as possible. While the numbers of elective and emergency caesarean sections was higher than in the background population, increasing numbers of women had a vaginal delivery and were involved in their blood glucose monitoring and control during labour.

The amount of insulin required during labour can be quite low, reflecting the energy required in the process of labour. After delivery there is a dramatic fall in insulin requirements, hence the recommendation to half the IV insulin infusion rate but continue the dextrose rate as before. The switch is made to sub cutaneous insulin when mother starts eating. The increasing use of continuous insulin infusion pumps and continuous glucose monitoring systems has meant the mother is more involved in the control of glucose levels throughout the process. Breast feeding is encouraged in all mothers who are made aware that blood glucose can fall from the start to the end of a feed, so a snack is needed to compensate.

Management of the infant of the mother with diabetes (IDM)

A range of specific conditions can affect the infant including polycythaemia, hypoglycaemia, and hypocalcaemia. Infants who had signs of respiratory difficulty secondary to hyaline membrane disease received ten per cent dextrose infusions with added sodium bicarbonate to correct any acidosis. Oxygen and respiratory assistance were given based on blood glucose and transcutaneous oxygen monitoring. A clear feeding schedule was set out for the next few days. Breast feeds were encouraged where possible. Adult physicians were regular visitors to the neonatal unit to check that insulin doses were appropriate after delivery.

However, the main focus of care at this stage was the newborn. A clear management plan was laid out to avoid hypoglycaemia in the newborn infant. Early feeding is encouraged to avoid neonatal hypoglycaemia and to stimulate lactation. Over recent years, routine admission of every infant to the neonatal unit is not considered necessary but access to such facilities at short notice remains essential.

Research and developments in care

Local research meetings (Aberdeen Diabetic Pregnancy Study Group) were held in the University Department of Obstetrics in Aberdeen Maternity Hospital.

Delegates attending the European Diabetes in Pregnancy Study Group (DPSG) at Aberdeen in 1997. Dr Joyce Baird is second from the left on front row, Prof Donald Pearson middle of front row and Prof John Stowers third from the right front row.

(Photograph courtesy of Professor Donald Pearson)

Since national or international guidelines were uncommon in the 1960s, there was much clinical debate about the most effective way to deliver care for women with diabetes during pregnancy. The 1950s model of care previously described which involved prolonged admissions was socially inconvenient but had produced better perinatal outcomes than the outcomes in the early years following the discovery of insulin. Changes in obstetric practice, developments in diabetes and advances in other specialties such as clinical biochemistry, ultrasonography and neonatal paediatrics were changing the way care was organised and presenting new opportunities and challenges.

A series of colloquia were held in Aberdeen in 1973, 1978, 1983 and 1988 and the proceedings of each meeting published as a book. The colloquium on Carbohydrate Metabolism in Pregnancy and the Newborn in 1973 attracted an audience from across the globe to Aberdeen. Presentations included detailed accounts on topics ranging from the renal handling of glucose to the types of glucose tolerance tests used in pregnancy.

Stowers and Sutherland appreciated the need to have different care plans for women who had different types of diabetes and thus differing needs during pregnancy. Programmes were developed to support women planning pregnancy, those with established type-1 and type-2 diabetes prior to pregnancy and those women who developed diabetes in pregnancy (GDM).

The outcomes recorded by Matthews Duncan for diabetes in pregnancy were very poor, and the outlook for the mother had improved dramatically following the discovery of insulin, but major challenges were still faced with adverse perinatal outcomes. Babies were born prematurely, late still birth was feared, infants were often heavy for dates and respiratory distress and other neonatal conditions were well documented. The Aberdeen team from across a range of disciplines developed clinical services which would transform these outcomes. The key player in the team was the mother. She was asked to achieve much tighter glucose control than was considered necessary at that time outside pregnancy. Tight control was achieved through more regular blood glucose and urine monitoring, careful adherence to diet and very frequent contact with clinical services throughout pregnancy so that intensive obstetric and metabolic assessment would improve the chances of a successful outcome. The combined clinic evolved as changes in clinical practice in all the specialties had to be introduced, but always with the pregnant mother and her offspring at the forefront.

Developing guidelines and sharing population data 1990–2010

Professor James Petrie was professor of Materia Medica at the University of Aberdeen and President of the Royal College of Physicians of Edinburgh when he established the Scottish Intercollegiate Guidelines Network (SIGN) in 1993. The ambitious aim of the programme was to coordinate national guideline development using a rigorous evidence-based methodology. The ninth SIGN guideline was published in December 1996 on 'The Management of Diabetes in Pregnancy' included the recommendation that 'all clinicians caring for pregnant women should audit their own practice and be prepared to share data at a national level'.

In each of the 22 obstetrics units in Scotland, where women with diabetes were having care, a diabetes nurse specialist or specialist midwife acted as 'audit assistants' who prospectively identified all clinically recognisable and recorded pregnancies, whether progressing to delivery, abortion, or miscarriage, among women with pre-existing type-1 diabetes.

Digital diabetes 2010–20

Although outcomes for pregnancy in women with type-1 diabetes had improved over the decades, the challenge of the St Vincent Declaration (1989), which was to achieve outcomes in pregnancies in women with diabetes similar to those in the background population, had not been met by the start of the 21st century. Further innovation would be required to achieve this target. The previous decades had seen progressive efforts to improve and optimise maternal blood glucose levels since the evidence had pointed to the importance of optimal glucose control throughout pregnancy. In the early years of the 20th century research had confirmed the limitations of urinalysis for glucose assessment, especially during pregnancy. The introduction of home blood glucose monitoring (HBGM) in the 1970s was a major advance and over the years the techniques for HBGM became quicker and more accurate, though uncomfortable, especially if women were testing six to eight times a day.

After the millennium, analysis of home monitoring results changed from examination of individual booklets or charts to downloading values electronically and reviewing a summary of results and identification of trends. Information technology was moving fast, and the combined clinic was often the area where new technologies to help mothers manage their diabetes more effectively were introduced, providing the advances had a good evidence base. Several companies developed equipment for continuous subcutaneous blood glucose monitoring (CGM) with the information available on mobile phones.

Continuous glucose monitoring (CGM)

Continuous glucose monitoring provides detailed data on the direction and rate of changes in the subcutaneous glucose levels. Real time systems display contemporaneous glucose readings. The subcutaneous values lag five to ten minutes behind blood glucose levels and the display shows arrows indicating if the glucose level is stable, rising or falling. Alarms can be set to warn if the glucose levels are falling or rising quickly and if the glucose is approaching the hypoglycaemic range. Users can find the amount of information overwhelming, so a supportive care team needs to offer advice about realistic targets and settings.

During pregnancy women learn a great deal about managing diabetes intensively and CGM provides much important information. Trends can be identified in early pregnancy about the types of food which can cause a high post-breakfast peak. The warning arrows for hypoglycaemia can advise if some quick acting carbohydrate is needed, especially if the appetite is poor in early pregnancy and food intake is reduced.

During pregnancy the timing of pre-meal bolus insulin usually changes. Many women need to progressively increase the interval between injecting to avoid a post-meal peak followed by later hypoglycaemia. Mid-pregnancy, CGM will improve confidence to increase insulin gradually and steadily doses as insulin resistance increases. Overnight blood glucose control has always been a challenge for women in pregnancy. CGM gives information about fluctuations and hypoglycaemia during sleep. In later pregnancy CGM patterns help optimise the timing and of pre-meal insulin doses. Systems are under development to combine the use of continuous monitoring and insulin pumps with the aim of developing a reliable artificial pancreas.

Studies of islet transplants and stem cell transplants continue but seem a long way from routine clinical practice.

Gestational diabetes mellitus (GDM)

Diabetes may come on during pregnancy.—James Matthews Duncan 1882

Matthews Duncan emphasised the importance of understanding the physiological changes which occur during pregnancy. Resistance to insulin develops as pregnancy progresses. In the first trimester women become more insulin sensitive but after the first trimester insulin resistance increases till at term. On average, women with type-1 Diabetes Mellitus require double their pre-pregnancy dose of insulin. Insulin resistance occurs in all pregnancies and if a mother has a reduction in the number of insulin-producing cells of the pancreas or more than expected resistance to the action of insulin, diabetes may develop during the course of the pregnancy. Gestational Diabetes (GDM) – diabetes which is first recognised during pregnancy – has been the subject of controversy and continues to cause debate. GDM can be defined as carbohydrate intolerance of variable severity with onset or first recognition during pregnancy. This definition included women with abnormal glucose tolerance that reverts to normal after delivery, those with undiagnosed type-1 or type-2 DM and, rarely, women with monogenic diabetes. If type-1 or type-2 diabetes was suspected (due to early presentation or grossly elevated blood glucose, for example), urgent action was required to normalise metabolism as previously discussed. However, most cases of GDM are asymptomatic and detected by screening. Publications from groups in the 1940s and 1950s suggested that, during the period of at least five years prior to the full clinical presentation of diabetes, foetal risk was as high if, not higher, than the risk in a known diabetic pregnancy. The concept of 'prediabetes' was developed. Procedures for screening, diagnosis and management of gestational diabetes would be a topic of much debate for the rest of the century and Aberdeen was often at the centre of discussions. In an article in 1961, John Stowers discussed the problem of late diagnosis of diabetes (considering in particular the condition which would now be classified as type-2 DM). He was concerned that one in four patients already had complications at diagnosis and argued that screening and early intervention could reduce the severity of the condition and reduce complications. An early diagnosis would allow the introduction of a sensible lifestyle to reduce the future risk of diabetes.

In the North East of Scotland during the 1960s, a screening programme was established to identify those women at increased risk of developing abnormal glucose metabolism during pregnancy. In a book chapter published in 1973 Stowers explained the advantage of a coordinated approach to the problem:

> There is a marked degree of central supervision of both the maternity and diabetic services for the North East of Scotland containing about half a million people, and approximately 50% urban and 50% rural. The data reflect that there has been an active screening process to detect the early stages of diabetes in pregnancy... Most of the pregnant diabetics attending the combined obstetric diabetic clinic have only chemical, that is sub-clinical diabetes (fasting glucose not exceeding 130mg/dl (7.2 mmol/l).

Those with chemical diabetes outnumbered the insulin dependent cases (type-1 DM) in a ratio of 6:1 in the combined clinic.

Screening for GDM

In the 1960s it was not feasible to perform a diagnostic glucose tolerance test (GTT) on the entire pregnant population so a methodology was developed to identify those at greatest risk of diabetes and to perform GTT on this subgroup. Thus, in Grampian, all women at booking had a careful history taken and, if a positive indicator was identified, a diagnostic GTT was arranged. Similarly, if an indicator developed during pregnancy a test was arranged. During their research, the group developed a pragmatic approach to the question of glycosuria which Matthews Duncan and others had commented on.

The Aberdeen team reported:

> From a practical point of view we found that fasting glycosuria has been a useful means by which the huge logistic problem of pregnancy glycosuria could be simplified i.e. by the use of clinistix to test the second fasting specimen of urine... Moreover we would recommend that a random blood sugar should be done as soon as second fasting glycosuria is found in pregnancy, because fasting glycosuria has been found invariably when overt diabetes has presented de novo in pregnancy.

Diagnosis of GDM

During the mid-20th Century there was much uncertainty about the optimal method of glucose tolerance testing to make a diagnosis of diabetes. If the random or fasting blood glucose was not in the clear diabetic range, but above normal, the individual was given a glucose challenge and the blood glucose measured over a period of time to assess how well the individual dealt with the glucose load. In the 1960s there was little agreement about the best way to perform a GTT. Different centres used differing amounts of glucose challenge, ranging from 25 grams to 100, and different routes of glucose administration (intravenous or oral) and different values to define abnormality. Outcomes of clinical studies were very difficult to compare between centres, even within the same country. In the early 1960s the Aberdeen group decided to use the intravenous glucose tolerance test (IVGTT) which they considered was more suitable than the oral glucose tolerance test (OGTT) in pregnancy. The IVGTTs were performed in the University Lab at AMH. Copies of all results were carefully recorded to ensure comprehensive records were kept of all the reasons for testing, the glucose values, and clinical outcomes (maternal and neonatal). Over the next few years data were carefully recorded and detailed studies of the IVGTT were published from Aberdeen. One major challenge identified was the lack of information about glucose handling in most pregnant women, such as those who did not have risk factors or indicators for testing. The 'Thousand Pregnancy Study' was published from Aberdeen. Nine hundred and seventeen randomly selected, non-diabetic pregnant women agreed to have an IVGTT at or about 32 weeks gestation. The main finding was that fasting plasma glucose and indices of intravenous glucose disposal were distributed unimodally with no evidence of a separate pathological group towards the diabetic end of the distribution.

Following a diagnosis of GDM, women were recognised to be at increased risk of developing diabetes in later life but also at increased risk of some adverse neonatal outcomes. At the combined clinic women had intensive dietary advice, instruction on home blood glucose monitoring (from 1977 onwards) and careful supervision of their pregnancy. Most interventions were introduced through the combined clinic as outpatients. Regular clinical examination and ultrasound scanning gave an indication of foetal growth and obstetric findings were considered along with metabolic assessments.

In overweight women, metformin was the drug of choice in gestational diabetes. Metformin was also occasionally used in addition to insulin if women were insulin resistant. Women with GDM were seen on a regular basis from diagnosis till delivery. Insulin was introduced if control was suboptimal.

Debates about the optimal methods for identifying and treating women with gestational diabetes continued into the 21st century. Norman Waugh of the

Aberdeen Health Technology Assessment Group and others produced a detailed Health Technology Assessment on 'Screening for hyperglycaemia in pregnancy: a rapid update for the National Screening Committee' in 2010 and national guidelines are still divided about the most effective way to manage this condition.

Perhaps a new approach in future will identify more accurately those pregnancies at increased risk and the optimal management of GDM when it is present.

17

Midwifery in the Community and in General Practice

Peter Duffus

IT MAY SEEM that obstetric practice has always been part of the General Medical Practice for the doctor working in the North East of Scotland. In fact, in historical terms, it only came about recently. Traditionally assistance at birth was limited to female companions, female family members and the howdie wife. Men were generally not allowed to be present. Medical men may have become involved occasionally when something went wrong, and instrumental intervention was required.

Gradually, however, man midwives became acceptable, but it was not until the 17th century that 'accoucheurs' became fashionable in France. In Scotland, they became popular with the aristocracy who always had births at home and would not mix with the common people in a hospital. Given the fact that in the early 1800s there was only one general doctor between Aberdeen and Peterhead and most poor people could not afford a doctor, even if one was available, it is unlikely medical help would be sought in childbirth. Up to the 1920s an estimated 95 per cent of all births at this period, among rich and poor alike, were home births. In fact, hospitals were feared. Gradually, however, local GPs became accepted for providing maternity care, although it was mainly intra partum care they practiced as antenatal care did not initially exist.

Payment to the GP by the mother was often difficult and many GPs were willing to forgo payment for confinements as shown in the following story about Dr Sinclair of Ellon (who did over a hundred cases a year, mostly among the cottar wives), told by Dr Danny Gordon:

Long weary nights he would wait with them. One night the patient's pains were few and far between, and old Sinclair was half-drowsing by the fire, well-stoked for the hot water and for burning the afterbirth. His eyes were closed, and the howdie wife, thinking he was asleep says, 'Look at him. Isn't doctor's siller easy won?' He opened his eyes and caught a quick glance from the lady in labour with her seventh. She reddened to the roots. She knew, as he knew, that not even the first confinement had been paid.

Maternity hospitals in Aberdeen did not exist until 1894 when a lying-in department was established in Aberdeen General Dispensary. In the county maternity beds did not appear until the 1920s. In fact, patients who were poorer could not afford hospital and they were frightened by maternal mortality related to infection. Country obstetrics was improved by the building of local cottage hospitals. In the 1920s and '30s there was a series of cottage hospitals built which also contained maternity units. In 1922, Insch Hospital was opened, with four male and four female beds, three maternity beds and an operating theatre. It is of interest to note that at that time Aberdeen only had 15 maternity beds. In fact, it was said that the outcome of a birth managed by an experienced community GP was as good as the hospital.

Dr James Gill of Inverurie wrote:

In the 1930s, the most important part of a doctor's practice, was midwifery. If he was thought to be good at that, his future was assured. He was expected to tackle anything and any attempt to persuade patients that their condition required hospital treatment, was answered by 'if I'm to dee, I'll dee at hame'.

The importance of obstetric practice is demonstrated in one case involving Dr Reid of Ellon:

Dr James Reid of Ellon in the 1860s, like many of his time, was a farmer-doctor in his prime. His son James, then a medical student, came home a few years later as assistant, but lost his first three midder cases with puerperal fever, and his father had to pack him off to London, because a good name as a howdie was essential in country practice, otherwise you were damned. Incidentally, in London the young James prospered to become Sir James Reid, beloved physician to the old Queen, a fame and fortune he would never have won on Ythanside.

Over time, childbirth was becoming more academic and technical with great advances improving the morbidity and mortality of both mother and child. The provision of hospital beds and hospital interventions increased. This increased greatly at the start of the NHS when doctors were separated into Consultants and GPs and also maternity care was free. In urban areas most of the intrapartum care passed to the hospital while the GPs retained antenatal and post-natal care. This, however, gradually diminished as the GP training scheme no longer had a six-month obstetric block. As older experienced GPs retired, younger GPs did not undertake antenatal care as this was being taken over by Community Midwives.

In the county areas, intrapartum obstetrics continued for much longer but again home deliveries gradually disappeared. However, the birth rate was falling, patients lived nearer hospitals and had better transport and older experienced GPs retired. Now it is uncommon to have home deliveries in the country.

In 2009, 78 per cent of deliveries in NHS Grampian occurred in Aberdeen Maternity Hospital, 18 per cent in Dr Gray's in Elgin and 4 per cent in Community Hospitals. Home births account for under 1 per cent of all births in Aberdeen City, and nearly two per cent of births in Aberdeenshire.

Home deliveries

Past practice for centuries and decades prior to the NHS, favoured home deliveries involving a dependency upon 'howdie' midwives, accoucheurs and family doctors. Dependency on the general practitioner continued particularly in rural settings until the very recent past. This section outlines some of the stories and challenges involved in the delivery of that service and is extracted from a wide range of sources detailing the experiences of family doctors and others involved in delivery at home.

The following extracts are taken from *Aberdeen Doctors*, Aberdeen Medico-Chirurgical Society, 1894:

> Social customs shed some light on the home lives of our forefathers. In great houses the doctor superintended the birth of the son and heir, but the midwife was in employment amongst all classes. It is not long since midwives were employed by royalty; and when a male physician was engaged for the first time, he was called a 'man-midwife'. The festival of the newly born had purely a feminine character in the country. The groaning malt and the mystic cheese or 'Kenno' made in secret and presented at the birth, was a women's symposium, which had its origin in ancient heathen rites. The men of the house were not allowed to interfere in the matter and made a grave pretence of not knowing what

was going on. The birth of the child was followed by a bath of cold water and crossing by a burning brand, for which the medical profession was not responsible.

* * *

Of Dr Joseph Williamson, an unselfish and devoted physician, a grateful recollection should remain in the city in which he laboured. He was for many years, secretary to the Medical Society, and his careful and valuable minutes are to be found in a large tome in the Medical Hall and speak for themselves that he had its interests at heart. He unfortunately died of heart-disease in middle life but bore his complaint with great resignation. It is told of him that on the last day he was out he visited a poor woman with a baby, who offered him a sovereign as all she could give for his professional attendance on her. He refused the fee, which with a spirit of independent pride was re-offered, and the doctor bent over the child's cradle and put the money under its pillow. What were the feelings of the mother when next morning, on hearing that the good doctor was dead, she found the gold piece where he had laid it! Welcome the gossip of a provincial town which tells such stories as this. Dr Joseph Williamson was not appointed a physician in the Aberdeen Infirmary, though a man of medical skill and worthy connection; but of his exclusion from what he might have claimed as a right he did not complain, any more than he did of the disease under which he so distressingly laboured, and of the symptoms of which he spoke as if it belonged to someone else.

Reminiscences from general practitioners serving the towns of Aberdeenshire in the 1920s and '30s are also recorded:

Now-a-days, you know the care and attention given to expectant mothers from doctor and nurse throughout the pregnancy – the blood tests, the weighing, the B.P. checks and so on, becoming more frequent as time goes on. When I started, very little antenatal care was done and, if an obviously pregnant woman waved to her doctor as he passed, that could constitute a booking. To begin with, my patients resented my antenatal attentions but, in time they came to accept them, though the care fell far short of what is considered necessary now. Preparations for the confinement were simple – baby's clothes, a clean night gown and sheets, plenty newspapers to put on the floor near the bed, a rubber sheet or brown paper to put under the draw sheet, 1lb Cotton Wool, a bottle of Lysol and a pint of whisky. The latter item was to resuscitate the mother if she collapsed and for the doctor, and neighbours to drink baby's health. The patient's mother or some other relative or neighbour was advised to be in readiness, and a 'skeely wife' was usually engaged to assist at the confinement.

* * *

The end of a confinement, with a smiling mother sipping hot tea and the baby bawling beside her, gave me a most satisfying feeling, though many deliveries were nerve racking to the doctor as well as to the patient... 'if this is what marriage means... the engagement is off!'

* * *

A difficult delivery, after an anxious wait of several hours, left me feeling like a wet rag. Occasionally, in a very difficult case, I might ask a neighbouring doctor to give the anaesthetic but otherwise I was expected to deal with any complication.

If nurse was in attendance, she gave me good warning of the confinement and, if only the patient's mother or neighbour were present, I often was called at the first contraction. Telephones were scarce and father had to walk or cycle for the doctor. So usually, especially through the night, I waited at the house. There was a good fire, abundant supplies of tea, which became stronger as time passed, and there, surrounded by nightgowns, nappies, towels etc airing, we sat and chatted and encouraged the patient. In this cosy atmosphere, I got to know my patients – and the gossip of the neighbourhood – far better than I ever did when I attended them in hospital. Many of the births took place in a box bed, an abomination, if ever there was one. My nurse had to climb into the back of the bed to hold up the patient's leg and, once in, she was stuck there. Children, dogs and cats had sometimes to be cleared out of the bed and bedroom, and sometimes the only place left for the anxious father to shelter, was a small wooden building at the foot of the garden.

Some of the confinements I had to attend remain more vividly in my memory than others.

Once, I had five in 24 hrs – an exhausting experience. From delivering a member of the travelling community in a caravan on the Market Green

– to getting a tractor from Meldrum Station in bad weather.

The picture changed completely in 1939 when war broke out – and there was a maternity unit at the newly opened Inverurie Hospital.

To cope with the increase in Hospital confinements, Haddo House was opened as an emergency maternity hospital. Oldmeldrum being near, it was decided to send a party of expectant mothers from Glasgow to stay in Meldrum till their time came – numbers of 100 to 150 were mentioned. Volunteers were called for to accommodate the patients and, when few offers were received, the Town Council decided to compel residents to take the evacuees. There was a great stir, and doctors were asked to give certificates to old ladies to say that having an expectant mother in their house would damage their health. The Town Councillors were even sworn at by lifelong friends. Finally, the great day arrived, cars were waiting at Inverurie the nearest station to drive the 150 to their billets and a canteen was mobilised to serve refreshments on their arrival. The train drew in and about 12 pregnant ladies stepped out. Fourteen had left Glasgow; one was rushed to the hospital at Perth and another at Aberdeen. The rest had refused to leave Glasgow. We had a mother with two children staying in our house.

Dr James Gill, Inverurie

I had just finished a ten days' locum for my uncle, Dr John Skinner of Skene and had now arrived to be assistant to Dr George Mitchell, his third, my predecessors having been Vincent Watson and Cecil Spark. After supper there was a call to a farm to see a lad of fifteen with pain in his tummy.

'Funny thing,' said George Mitchell, 'when I started practice here in 1909, I had a call one night to this same farm. The patient was the farmer's daughter who had pain and a swelling of the abdomen.'

The young doctor found she was pregnant and starting labour. He came downstairs in some trepidation wondering how he would break the news to her father sitting at the kitchen fireside smoking his pipe.

'O that's a' is't doctor' he remarked when told, 'I thocht it might be one o' thae knots that would ha to be cut awa.'

The 15-year-old we had been called to see was the 'knot.' He had an acute appendix. We took him in the back of the car to the Insch War Memorial Cottage Hospital, I gave my first of many anaesthetics, and George Mitchell, one of the best GP surgeons in the North, had the appendix out without any bother.

His favourite story and best known one was of one week in March, about the turn of the century, when he delivered three babies on the wrong side of the blanket to three farm quines, one at Collieston, one at Belhelvie, and the third at Tarves, and all three named Jock Watt as the father. The doctor took the first opportunity to speak to Jock, the foreman at Hillies, as he was watering his horses at the farm trough, and asked him how he managed this feat, to which the sheepish Jock replied, 'I have a bicycle'.

Dr Theo Goodbrand, Longside

It was the occasion of a maternity attendance that led Dr Theo Goodbrand to commandeer a train. In the days prior to the Dr Beeching cuts, a branch line ran from Maud to Peterhead stopping at Longside and Mintlaw. A call came in from a patient of the practice who was in Peterhead about 10 miles away, and who was in labour. It was winter and snowing and all the roads were closed. Despite having a Morris Minor, it was no match for the snowy roads. Theo contacted his trainer Dr Burgess for advice. It was now about 3am when Dr Burgess looked out of the window and saw a light in the distance. It was the signal box for the railway branch line. Dr Burgess suggested that there might be a train out early in the morning. Theo made his way to the Signal Box and let the signalman know of his predicament. Yes, there would be a train with a snow plough coming past shortly and

Image of a steam train with snowplough as would have got Dr Goodbrand to Peterhead for his delivery.
(Image courtesy of Waverley Route Heritage Association Archive.
https://whra.org.uk/the-waverley-route/photograph-archive)

yes it could be stopped for Dr Goodbrand.

When the engine with the snow plough arrived, it stopped at the signal box and Theo rode to Peterhead on the footplate alongside the engine driver. On arrival at Peterhead he trudged through the snow only to find that his patient was not there she had gone to stay with her mother at the other end of Peterhead. More walking through the snow finally took Theo to his patient. Fortunately, after that all went well and a healthy baby was delivered. Theo then took the regular train back to Longside.

Dr GP Milne – birthing in the Cairngorms

In the late 18th century, the countryfolk in the Cairngorm area had a form of therapy which was thought to be effective in producing easy childbirth. Part of Ben Avon, one of the highest mountains in the Cairngorms, is known as the Sandy Hill and on it is a wart or tor, known as Clach Ban or Woman's Stone. It has been worn away in parts by the elements to form a chair. Down to the middle of the 19th century, women who were approaching confinement used to sit on the Clach Ban for the purpose of being chaired in this worn-out pothole, the belief being that this ensured an easy labour. Alexander Smith, in a *New History of Aberdeen Shire* published in 1875, says that in August 1836 he witnessed the chairing of 12 women who had that morning come from Speyside over 20 miles to undergo the rite, and the custom is said to have lingered on even as late as the 1860s.

As can be seen from the above, midwifery particularly in the rural communities was a varied and periodically challenging practice but was a service much appreciated by those who had to partake in it, retaining a unique identity character and appreciation for all concerned.

Further Reading

Aitken-Swan, J, *Fertility Control and the Medical Profession*, Croom Helm, 1977.
Debenham, C, *Birth Control and the Rights of Women*, EB Taurus, 2014.
Elliott, K, 'Birth Control Clinics in Scotland 1926–c.1939', *JSHS*, vol 34, issue 2, 2014.
Horsburgh, F, 'The back street beginnings of birth control', *Press & Journal*, 4 December 1972.

Milne GP, *The Aberdeen University Review*, vol. 142, 4, no. 160, 1978.

Rodger EHB, *Aberdeen Doctors at Home and Abroad*, William Blackwood & Sons, Edinburgh, 1893.

Family Planning and Marriage Guidance pamphlets, University of Aberdeen MS 3179/8/5.

Family planning services in Aberdeen archive, University of Aberdeen MS 3179.

Lecture notes on medical jurisprudence and on public health by Matthew Hay and taken down by John Stuart, 28 April 1896 – 14 October 1899, University of Aberdeen MS 3128/2.

PART 4

Stories, Tales and Memories

Here we bring together a record of the past and the living history of the maternity hospital, the contributions of Sir Dugald Baird and how they were valued by others, along with the memories of women who used the service, including some of their stories and anecdotes. We identify some examples of the drivers for change which might have motivated Sir Dugald Baird, such as the illegal practices in termination of pregnancy which resulted in septic complications.

The commentary on Sir Dugald 'the Maty' and the service, have been gathered from files, documents and papers found in the back of old shelves and desk-drawers, as well as by invited contributions from clinicians who worked in the hospital. The stories and other narratives were captured by word-of-mouth and from articles published in the local press. Quotes about and some reminiscences of Sir Dugald Baird highlight his immense contribution to midwifery. Some quotes are attributed to their originator, others simply speak for themselves.

Recollections of the maternity hospital from those still living – albeit, on occasion, reporting the memories of forebears or friends – chart some recent and not so recent anecdotes and stories, providing a reflection on how the hospital is valued by those in receipt of its services.

Our aim is to preserve a history that might otherwise never have been recorded.

18

Memories of Sir Dugald Baird, Lady May Baird and Mary Esslemont

Lesley Dunbar, Alison McCall, Fiona Rennie and George Youngson

Sir Dugald Baird

SIR DUGALD BAIRD who was Regius Professor of Obstetrics and Gynaecology in the University of Aberdeen from 1937, died on 7 November in his 86th year. He came from Glasgow with the reputation of a firebrand who would upset the apple cart in Aberdeen. And so he did; only his motives were so clearly humane and not self-seeking that it made him more friends than enemies. He had practised as an obstetrician in Rottenrow and was deeply affected by what poverty did to women giving birth in Glasgow. He was determined that Aberdeen should do better. During his regime, our region achieved the lowest perinatal mortality in Scotland.

Dugald made a great contribution to obstetric science but the first recollection of him that springs to mind was of his role as a clinician. He reorganised the hospital practice, building up services such as blood transfusion and contraception. Later he led the way in doing terminations of pregnancy for social reasons. His brave stand on issues such as contraception, sterilisation and abortion were part of his drive to rid women of the burden of unwanted fertility. He lived to see his teaching taken up in medical practice and the law of the land. The women of this country owe him much. In the full flow of his reforming crusade, his wife, May, became Chairman of the Health Board. It added greatly to his power to influence policy and appointments. Many of the people who moulded hospital practice in Aberdeen in the 1950s were picked by Dugald. (Anon)

Dugald was a magnet which drew not only scientists but also young clinicians from far and wide. Under his hand was trained a generation of men who now command the heights of obstetrics in this country. In his last few years in the chair he had much power in the faculty of medicine. He used it for change to great effect. But always with humility. He used to scribble ideas on the back of an envelope and would buttonhole the most surprising people in the hospital corridor to ask what they thought of his latest notion. (THE LATE PROFESSOR EMERITUS ARNOLD KLOPPER, PROFESSOR OF REPRODUCTION OF ENDOCRINOLOGY, UNIVERSITY OF ABERDEEN)

By creating complete clinical coverage and a unified record system for a total obstetric population, Dugald Baird produced a milieu, not only for epidemiological studies, but for nutritional, metabolic and endocrine investigations into the physiological and pathological changes in pregnancy. He collected together and inspired the staff which, under his direction, showed the influence of lifestyle and physical characteristics on reproduction of performance.(PROFESSOR EMERITUS IAN MacGILLIVRAY, REGIUS PROFESSOR, OBSTETRICS AND GYNAECOLOGY, UNIVERSITY OF ABERDEEN)

Sir Dugald was an incisive, though gentle critic. A person of great stature, we shall perhaps not see many of his like again. (DR BILL FULLERTON, CONSULTANT, OBSTETRICS AND GYNAECOLOGY, ABERDEEN MATERNITY HOSPITAL)

It was no surprise when in 1937 he was appointed Regius Professor of midwifery at the University of Aberdeen. In congratulating him on his appointment to my home university, I said: 'You will find that the facilities are fairly basic and that the Aberdonians are a tough lot.'

'Yes,' he replied, 'I know well that the facilities are even less than basic; and that the Aberdonians are a tough lot who do not welcome change. But I am not a weakling.' (SIR JAMES HOWIE, MD, FRCPE)

I had a high regard for Sir Dugald who, by example of his compassion towards mothers living in difficult circumstances, taught us as midwives to respect the young anxious mothers in our care and to give them both encouragement and kind attention.

As a midwife sister in his wards, he always asked your opinion
and he appeared to consider the midwife's observations as important
as medical opinions. This was a tremendous boost to one's ego and
encouraged one to try and further improve the midwifery care in the
unit. (MARGARET NAIRN, SISTER, ABERDEEN MATERNITY HOSPITAL)

He was such a genuine person. I felt for him at our first meeting. He was
absolutely honest and never shrank from facing up to the evidence even
if this meant abandoning a cherished conviction. I count myself lucky
to have had dealings with him. (THE LATE SIR HAROLD HIMSWORTH,
CHAIRMAN OF THE MEDICAL RESEARCH COUNCIL)

There is another very great achievement of Dugald Baird – sadly much
less known-namely, the establishment of a first-rate contraceptive clinic
in Aberdeen.

The dangers of increased parity to a woman's health were felt very
strongly by Dugald Baird. The only facility available to deal with this in
late 1939 was a Marie Stopes clinic in Gerard Street in a poor city area.
It was staffed by one or two dedicated ex-midwives or nurses.

Strong views on the need for contraception were frequently expressed
by Dugald Baird. I admit I was deeply shocked and embarrassed at first.
The subject, as far as my six-year medical curriculum was concerned,
was completely taboo and the public always avoided any mention of it.
In the eye of the average Aberdonian, a Marie Stopes clinic was a den of
iniquity – the equivalent of or even worse than a venereal disease clinic.
Few Aberdeen women had the courage to visit the place. One of the
first things Dugald Baird got me to do was visit the place from time to
time, give advice, support and encouragement to the staff. I do not mind
admitting each time I enter Gerard Street, I would pull my hat down
over my eyes and hope I was unobserved.

Dugald Baird recognised that the situation was ridiculous and
decided that a clinic with properly trained staff including a doctor,
must be set up in a more acceptable area such as the Woolmanhill
Hospital precincts. This meant obtaining adequate funds from the city
council and reducing public prejudice. It was a very hard battle (not
helped by unsympathetic medical people such as the Medical Officer
of Health) and took all of 15 years. In the end, in the mid-50s, a first-
class clinic with an enthusiastic medical officer, Margaret McGregor,
and appropriately trained nurses was established at Woolmanhill.
The purpose of the clinic was camouflaged by the euphemistic title

'Gynaecological Advisory Clinic'. I know this must all sound ludicrous today when children are being offered condoms at school. (ANON)

During the 1950s, Sir Dugald Baird raised the standard of research in obstetrics and gynaecology in Britain by an order of magnitude-in effect, he laid the foundations for modern evidence-based clinical care. He introduced scientific method – statistical and epidemiological – into the analysis of clinical outcomes. Studies had to be large enough to produce significant results and all analyses had to take into account the confounding effects of age, parity and social class. He stressed that clinical research was a professional activity that must be motivated by a genuine desire to know. To contribute effectively, junior doctors needed to be taught and supervised by full-time academics with a track record of research achievement rather than left to develop projects on their own.

Sir Dugald was also a pioneer in demonstrating that health and illness are strongly influenced by social factors. He considered assessment of a woman's socio-economic circumstances as much a part of a consultation as taking the medical history and making the examination. He showed that deprivation had measurable effects such as reduced growth in childhood leading to low adult stature, and higher perinatal mortality that was independent of the quality of medical care. He was particularly concerned about the increase in deprivation that resulted from the difficulty poor women had in regulating their fertility. He supported the provision of free contraceptive services by the Aberdeen local authority many years before such services became available nationally, made sterilisation available on request to women who had completed their families, and considered that termination of pregnancy by doctors was both ethical and beneficial when women felt they could not cope with a further child. (THE LATE DR DAVID PAINTIN FRCOG, EMERITUS READER IN OBSTETRICS AND GYNAECOLOGY, IMPERIAL COLLEGE SCHOOL OF MEDICINE, LONDON)

Stories told by Sir Dugald Baird
Extracted from an interview with Sir Dugald Baird in 1980

Family planning

I said to another woman, 'you have only had three children – all you wanted, how did you manage it?'

'Well, I have a very good husband he disnae bother me very much Professor.'

'Oh what do you do?'

'Well, you see, he goes to the football on Saturday and on Saturday night I just hand him a condom and that is that.'

'How do you get condoms?'

'Well,' she said, 'you see, I have an understanding with the chemist. I go and ask for cough drops and I hand him the money and he hands over the "cough drops" and there is no questions asked or anything. If the shop's full of people, it disnae matter.'

Becoming an obstetrician/gynaecologist/epidemiologist

Two years after graduation I had held a variety of house appointments, all of which were unpaid. It was then suggested to me that I apply for a post of resident registrar which was being created by Professor Munro Kerr in his department of gynaecology in the Glasgow Royal infirmary. This may well have been the first paid post (£250 per annum) in Scotland. The Professor happened to have seen me play in an international rugby trial and is alleged to have said that 'if he turns out to be as good an obstetrician and gynaecologist as he was a footballer, then they have made a good appointment'.

Early use of antibacterial medication

Leonard Colebrook rang me up from Queen Charlotte's Hospital one day in 1936 and said 'Dugald you must come to London, I have something I want to show you.'

'Oh' I said, 'do I have to come?'

'Yes,' he said, 'you will enjoy it once you get here.'

So I travelled to London and to the isolation block at Charlotte's. They showed me the temperature charts of many women who had septicaemia due to the dreaded haemolytic streptococcus and were successfully treated with 'Prontosil Rubrum'. In many cases the temperature was normal in 48 hrs...

The realisation... was that this was the beginning of the end of maternal mortality, this was one of the most memorable periods of my life.

Prontosil was one of the earliest antimicrobial drugs used to treat infection.

Memory of Lady May Baird

I spoke to May Baird in St Katherine's Club, West North Street Aberdeen in 1947. She came one afternoon to the afternoon sessions for mother and babies. A creche was available. Miss Walker, who ran the St Katherine's Club came at our social time after classes to tell us this lady was coming to tell us about 'childbirth'. A few young girls had met her husband Dugald Baird when in ARI having minor operations after giving birth. He was the 'gynae' head. We went along to the small hall. It was packed with young women some 18 plus, some single, some widows.

Our group was single and young married women. I remember it well, the hall was packed. 'Childbirth' – well the intimate side of this was never discussed in 1947 and certainly not in school. May Baird, Miss Walker and Miss Moffat were on the stage. Miss Walker introduced May Baird. She was a petite, bonny woman and all smiles. She came down from the stage and spoke to us. She told us of this cap. It did have a proper name. I can't remember it now! She passed it around us, she told us the place where we could go and buy one. It was in Charlotte Street near the Hutcheon Street end – a narrow street lined with tenements. I think it was called the Marie Stopes Clinic. It cost seven shillings and sixpence not a lot in today's money, but the war had just finished and many men had no work and also no homes.

At the end of the meeting, we went to the canteen with Miss Walker, Miss Moffat and May Baird. May Baird came into the canteen and approached several tables. She said she had been to the creche and had seen all the babies and small children and they were a credit to us. She seemed a truly honest, unassuming lady. May Baird I heard often came to the club. Another meeting was held for the benefit of new members. Many of the girls attended a mother and baby clinic in the old infirmary, through from the Salvation Army. (ANON)

19

Maternity Memories

Midwives' memories

A midwife from the '50s

HAVING QUALIFIED AS a General Nurse, I went to Aberdeen Maternity Hospital in 1959 to train as a Midwife. The course was a year long and in two parts. Some of my colleagues chose to do Part 2 in other hospitals. During training, we worked at the main hospital at Foresterhill and also at Fonthill, Summerfield and Queen's Cross Nursing Homes. The latter was on Carden Place. The Antenatal Clinic was at Castle Terrace. I recall a senior doctor who was a woman saying how she liked to see the Mums-to-be wearing bright, colourful smocks even though they were bought on the 'never never'. In her younger days, she said that all the pregnant women were draped in dark clothing. One lady, on her way to the clinic, had an item stolen from her fashionable 'bucket' bag. She had put her urine sample in a miniature whisky bottle!

We had, as pupil midwives, to attend ten home confinements. The medical students also had to have that experience. As home confinements reduced, this became competitive. Sometimes it had to be at out-of-town deliveries. The Special Nursery really was special, overseen by Sister Hogg who was strict but really knowledgeable, being able to diagnose a problem at a glance. I had a turn of preparing the milk bottles for those who weren't breastfed. The flat-sided bottles went into crates of eight, all stacked in a massive steel steriliser. During my time there, I recall feeding, amongst many others, a very tiny, premature baby, night after night. His name on the cot label was imprinted on my memory. Imagine my delight, when, 16 years later, our paths crossed, and he had just gained A grades in his 'O' levels.

When, 'on district', we lived at 32 Carden Place, and had a rota. During the night once you took your phone call, you booked your taxi to join the Qualified Midwife at the address of the home confinement. You then woke the next pupil midwife on the rota. My first home confinement was very early in the morning. The father went to the newsagents as soon as it opened, to get 'kindling' to light the fire so we could boil up our cotton wool balls.

After having my own family, I did a refresher course at Gorebridge and returned to midwifery. How things had changed! Everything was now handled at Central Sterilisation, everything pre-packed and disposable. Terry towelling nappies were gone in favour of disposables. And the new cots, on wheels, rather than those suspended from the mother's bed. In the 50s we were very proud of our still new hospital. Our training was from Maggie Myles' *Textbook of Midwifery*. I did not know her Aberdeen connections at that time. Our tutor, Sister Cook, had no modern teaching aids. She used flannel graphs to teach us anatomy and we recall her searching in a box, asking if anyone had seen her uterus! She taught us well and I believe we all qualified. (ANON)

A midwife in the early '60s

I always wanted to be a nurse and I trained for three years at the Royal Infirmary, Foresterhill in Aberdeen. During our first two years, we had to stay in a nurses' home and were allowed to sleep out in our third year. Throughout the three years, we were placed in different wards and operating theatres for experience. Woodend General Hospital had amalgamated with the Royal Infirmary, and we were sent there too. Night duty on a rota basis was included. Study blocks were organised, and we had to attend lectures given by the Sister tutors. After each block, we had an exam. At the end of our third year, we had our big exam, which consisted of an oral and written paper. On passing, you were a Registered General Nurse and could apply to be a staff nurse. Some nurses would opt to leave and do further studies in either midwifery, sick children's nursing or even decide to leave to get married.

I applied to work as a staff nurse in a surgical ward at Woodend. It was very busy, especially on theatre days and admission days. Even in those days, we were short staffed. It was very satisfying to see patients improve and go home.

In 1960, I applied to do the midwifery course, which lasted one year. You could do the whole year at the one hospital or opt to go elsewhere for the second six months. I decided to stay at Aberdeen Maternity Hospital, Foresterhill. Throughout the year, we were learning all the time, either at the bedside or in lectures. We were advised to buy a midwifery textbook written by Maggie Myles, who was known far and wide for her books on midwifery and also locally for her hats. The majority of midwives used these books for study. We were given a 'blue' book to record deliveries. We had to get 20 hospital and 20 district confinements. Some student midwives found it difficult to get the necessary amount of births, owing to medical students also requiring deliveries in their training. Eventually, it was reduced to ten hospital and ten district confinements. Each delivery had to be signed by a trained midwife present at the birth. We had to observe a few births before we were permitted to do a delivery. When on duty at the antenatal ward, pregnant woman would be admitted with high blood pressure (pre-eclampsia), hyperemesis (sickness) and diabetes. Multiple pregnancies could be admitted from the GP, home or another clinic outside Aberdeen. The women would be assigned a consultant, such as Professor MacGillivray, Dr GP Milne and Professor Baird, who would come and check how the pregnancy was progressing. There were darkened single rooms which were used for women with severe high blood pressure and headaches. They would be monitored and observed very closely. Women in early labour would be admitted and to encourage labour, they would be given an OBE (Oil-Bath-Enema). The labour ward was situated close by.

For home confinements, we had to stay at 32 Carden Place, Aberdeen. This was a house that was used by the hospital to house the student midwives. A trained midwife would stay there to oversee the students. When on call, the student who was first on call had to listen for the telephone, whatever the time. A community midwife would phone us to say a woman was in labour and we had to phone for a taxi first, then get dressed and go to the address. The midwife would be already there. The student did the delivery and got the blue book signed. We did daily visits with the community midwife, checking mothers and babies, sometimes bathing babies if need be.

We also did antenatal clinics, one of which was situated at Castlehill, Aberdeen, and was very popular with expectant mothers. A doctor would attend from the maternity hospital to check the women, the midwife would take students. There were always queues waiting to be seen.

There were three maternity homes, as well as the maternity hospital in different areas of the city: Summerfield, Fonthill and Queen's Cross. I worked in Fonthill and Queen's Cross. I enjoyed Queen's Cross; it was my favourite. It was very homely and the sister in charge was nicknamed Queenie after the home. She ran a tight ship but was fun too. After a delivery, we had to carry women to their beds to prevent haemorrhage. Mothers and babies would stay for seven days to establish breastfeeding and baby bathing. A doctor would visit from the hospital if there were problems. If an emergency occurred in the maternity homes to do with a delivery, the Flying Squad would be called. The staff had a special number to phone directly to the Labour Ward at the maternity hospital. A team consisting of consultant, anaesthetist and paediatrician would attend with blue lights flashing to the destination. The mother and baby home was near to Queen's Cross. Young, unmarried girls came to give birth and get postnatal support. We also had a cook in the homes, who would prepare all the meals for the staff and mothers.

On the day of the final exam, we took our blue book and went to the antenatal ward, at the maternity hospital, where the exam took place. An expectant mother was asked if she was happy to participate in the exam beforehand. Consultants were there to question the students. We had both oral and written papers to pass. I became a staff midwife and worked at Queen's Cross.

In early 1963, I started the District Nursing course. At that time, it was known as the Queens Institute of District Nursing. We were based at Ingleboro House, which was on Castle Terrace in Aberdeen. We went there every day to get our duties. The nurses each worked in an area in town, for example, Holburn, Northfield, Tillydrone and more. The training lasted one year, and we had lectures and tests. One of the lecturers was Dr Ian McQueen, who was the Medical Officer of Health. During my time as a district nurse, in 1964, a typhoid outbreak occurred, and having midwifery experience, I was assigned any pregnant ladies, leaving the other nurses to carry on with their duties.

While on District, I got married and in time had a daughter and left District Nursing. I resumed part- time nursing again, working at Woodend General Hospital, doing relief duties in various wards, until I eventually was back in the surgical ward, where I had first started as a staff nurse. Nursing had changed. Instead of washing and powdering gloves or washing and sterilising instruments in autoclaves, they were all sent to the Central Sterile Services Department.

In 1970, I resumed midwifery as a sister based in the Health

Department at St Nicholas House, along with community midwives that I had known when I was a student. We were area based and did mainly home visits, antenatal and post-natal and clinics based in town. One clinic in particular at the Beach Boulevard was supposed to be a temporary building but lasted over 20 years. Midwifery in the community was changing, as women opted for hospital delivery. Home deliveries diminished. In 1974, there were only four community midwives left, and we were transferred to the Aberdeen Maternity Hospital. We still did postnatal and antenatal visits and clinics in the community but midwifery was changing, as General Practitioners were doing clinics at their surgeries. The community clinics were no longer required instead the midwives did clinics at the doctor's practice.

In 1976, more midwives from the maternity hospital gradually joined the community team. Women were offered Domino as well as home births. A Domino birth is when a woman is assigned a named midwife. The woman is checked at home and when labour progresses, the woman, partner and midwife go into hospital, the baby is delivered, then, six hours later all being well all can go home. The midwife then visits twice a day for the first three days and then daily until the tenth day and then discharges them to the Health Visitor. If there are any problems, the midwife continues to visit until she's happy to discharge them. Student midwives gained experience by accompanying community midwives. I still keep in contact with some of my students to this day.

While working in community, I set up a clinic in the Powis area of Aberdeen. A ground floor council flat was used, and I got the necessary items, such as a weighing machine and a couch. I carried my own Sphygmomanometer for measuring blood pressure and a Sonicaid for foetal monitoring. The Powis Clinic proved very popular with the expectant mothers. If they had other children at nursery or school, it was easy for them to pick them up and there was no expense on bus fares either! There was a great community spirit.

In 1989, a mother requested a water birth. I knew the lady, as I had delivered her first baby as a Domino. Never having done or seen a water birth, I had to get literature and films to study. Early one February morning, with snow on the ground, the lady's husband phoned to say his wife was in labour. I had already prepared everything in the house prior to this. She had hired a birthing pool. I placed thick polythene under the pool to save the carpet and added extra heaters. Another midwife and two student midwives were called as the labour progressed. A healthy boy arrived. Mother and baby were well. The following year, the 5th May 1990, was the International Day of the Midwife. I was asked to present in the MedChi Building at Foresterhill on the water birth. The photos I had were put onto slides. A lot of midwives attended, many from outwith Aberdeen, all enjoyed the presentation and questions were asked. Water births are now being done throughout the country. In the hospital, they now have a pool that the women can use if they wish.

When I retired in March 1996 trousers and tops were beginning to be worn.

Many changes have taken place in midwifery since I was born. My mother delivered me at home, there was six feet of snow and the doctor came on horseback. I arrived feet-first!

Being a midwife, I felt it an honour to be involved with families and each baby I delivered was special. I still keep in contact with many of my ladies and enjoy hearing about the babies making their way in the world. (EMMA CLARK, MIDWIFE)

A student midwife's perspective: learning from patients

I was very grateful that her most recent mother had spent a lot of time explaining her diabetes to her. The 29-year lady had delivered a few days earlier and was preparing for discharge from hospital. The delivery had gone smoothly and her baby's glucose levels and breathing had been fine post-delivery so there was no need for admission to the neonatal unit. Baby was sleeping and mum was able to chat to her all about her diagnosis of type 1 diabetes at age 15 and her challenges over the years. A structured education programme and her insulin pump had made a big difference a few years ago; as well as the pump she had a small device on her arm to monitor her glucose continuously.

She and her partner had appreciated the reassuring advice and the screening tests at the pre pregnancy clinic. When control was optimal, she had discontinued contraception and then attended the combined clinic just after her positive pregnancy test. Although she needed to attend the combined clinic monthly and then weekly, she had not needed admission during pregnancy. She got to know all the staff at the combined clinic well. The consultants Dr Shearer and Dr Watson had been very supportive, and she had a great rapport with all the staff at the clinic. The lab staff would download all her home monitoring results and feedback on her glucose and HbA1c results, the midwives kept a close eye on all her pregnancy recordings, the dieticians always had practical advice, especially when she had hypos in early pregnancy, and the diabetes specialist nurse supported her use of the pump and continuous glucose monitoring. Consulting the diabetes and obstetric teams together meant she and her partner could discuss issues with them and get answers to their queries. The student moved to her next case since the lady was having a snack just before she started breast feeding her baby. (ANON)

Mums' memories

A *diabetic mother's perspective*

In 1986 I was 28 when I was diagnosed with diabetes. It is a hereditary condition in my family. I was keen to have children and mentioned this while at the diabetic clinic. They suggested a Pre-pregnancy Diabetic Clinic at the Maternity Hospital. I dutifully went every Tuesday afternoon where they would check my health, folic acid levels and get me to do a weekly diary to get my glucose levels lowered. As my diabetes was very erratic, this was challenging to get under control. I had a good week where my glucose levels were low and then eat exactly the same the following week and they were high. For nearly two years I went to the Pre-pregnancy clinic. I wasn't getting any younger and was classed as an older mum. I decided to become pregnant and take the consequences as the medical staff would sort it out.

I was 35 when I fell pregnant in 1993. I went to the hospital for the pregnancy exam and they couldn't hear a heartbeat. I was told to come back the following week. Seemingly in diabetic women, it is longer to pick up a heartbeat. I had an internal scan, and they found a heartbeat then. It was starting to become a reality this was going to be some journey. I hadn't understood when attending the pre-pregnancy clinic how getting my sugars level down was so important. What I had eaten even down to the colour of a banana was recorded. I had found out while pregnant if sugar levels are high it affects the internal organs of the baby.

Between six weeks and 12 weeks, I started bleeding. I went to the hospital and had a scan. I'd also had a hypo but everything was fine. I really didn't have much sickness, but it was only at night. I felt fine. I attended the hospital weekly or fortnightly for appointments. At four months my whole body began to puff up. My legs were like tree trunks. At six months I was phoned by the hospital, I left work and by the afternoon I was in hospital and stayed there till I gave birth.

I was monitored every day. A couple of weeks after being admitted my mother-in-law took me down to the beach. When I came back the Sister said I was not allowed out the front door. It was dangerous, my baby could come at any time, it would be so quick the cord would wrap around the babies neck and strangle it. I was in a four bedded room downstairs in the maternity hospital for problem pregnancies but as time progressed, I was put in a single room. By now I was not sleeping, I was getting bigger and bigger and at night I would sit with wet j cloths on my legs trying to cool them down. They were on fire and itchy. My skin felt so tight.

Six weeks before the due date was the day I went to the theatre to have my baby. He was a healthy 7lb boy, big for a premature baby. I had insulin throughout my pregnancy, more than I usually take. I put on seven stone during my pregnancy. Our baby's father was the only one that saw him in the special nursery. They brought a photograph to me. I was getting monitored closely with one-to-one care. It lasted for three days. Later the following day I went in a wheelchair to the special nursery to see my son for the first time. We were both in hospital for three weeks and a couple of nights before going home we were together.

When he was born the heat and itchiness in my legs went away. Given all I went through it was still worth it, but I was advised not to have any more children and I didn't. (HAZEL ADAM)

Mums from the '50s

When I left school I went to Websters Business College for Young Ladies and from there was offered a job at the Rowett Research Institute under Dr Leitch. Two of us were compiling the index for the book Nutrition Abstracts. I left the Rowett in 1940 and was married in 1946 when married women did not work. In 1948 Dr Leitch came to my door asking me to contact Professor Baird who was looking for someone part-time to collect data on primiparae women in their first pregnancy.

Professor Baird had two dieticians who gave out notebooks and scales to the women to weigh and write down every morsel they ate, even a sweet eaten at the cinema was calculated. After a week these books were handed back to me to calculate the calories in their diet.

The project was to check if the amount they consumed had any relation to the weight of the baby. It did. Unfortunately, I had to leave before the project was completed since I had now become a primiparae.

If you wanted your own GP at the birth you went to a private nursing home. My son was born in June 1949 in Rubislaw Nursing Home at a cost of a guinea a day. We were mostly kept 14 to 21 days. My daughter was also born there in 1952. The lady in the next bed also had a daughter, Maureen, and we struck up a firm friendship which indeed continued and Maureen, I am happy to say, has now been my daughter-in-law for 40 years. (FREDA ROSS)

Mum from the '70s

In 1978 I fell pregnant and was classed as an elderly mum as I was 31. All antenatal appointments and the birth would be at the Maternity Hospital at Aberdeen Royal Infirmary, Foresterhill. Later, into my pregnancy around 5 months, I was asked by the research team if I would like to be part of a study. They measured how fast blue dye would go through the body in pregnancy. This would mean more appointments. I remember work at the time didn't like the extra appointments. I went home with tubs to collect the urine. This was only done once as my baby was early by 7 weeks.

When I went to ARI I had the baby in the research ward on the top floor. The rooms were two mums per room with a lovely separate dining room. I was in for ten days. I had a Caesarean section at birth and half the stitches were removed after seven to eight days. The last were removed on day ten. After doing the research I was told if I was pregnant again to get in contact with the research team.

In 1981 I was pregnant again. I contacted the research team, but it was too late into my pregnancy to join the latest study. As I already had previously contributed to a study however, I was able to have my baby in the research unit once again.

I noticed coming back in 1981 it was still the same staff from my first pregnancy. The research team were Professor McGillivray, who had a very nice bedside manner, Dr Doris Campbell, Dr Sheena Tuttle, and Dr Jandial. I was very well cared for, with even an auxiliary nurse waiting past her shift's end for me to pass urine after the birth. (ANON)

The '90s – The Domino Scheme

In 1993 I was 29 and expecting my first baby. At the 12-week appointment, I said that I didn't want the AFP (alpha-fetoprotein) blood test. I knew that it was only indicative and that if I had raised AFP I would be offered a definitive result by drawing some amniotic fluid, which carried a small risk of miscarriage. As I wasn't prepared to have the definitive test, there seemed no point in having the initial indicative test. The midwife said that it seemed as though I'd thought it all through, and on that basis invited me to have a midwife-led pregnancy.

I was part of a trial extending the Domino Scheme (early release) to first time mothers. Domino stands for 'Domiciliary In and Out'. The idea was to minimise the time spent in the hospital and to stay at home as long as possible, then return home as soon as possible. When the woman goes into labour, instead of going into the hospital, the midwife visits the woman in her home. The woman doesn't go into the labour ward, but straight into the delivery suite and has the baby. Then afterwards the woman goes home, rather than going onto the Labour ward. The benefits are that it reduces the chance of a hospital-acquired infection, and breastfeeding starts better because the woman is at home and relaxed. It had been available to women who had had previously had easy, straightforward births. Being part of that study was one of the best decisions I have ever made.

Throughout my pregnancy, I had a named midwife, Jean Mosedale, who was brilliant. She inspired confidence and trust, and she made me laugh. 'I recommend breast-feeding to all mothers,' she said, 'but I particularly recommend it to you. You'll pass on all your immunities and, judging by the state of your kitchen floor, I'd guess you've built up quite a range of immunities.' I had the first twinges on the morning of Sunday, 20 February 1994. When I went into labour with my son, Jean came to my house and stayed with me through the early stages, then we went into the hospital, to the midwives unit, around 10 pm. My son was born at 4 am, and we went home at 11 am – I was only in the hospital for 13 hours. My husband and I felt a bit shell-shocked when we walked our flat with our seven-hour old son, brand new parents, and thought 'What now?' The answer was to get the kettle on and settle down to admire our son: I couldn't take my eyes off him.

In 1995 I was expecting again. I wanted another Domino delivery. My midwife would be Elaine Mitchell. The second labour in 1996 progressed more quickly and I went straight into hospital with no jolly time at home. My waters didn't break, and my daughter was born in the bag – a lucky caul baby. We went in just after midnight, my daughter was born at 4.20am, we were home by 12 noon to introduce my son to his new sister. I was in the hospital for less than 12 hours. (ANON)

Memories of places

Mother and baby clinic, Castle Street

At a works' medical examination, I was told, for the first time, that I should not consider becoming pregnant. This was because I had a heart condition, which was thought to be the result of rheumatic fever when I was 13 years old. However, in 1959 I became ill and when I consulted my doctor, she told me that I was pregnant. I was then referred to the Mother and Baby Clinic at Castle Street, where my care was taken over by Dr Dugald Baird and the clinic staff. They estimated that the birth was due in the December but, because of my heart condition, I was told that I would have to stop work in the July. I regularly attended the clinic, and they monitored the situation until the birth in November 1959. Because of the birth being earlier than anticipated, the allocated consultant was not available as he had taken an early vacation so he would be available for the predicted birth in December. This caused some consternation because my heart was giving problems at the time and my condition was deteriorating. In the event, a forceps delivery was necessary, and the birth of my daughter was successful but was not an early birth as had been presumed. In fact, it was realised that the birth was late. I immediately asked that my baby's heart be checked. Her heart was fine, however she had to be cot-nursed in the nursery and I was not able to see her for two days.

The facilities of the clinic then were basic compared with those of today. There was not the same privacy as there is now and during one of my visits to see Dr Dugald Baird, from one of the two changing cubicles which led to his room, I could hear his conversation with another patient. Owing to her frail condition he was obviously not happy at her having become pregnant once more. She already had a few children and he said that her husband was being irresponsible, and it was he who should be present. I wondered what was in store for me. However, he was very kind to me.

At that time, pregnancy and labour were not openly discussed but my mother-in-law did warn me after I had eaten some beetroot that I should not panic if I noticed that my urine later became red. And it did. But in fact, my waters had broken, and labour had started. However, when the contractions became ten minutes apart, I thought I'd better get to the maternity hospital. The receiving nurse said that if I could walk in the high heeled shoes that I was wearing, there was no way that I could be as far on as I thought. However, my daughter was born three hours later. My postnatal care was at home until my six-week check-up. The doctor asked about the baby, and I said she was not sleeping at night as she had already been test fed at the clinic as I was breast feeding. It transpired that I was not fit for the last feed at night. I was advised to buy a bottle and give the baby a feed of half Co-op milk and half water. Problem solved. I was also told to attend the Family Planning Clinic as any future pregnancies were not advisable. This I did. (ANON)

Cults Convalescent Home

When I became pregnant with my first child in 1956 I attended Castlehill for antenatal check-ups. I was advised that I would be having my baby at the Maternity Hospital at Foresterhill. I was an 'elderly prim' meaning I was over 25. I was two weeks overdue when labour pains began and in his lunch hour, my husband dropped me off at the hospital and went back to work. In those days men didn't get to stay for the birth of their children. He came to visit in the evening but again had to leave. I went into the labour ward at midnight and my daughter was born around 4 am. A little later a nurse came and said that as we were both healthy we would likely go to the Cults Convalescent Home, as Aberdeen Maternity Hospital was being renovated. This was July 1957. We were put in an ambulance and transferred to Cults.

The bus to Cults was run by Alexanders and their drivers were on strike. Luckily for me, my husband had access to his father's car and was able to visit in the evening but only for an hour. He brought my mum the next day. My husband's parents came in a separate visit as only two people per visit were allowed. Cults was very homely. We had lovely meals as they grew their own veg and some fruit. My next three children were born in 1959, 1961 and 1969 at Fonthill Maternity Home. Each time I was dropped off there and my husband was told to phone later in the morning. When he did phone, he was told the sex of the child and that we were both well and once again he came to visit in the evening. Fonthill was a lovely maternity home the nurses were not only friendly, they were very efficient and we were very well looked after. (ANON)

Cults Convalescent Home at Craigton Road, Pitfodels Hill in Cults was more recently Aberdeen Waldorf School.

The family planning clinic

In 1959 I was four and my wee brother was only a couple of months old. My mum was a private person when it came to women's issues. My mother explained where we were going to – Castle Terrace – to the family planning clinic. Well what she said was that she that she didn't want any more wee brothers or sisters for me. On the day of the visit it was only me that would be accompanying my mum. My brother was looked after by my great gran, who had a flat in Crown Street. I remember going into the Castle Terrace building. It was white and sterile. I was left by my mum for her appointment and was chatted to by some nice ladies who were there.

I'm glad I have this early memory of my mum as I cherish her memory so much.

Also, when I was growing up, I heard about my Great Grandma and how women came to her flat to have babies. One time my mum when she was 12 was put on the bus to Gourdon by her grandma to tell a woman's husband our family knew that his wife had had a baby and they were both safe and well. This was around 1947. (DENISE SAVILLE)

The Rubislaw Ward in Aberdeen Maternity Hospital is very special. It's not a ward with lots of beds; each bed is in a separate room. It must be a difficult ward to work in, but all of the staff are amazing. I was in the Rubislaw Ward three times, for miscarriages in 1998 and 2001 and a stillbirth in 1999. Everyone was very kind; I remember a cleaner giving me a bosie, at a time when I really needed a bosie! (ANON)

Memories of the services

Dr Mary Esslemont's memories

In the summer of 1969, Dr Mary Esslemont, now retired, was approached by Lady Vera Dawe, editor of *Mother and Child*, a health education journal and requested to contribute an article for the forthcoming autumn edition. It was 'to be devoted to the splendid maternal and child health and welfare services in Aberdeen to include general health education measures and the medico-social research which is being done in the University.' The following are some extracts from Dr Esslemont's article.

My memory goes back to the first decade of the century which saw the beginnings of The Aberdeen Maternity and Child Welfare Scheme. It was always a great satisfaction to my late father (George Esslemont) that the first Health Visitor was appointed when he was Convener of the Local Health Committee. We were fortunate in having as our Medical Officer of Health that most distinguished man, the late Professor Matthew Hay, respected and revered by all his medical colleagues throughout Scotland and beyond, and even today we still reap the benefit of his forward-looking planning in public health, and hospital development.

   The first Health Visitor was soon joined by another and another, but the staff was much too small to cope with the many problems of the underprivileged in our community, and in the second decade of the century, the Voluntary Association for Maternity and Child Welfare came into being. This was an Association of comparatively leisured and well-to-do women in the city who raised the money to start Child Welfare Clinics, helped at these Clinics and visited problem families under the guidance of the Health Visitors. They also attended classes held in the Public Health Department of the University and conducted by members of the Public Health staff and interested General Practitioners. Again, we were fortunate in the appointment of the late Dr Stephen as the first whole-time Medical Officer for Maternity and Child Welfare. He had excellent liaison with General Practitioners in the city and was literally adored by the mothers and children who attended his Clinics. The medical Officers at the Voluntary Clinics were originally General Practitioners, and outstanding help was given – completely voluntarily – by two of our pioneer women doctors, the late Dr Laura Sandeman and the late Dr Agnes Thomson. They continued to help at the Clinics until gradually more whole-time public health medical staff were appointed and voluntary help was not required. With this development a gap between the public health doctor and the general practitioner began to appear.

After about 40 years of voluntary work, the Maternity and Child Welfare Association, (of which for practically the whole time of its existence, my late mother (Clementina Esslemont) was the President) became redundant because of the very great increase in the number of Health Visitors and trained Social Workers. These trained workers were of course very much more efficient than their voluntary predecessors...

Great changes have taken place in the past few years in the Domiciliary Midwifery Service. Practically all women are now confined in hospital. In Aberdeen in 1968 only 31 women were confined at home. (When I started general practice in Aberdeen nearly 50 years ago, I myself had an average of almost 150 home confinements yearly for many years.) The hospitalisation of pregnant women for confinement has put a great strain on the resources of our maternity hospitals, and early discharge has become a real necessity. In Aberdeen in 1968 an interesting, combined care scheme was started. The case is 'booked' by the general practitioner, and is then sent to the Maternity Hospital for acceptance for delivery. The ante-natal care is undertaken by the General Practitioner and the Domiciliary Midwife, but in addition the patient is examined periodically by specialist hospital staff. If no specific abnormality or difficulty arises in the case, the woman is confined by the general practitioner or domiciliary midwife, looked after by the hospital staff for 48 hours and then discharged home to be under the care of the general practitioner and domiciliary midwife. This makes for very good liaison between hospital staff, general practitioner and midwife and ensures continuity of care. Home helps are provided where necessary for the puerperium (six weeks after childbirth...

Aberdeen Health and Welfare Department was pioneer in the investigation of accidents in the home and also in educating the public in ways of preventing such accidents. The first Home Safety Campaign in Britain was in Aberdeen in 1954. These investigations are time consuming and costly, and one hopes that this will be easier with the co-operation now existing between General Practitioners and Health Visitors in the attachment scheme...*

As has already been said, most people feel that some changes in the administration of the Health Service are needed to make co-ordination easier and to increase efficiency but the greatest improvement of all will come from an increase of goodwill and mutual understanding not only between the branches of the Service but also between patient and doctor at all levels.

* Today our homes remain the place where accidents, potentially fatal, are most likely to happen for young children under 24 months. Aberdeen City Council continue to provide a free Home Check service to anyone living in Aberdeen.

A memory after a visit to the dispensary, Guestrow

When I was a bairn, back in the '30s, I lived in Fittie (Footdee) with my family. One day my mother told me to go a message for her and she sent me up to the Dispensary at the Gushie. That's what we called the Guestrow. I'd to get a bottle of ipecachua mixture for my wee brother. He was bedded with a bad chest.

So up the road I go, gets to the Dispensary, and gets the bottle of mixture. Now I'm on my way back home to Fittie. I think to myself, I'll try a scoof of this. See what it's like. So I take off the top of the bottle and take a swig. Oh gads! I spit it out immediately. I head back home with the mixture and hand it over to my mum. I never let on I'd had a wee taste on the way home. (BILLIE ARTHUR, AS TOLD TO HEATHER SPENCE)

A Shetland mum

On 25th August 1976, I went into early labour, I was home in Lerwick, Shetland. As there were no scanning facilities in our local hospital in Lerwick, I had an x-ray that morning and discovered I was going to have twins. My labour had progressed too far to be flown to Aberdeen, our nearest maternity hospital. Our identical twin girls were born later that afternoon. They weighed just, 3lb 11oz and 5lb

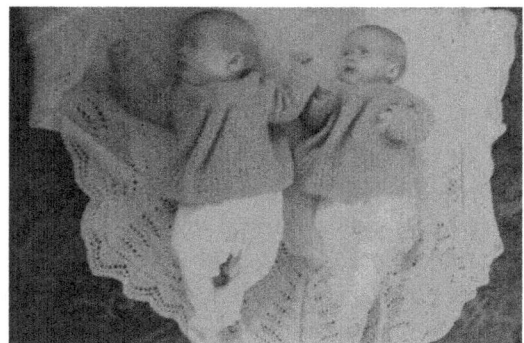

Twins delivered in Shetland and subsequently transferred by air to Aberdeen Maternity Hospital because of their low birthweight.
(Photograph courtesy of Elizabeth Smith)

1oz. The doctors decided they would need to be transferred to Aberdeen Maternity Hospital because of their weight. They were flown on an ambulance flight to Aberdeen, accompanied by a midwife. My husband and myself went a few days later to Aberdeen. They were in the special care baby unit and were perfect, apart from their weight. We were told they would have to reach five and half pounds weight before we could take them back home to Shetland. We were allowed to go in each day to bath and feed them and hold them.

Everyone on the unit was lovely and helped us a lot. They kept us up to date with everything that was happening. We were lucky as their Auntie stayed up the road from the hospital, so we did not have to look for accommodation when we were there. After several weeks we were able to return to Shetland with our daughters. (ELIZABETH SMITH)

Shetland midwife comments on a transferred mother

My observations are that Sarah was quite a young mum having her first baby in very unfamiliar surroundings with no familiar faces around her and without her own mother or somebody else to provide advice and support. She had been prepared during her pregnancy to expect delivery in the Community Maternity Unit in Shetland then all of this seemed to come out of the blue at a time of heightened anxiety leading up to the birth of her first child. Also, although only 19 years ago, maternity care in a large hospital was still a fairly clinical (and at times cold) experience compared to the wrap around mother/baby care we have nowadays.

Sarah's story

At the end of May 2001 we were sent down to Aberdeen when I was roughly 38/39 weeks pregnant, very last minute as it was the last day I could fly on a normal flight. I was sent down as the baby's head wasn't engaging and there were concerns my pelvis was too small to deliver and it was safer to be in Aberdeen in case there were problems. We got accommodation in the Shetland rooms on the hospital grounds, next to the maternity ward, which was lucky as there wasn't always space available. I seem to remember it costing a lot to stay there as the only shop nearby was a small corner shop and the nearest supermarket was a bit of a trek for someone in the later stages of pregnancy.

I wish I had fonder memories of my hospital experience, but I just seem to remember being 'told off' a lot – for carrying our babies around the ward or not filling in notes about last feed in the middle of the night. We were only allowed to put the babies in ARI babygrows, but then they would run out of those over the weekend leaving mothers to re-use. I guess there were staffing difficulties back then as I rarely seemed to see the same nurse or midwife twice.

It was a very different experience to when I had my second baby in Shetland in 2002 where the care seemed much more personal, the ward was much more mam and baby focused, if you fell asleep breastfeeding they sneaked into your room and put a guard on the bed, so the baby didn't fall out rather than wake you up to tell you off. (SARAH IRVINE)

An IVF memory

I walked through the front door of Aberdeen Maternity Hospital past the expectant mothers and up to the first floor. Before I arrived for this appointment; I had liaised with my doctor to get on this programme. There were not just couples from Aberdeen city, they were from as far afield as Moray and right down to Fife. The process started with counselling as it was explained it would be an intrusive and long process. It might not be successful with disappointments on the way. Having successfully come through the counselling, I'd be getting my eggs fertilised. During the process I'd have injections to get my hormone levels up to produce eggs. They were inserted and you went back in ten days. We knew then if the treatment was successful.

There was a Waiting List for IVF. It included those who qualified for free treatment. Those who paid, older women over the qualifying age for free treatment and those willing to pay to get treatment sooner. Also, those who didn't qualify for free treatment, but who couldn't afford to pay to get treatment sooner. Our doctor was very nice and because we were self-funding, we had IVF treatment for an extra year over the upper age limit. (ANON)

20

Old Stories Retold (and other Old Wives' Tales)

Getting better

AROUND 40 YEARS ago or more, 'getting better' was still a term being widely used by older women in the North East of Scotland. A pregnant woman wasn't asked when her due date was but when she would 'be better'. Also, around this time on meeting and seeing a new baby in their pram with their mother in the street a silver coin, or even a pound note, was offered for the bairn. This was regularly done and considered to be good luck, an omen that the bairn wouldn't want during its life.

Extracts from the press

Concealment of pregnancy and mother of stillborn twins 1754

They write from Aberdeen, that on Saturday fortnight, one Mary McKenzie, a servant girl in the parish of Old Meldrum, was found in a park near that place, with two newborn dead female children by her. Upon examination before a Justice of the Peace, where the Minister of the parish, two surgeons and the midwife were present, she declared the children were dead born: and the surgeons and midwife unanimously agreed, that they seem to be born on the 7th month and that there appeared no marks of violence upon their bodies. The woman in the meantime is kept under proper guard till she is in a condition to go to prison. (*Leeds Intelligencer*, Tuesday 20 August 1754)

In the early part of the 20th century, Aberdeen was no different from any other Scottish city where there was an underbelly of illicit practice in termination of pregnancy which part served as a driver for Dugald Baird to encourage a rethink on how unwanted pregnancies be managed. The following is an example of such a practice reported in Aberdeen journals.

Forest Avenue Nursing Home

In 1941 there were four charges against Miss Christina Ross and Mrs Mary Patton and a further one against Mrs Patton. All charges were for illegal operations between 1935 and 1940. Both women pleaded not guilty to the charges against them. During the trial, a procession of women entered the witness box saying they were no longer able to have children after having had an operation to terminate a pregnancy. The charges were found not proven. The jury had been directed that they had to be satisfied an instrument had been used during the operations before finding the two accused woman guilty. The fourth charge was found not guilty. Mrs Patton had a further charge of an illegal operation at her residence, was found guilty and sentenced to 18 months in prison. She was 67 years old. (*Evening Express* and *Press & Journal,* 1941)

Taking caudle with gossips

Across Britain for centuries a drink called caudle (or caudel), a kind of fortifying porridge or eggnog prepared by the gossips, who were family and friends, and was commonly drunk by the mother to keep her strong and dull the pain during and after childbirth. 'Caudle' means hot. The *Oxford English Dictionary* cites the earliest use of the word in 1297. The earliest surviving recipe, from 1300 to 1325, is simply a list of ingredients: wine, wheat starch, raisins, and sugar to 'abate the strength of the wine'. Caudle had its own vessel, a caudle cup, a traditional gift for a pregnant woman. In Scotland a caudle formed part of the Beltane (May Day) fire festival celebrations as collated by James Frazier in *The Golden Bough*.

As caudle was served to new mothers to build up their strength, so it was offered to their visitors. 'Cake and caudle' or 'taking caudle' became the accepted term for a 'lying-in visit' when women went to see their friends' new babies. These were all-female occasions and continued into the 19th century with Queen Victoria's reign. The day after she gave birth to the Prince of Wales.

Many of the female nobility called at Buckingham Palace, and were received by Lady Charlemont, the First Lady of the Bedchamber, and after taking caudle were taken to the north wing to see the infant Prince.

A recipe for caudle – one serving

Ingredients:
1 cup milk
1 tbsp oatmeal
2 eggs, beaten
honey
salt
grated fresh nutmeg
wine, whisky, or ale

Instructions: Heat the milk in a pan with the oatmeal and a pinch of salt. Bring to a boil, stirring with a wooden spoon, then turn down the heat and simmer until it starts to thicken. Whisk in the eggs, plus honey and nutmeg to taste and simmer for about five minutes, constantly stirring to avoid sticking. Remove from the heat and stir in wine, whisky, or ale in the quantity you want. Serve hot.

Expectant fathers

The involvement of fathers and partners in the delivery process has changed enormously over time from a prolonged period of exclusion from the labour suite to a more recent view of them as an obligate partner and support in the birthing process. Likewise, involvement in antenatal care and preparation for delivery has changed substantially.

However, the following is an extract from the written advice given to fathers at the antenatal clinic at AMH as recently as in 1994.

You have to try and understand the feelings and emotions of yourself as both a husband and a father and not to forget that your wife may not become a 'mother' immediately. She too needs time to adjust and accept a new role in life...

If your tea is not ready when you get home or if the bed has not been made, do not react with criticism or anger, but offer her up the time to express her feelings and to explain how she has coped with her days...

During labour your wife may feel distressed and will need your support and encouragement. Do not be angry if she snaps at you or is really offhand – she will be trying to cope with this new experience. Help with the breathing patterns and assist the nursing staff when they ask – a sensible cooperative father can be of great help in the labour room.

The hospital offers a very false picture of parenthood as the staff are ready to step in when the mother gets tired. It is very different once home and the various pressures of normal life return. Please accept that she will be tired and that normal routines will be upset. It is your place to help a regulated new routine and you should offer to do many of the household chores... Even if you feel it is not your place i.e. doing the dishes... The baby is your responsibility too and mothers do not always have the magic cure for silencing a crying baby...

Take turns at feeding during the night and at bathing the baby. You will soon find enjoyment in this... Encourage your wife to keep up our postnatal exercises and she will soon regain her figure... It is important that you accept the problems along with the joys in creating a family.

Further Reading

Oakley, A, *The Captured Womb: a history of medical care of pregnant woman*, Basil Blackwell, Oxford, 1984.

Frazer, James, *The Golden Bough*, Macmillan, 1890.

PART 5

Then, Now – and a New Future

As these chapters come to a close, so do new ones open for the care of mothers and babies in North East Scotland. The truism that the problems of today become the history of tomorrow certainly applies to maternity and neonatal services in Scotland at the present time. Sir Dugald Baird might never have imagined how the obstetric and neonatal services he helped to create, have expanded and how Aberdeen's neonatal and maternity services have evolved. He would have approved of many of these changes. Indeed, considering mother and baby as a single entity is a feature which is well represented by the development of the Baird Family Hospital. Today, the focus is not just on the mother's and baby's clinical needs but also the needs of the entire family as well as several new considerations.

But whilst some of the challenges of the past have been resolved, others have not and have simply presented in new ways which require continued address by his successors. Moreover, some of his initiatives which had a local focus are now national imperatives and other themes in his research have progressed to a global level. Indeed, the world has been taken by storm with the COVID-19 pandemic, and its impact on pregnant women, newborns and maternity services locally and globally is a stark reminder of what Sir Dugald Baird championed – the need for resilient and responsive health systems. The pandemic has focused attention on the safety of mother and baby being the overarching consideration when all decisions on care are being made; but added to that foundation is an increasing appreciation of the importance of choice for women about how their care is given. Around the world today, we see large proportions of pregnant women opting not to seek care owing to fear of COVID-19 – this is indeed their choice, but services and providers must win back their confidence to attend. The need to include and blend safety and choice along with a high-quality service is implicit in planning now and for the future.

21

What Women Want: Safety, Choice and Advocacy

Lesley Dunbar, Alison McCall, Fiona Rennie and George Youngson

BY THE EARLY 19TH century, the poor and deprived in the city were encouraged to use hospital services since the hospital provided a cleaner and safer venue for childbirth and homebirth was a 'luxury' only afforded well-to-do women. The 'u-turn' came about gradually over time whereby home births reduced, and hospital was perceived as a 'better and safer' place to have your baby. In the view of many, however, that trend 'medicalised' a natural process, the trade-off being a safer environment for many, if not most. That trend in hospital delivery continues to the present time with only 2.6 per cent of women giving birth at home in Scotland and a more surgical interventionist attitude continues to grow, with an approximately 30 per cent rise in caesarean section delivery across Scotland.

In an attempt to balance this, stringent attempts have been made to provide alternative venues for delivery outside the labour suites of maternity hospitals and midwives have committed to expanding community-based facilities, either freestanding or adjacent to a hospital as an important alternative facility – available at the choice of women involved but also without compromising safety of mother or baby. Additionally, Grampian's home births service continues to develop that option increasingly as befits both suitability for and the choice of mothers.

Choice also extends to modes of delivery as well as place of delivery and the planning process tries to avoid any contest or conflict between the safety profile and responding to the mother's wishes. Additionally, a strong policy is emerging such that irrespective of place or mode of delivery, there are plans put in place to ensure continuity of carers, so that a mother, if needing to deliver in hospital, can have her midwife accompany her from her community base into that clinical environment thus maintaining good communication, good trust and good confidence on her part.

Advocacy by mothers and the views of women are being better heard than ever before and acted upon but it is also vital that additional needs are met when additional care is required. In that instance, high quality information needs to be made available so that choice can be fully informed.

> I am not sure what impact my involvement had but they were (seemingly) very receptive and the opportunity to try and improve things for future was very welcomed. I was heartened to hear their language of patient-centred care and respect high on the agenda in the new design, I hope this translates into the final product. Perhaps feedback that the outcomes from public participation could be better communicated would be relevant. (LAY MEMBER OF PLANNING TEAM)

Advocacy, however, can sometimes only be voiced by those with a confidence and an ability to articulate their thoughts and wishes. For others, access to choose is seen as a right that is not shared equally by all sectors of society and measures to support choice for disadvantaged, socially isolated, and impoverished members of our community are actions that require the continued commitment and support shown in such an exemplary fashion by the Bairds.

New aspects to maternal health

The features of periconceptual and antenatal health – features that Sir Dugald Baird was so passionate about and strived to improve, now take on new considerations. Health inequalities still exist in society. Substance abuse, alcohol abuse, smoking, and obesity impact negatively on maternal wellbeing. The need for high quality antenatal care has never been greater given the potentially devastating consequences of the above health problems. Indeed, the need for high quality family planning is similarly more important than ever but, at the time of writing, these services are under constraint because of the considerations imposed by the COVID pandemic, and access to contraceptive measures appear to have been relegated in importance – with unwelcome consequences.

22

Care for the Future

Lesley Dunbar, Alison McCall, Fiona Rennie and George Youngson

NEW THEMES HAVE come to the fore whilst the existing ones take on new priorities.

Privacy remains increasingly valued as a feature of care delivery for all and its importance increases during some particularly sensitive phases of care when the communications and emotions involved may be trying for patient and carer alike. The configuration of the new hospital, through provision of single rooms in wards, will allow a premium to be placed on private conversations in a private environment and private consultations taking place in a confidential manner.

At the same time, however, there is recognition that support can be had from sharing experiences with others, particularly if facing similar or the same type of problems and a 'peer group' can usefully develop in wards (even when split into single rooms) with a sense of community developing, which can be reassuring, sympathetic and encouraging. A balance needs to be struck between the privacy required, the need for clinical observation during the provision of care whilst at the same time avoiding isolation even in the midst of the company of others.

One particular time when privacy may be considered essential is during pregnancy loss – be that stillbirth or miscarriage. The facilities which currently exist for this service in the bereavement unit of the AMH will be improved and enhanced in order to provide compassionate and sensitive pathways of care in an attempt to recognise and reduce the distress that features at such a time. The physical separation from other mothers and their babies will be ensured. Dedicated exit facilities will also be introduced. The ability to take a stillborn baby into the 'open-air' and outside environment will be accommodated. A bereavement recognised and supported is possibly one better tolerated or endured.

Pregnancy Loss and Stillbirth are not always seen as important, however the care received when a baby dies is vital for bereaved parents, so that they can create memories of their precious lost baby in the little time they have. Their experiences and the care they have in hospital can have a lasting effect on their mental health going into the future. During the Covid19 pandemic government restrictions severely isolated bereaved parents, unable to get support from their friends and families, where charities such as SANDS (Stillbirth and Neonatal Death Society) have tried to support them through this difficult time. SANDS is a group of parents who have experienced similar and have learned to live with their loss.

* * *

Our roles were supported, we felt really listened to, we felt involved in every decision being made on the design and our thoughts of what we would provide good safe patient centred care, for future bereaved parents in a dedicated space to spend the little time they have with their precious babies. We requested quiet peaceful separate area, sound proofing, outside veranda and access-controlled lift entrance. We also shared our thoughts on the scanning department on the floor below as often bad news is given in this area.

An increasing awareness and sensitivity to the mental wellbeing and possible morbidity that can complicate a pregnancy, delivery and postpartum periods is also important.

Being exposed while trying to recover physically and while amid a mental health crisis was excruciating. My traumatic experience led me to develop PTSD so the noise of the ward coupled with my hyper vigilance and panic when any visitors arrived for the other occupants meant that meaningful rest was impossible until I was allowed a private room – this will hopefully be a thing of the past when the Baird opens its doors.

The availability of family suites for NICU stays will also have a massively positive impact on mental health, I cannot impress upon you quite how long the walk from the post-natal wards to the Neonatal ward is when you have just given birth, particularly if that birth was physically or mentally traumatic. This change will have a tangible benefit on bonding and attachment. (ANON)

Whilst the architecture per se cannot provide care, the right environment can facilitate the delivery of the right care and that extends to mental wellbeing as its much as it extends to obstetric considerations.

Where women live

Some women by virtue of where they live are distant from specialist care which may be required and, on occasion, required for a lengthy period of time. A prolonged hospital stay imposes many pressures on mothers and their partners, so it is important to have that prolonged stay only imposed when absolutely required. Providing accommodation for partners as well as the mother (as clinically appropriate), is a new facet to the package of care to be made available and is one which a holistic program should include. The ability to engage partners in all phases of maternity care encourages confidence and builds a stronger space for future family life and optimises parenting skills, and the provision of hotel-like accommodation should help to maintain closeness of the relationship instead of families being separated by distance.

However, distance need not always impose barriers to care and maximising the use of digital communication can allow women to remain in the home environment when that location also provides a safe one. Maintaining access to local care when possible, will be an important feature of midwifery services for the future.

Other benefits

Many other benefits are anticipated as emerging from the development of the Baird Family Hospital. Ambulatory care should be the norm when possible, thereby reducing inappropriate admissions to hospital. Similarly, a number of babies are currently managed in the Neonatal Unit who could receive parent led care from a transitional care unit and these babies will be suitable for the new Neonatal Unit's family-led transitional care unit as opposed to being an inpatient in the Neonatal Unit.

The ability to transfer patients to other parts of the site such as intensive care facilities or other operating theatres should be much improved with the new collocated architecture. The current transfer time of the neonate from the Neonatal Unit into the operating theatres should reduce from the present time in excess of an hour and dependent upon the availability of ambulances to a 15-minute journey, all within the confines of covered areas. And indeed, the new arrangements for improved capacity should reduce the requirement to transfer patients out of the region to other health board areas when not clinically indicated.

Currently, several women remain in post-natal beds unnecessarily because the baby is receiving care in the Neonatal Unit. The availability of a transitional care unit should minimise inappropriate hospital stays for well mothers wishing to be beside their babies.

While much of the above is about the buildings and physical environment, it is the quality of the staff that determines the quality of the service on offer. And in that regard Aberdeen has dedication and commitment from its healthcare community ensuring that the best care is available to all concerned, when and where required.

23

From Local to Global

Professor Wendy Graham

THE STANDARDS OF care of pregnant woman advocated by Sir Dugald should have no geographic restriction and whilst North East Scotland provided the footprint for his research and its implementation, these are fundamental rights which should be universal – across borders and socio-economic divides. Sadly, in 2020 an estimated quarter of all births in the world take place without any care – a statistic which no doubt Sir Dugald Baird would abhor. Indeed, the value and importance of working locally and globally became enshrined in the activities of the centre established in his name and under its first Director, Professor Wendy Graham, Emeritus Professor of Obstetric Epidemiology at the University of Aberdeen and now Professor at the London School of Hygiene and Tropical Medicine. The Dugald Baird Centre sought to improve the evidence base for maternity care and interventions both in Scotland and in low-income countries. This global remit brought collaborative partners to the Centre from far and wide – from Angola to Zimbabwe, and from major UN organisations to international agencies such as CDC and WaterAid.

The largest project to be co-ordinated by the Centre was IMMPACT (the Initiative for Maternal Mortality Programme Assessment) – a multi-million-dollar initiative funded by the Gates Foundation and other major donors, led by Prof. Graham but with a team of over 200 researchers spread across Burkina Faso, Ghana and Indonesia from 2000 to 2006. This initiative revealed huge gaps in the quality of care at birth received, particularly by the poorest women and engaged with local policymakers and service providers to address these gaps. The IMMPACT project placed the Dugald Baird Centre on the international map, and catalysed further research on quality improvement in many other low-income countries. Today, it's the legacy from Aberdeen which goes right back to 1795 which has influenced Professor Graham's current work – namely on infection prevention at birth. The Aberdeen-based doctor Alexander Gordon was the first to demonstrate the link between the poor hygiene practices of birth attendants (including himself) and the occurrence of the deadly infection called puerperal sepsis – or childbed fever in Gordon's day. Through a unique collaboration between NHS Grampian, the University of Aberdeen and overseas partners, Professor Graham established

Professor Wendy Graham presenting Dr Tedros Adhanom Ghebreyesus, Director-General of World Health Organisation with his honorary 'mop' to promote cleanliness. (Photograph courtesy of Professor Graham)

The Soapbox Collaborative – an evidence-based trust which revealed both the unacceptable healthcare settings in low-income countries in which women are delivering and the opportunities for low-cost interventions to change this, such as training hospital cleaners. And as the world grapples with the COVID-19 pandemic, the crucial importance of hygienic care environments and practices is ever more obvious. The work of Soapbox had a major influence on the World Health Organisation, leading to a global commitment to improve infection prevention in maternity units which was endorsed by the WHO Director General in May 2019 at the World Health Assembly – and captured in a photograph with Professor Graham presenting the Director General of the World Health Organisation with the mop of honour! Sir Dugald Baird was also a strong advocate for the most basic of interventions to improve the wellbeing and care of pregnant women and newborns, and although we have no record of his promoting cleaning equipment, he is well-remembered for his attention to hygiene at birth on the labour ward and in theatre. The new Baird Family Hospital will provide a respectful and safe care environment for mothers and babies in North East Scotland, but these same lessons which Gordon, Baird and Graham taught have much wider influence.

Further Reading

The Best Start: A five-year plan for maternity and neonatal care in Scotland, published by the Scottish Government, January 2017.

Epilogue

Let us be thankful that we live in an age when the art of printing has
rendered it impossible that any valuable discovery, once published,
should be lost; when every onwards step in scientific knowledge is
speedily communicated to the most distant parts of the world, and
when only what is visionary and useless connected with the healing art
is doomed to perish, while that which rests on a stable foundation will
remain, as far as human foresight can predict, a permanent record for
all succeeding ages.
(From *Introductory Address on Midwifery* delivered at Aberdeen University
October 27, 1869. Andrew Inglis MD FRCS Ed, Professor of Midwifery)

ABERDEEN AND ITS neighbouring communities have served its mothers and
babies throughout its history. There were times when no dedicated hospital
existed to act as a base from which midwifery and neonatal care could be
provided. Leaders emerged from 'town and gown' to ensure that the next
generation could build upon the gains and successes of the previous one. That
remains the case now. The Baird Family Hospital provides a new chapter in
the history of the care of mothers and their newborn to ensure that new lives
can be safely brought to the city.

In writing this book we pay tribute to the legacy of some of the giants of the
art and craft of midwifery, neonatal and early years services including David
Skene and Alexander Gordon from the distant past and Maggie Myles, Dr
Mary Esslemont. Sir Dugald and Lady May Baird from the more recent past.
Their work served the wellbeing of mothers and their babies over the centuries,
but more than that, they inspired others to follow in the same vein and to
encourage that leap from local to global standards of care as well as strive for
improvement in care for mother and child.

APPENDIX 1

List of Commemorative Plaques in Aberdeen Recognising Contributors to Midwifery

Dugald Baird (1899–1986)	38 Albyn Place
May Baird (1901–83)	38 Albyn Place
Mary Esslemont (1891–1984)	30 Beechgrove Terrace
Alexander Gordon (1752–99)	17 Belmont Street
R D Lawrence (1892–1968)	15 Ferryhill Place
John J R Macleod (1876–1935)	32 Cairn Road, Bieldside
Margaret Myles (1892–1988)	Aberdeen Maternity Hospital
Agnes Thomson (1880–1952)	13 Albert Street
Laura Sandeman (1862–1929)	20 Waverley Place

APPENDIX 2

Streets Named after Contributors to Midwifery

Lady May Baird
May Baird Avenue; May Baird Gardens; May Baird Place, Aberdeen,

Professor Sir Dugald Baird
Dugald Baird Court, AB12 5RU; Dugald Baird Square, Kincorth, Aberdeen

Dr Michael Tunstall
Michael Tunstall Place, Newtonhill, Aberdeenshire.

Contributors

SOHINEE BHATTACHARYA MBBS, PhD Sohinee is an Obstetric Epidemiologist with a special interest in pregnancy loss. Having trained in Obstetrics and Gynaecology in India and the UK, she is currently employed as Senior Lecturer at the University of Aberdeen and is the academic lead for the Aberdeen Maternity and Neonatal Databank. She also has an interest in global health and is the programme director for MSc in Global Health and Management at the University of Aberdeen.

DORIS CAMPBELL MB ChB MD FRCOG is an emeritus Honorary Reader in the Department of Obstetrics and Gynaecology having retired from the NHS in 2007. She graduated from Aberdeen's Medical School in 1967 and continued her career there. Her major research interests focused on the maternal physiological response, including nutrition in pregnancy (particularly in respect to foetal growth and development), multiple pregnancy, pre-eclampsia and hypertensive disease obstetric epidemiology including intergenerational studies and the obstetric antecedents of adult disease. During her professional life she participated in clinical obstetrics, including, latterly, an interest in substance misuse in pregnancy, and medical education.

MAGGIE CRUICKSHANK MB ChB MD FRCOG is co-lead of the Aberdeen Centre for Women's Health Research and an honorary consultant Gynecologist. After graduating from Aberdeen medical school, she trained in Leicester and Glasgow before returning to Aberdeen to develop her clinical research into the prevention of cervical cancer and lower genital tract disease.

PETER DUFFUS MB ChB, DObtstRCOG was educated at Robert Gordon's College and University of Aberdeen, graduated MB ChB., 1970, D.Obtst.R.C.O.G.1973 and NEGP Voc training Scheme 1971–74. He became a General Practitioner and GP Trainer in Aberdeen 1974–2009, Fellow of RCGP, Forensic Physician Grampian Police 1976–2010 and Member of Faculty of Forensic Medicine. He was Referee for Aberdeen Crematorium 1986–2020. Member of Med-Chi Heritage Committee and Administrator of NE GP History web site.

LESLEY DUNBAR MEd was born in St Joseph's Hospital in Hamilton, Ontario, Canada and came to Aberdeen as a baby to grow up in the Middlefield area. On leaving Aberdeen High School for Girls, she trained as a bookseller. She trained and taught as a primary school teacher for three years. Lesley was a founder member of Aberdeen Women for Peace in the early '80s after Greenham Women's Peace Camp was established. As member of the Invisible Bouncers Community Theatre Company, she co-produced and wrote 'Fit a Turn Oot!', a play about a women's factory worker strike at Broadfords in 1834. She worked at Aberdeen Women's Centre 1994–2002 and undertook various community learning jobs with Grampian Council, then Aberdeen City Council. She is a founder member of the Aberdeen Women's Alliance Women's History Group (2013) and was elected as a Labour Councillor for the Woodside, Hilton, Stockethill Ward to Aberdeen City Council in 2012 and again in 2017.

FIONA GIBB RM BMid PGCert MRes has 16 years of midwifery experience and studied and worked in Aberdeen Maternity Hospital 2004–13, latterly as a Senior Charge Midwife in Labour Ward before moving into an educational role. She now works as the Lead Midwife for Education at RGU and assists in the design and delivery of education for midwives, nurses and paramedics. Nationally, she is a member of the Scottish Future Nurse Midwife board, Scottish Lead Midwives and represents Scotland on LME UK (Lead Midwives for Education), assisting in the development and implementation of the NMC standards for education.

WENDY J GRAHAM DPhil is Emeritus Professor of Obstetric Epidemiology, Dept of Infectious Disease & Epidemiology, London School of Hygiene & Tropical Medicine (LSHTM) and an advocate for maternal and perinatal health improvement, particularly in low- and middle-income countries. Her career spans over 30 years, having trained at Sheffield and Oxford universities. Wendy was the first Director of the Dugald Baird Centre for Research on Women's Health at the University of Aberdeen, a post she held 1995–2005, and is now Emeritus Professor having left the University in 2015 to return to LSHTM. The initial focus of Wendy's work was the prevention of maternal deaths – a subject which Aberdeen health professionals and scientists have been addressing for over two centuries. Her research today centres on the reduction of healthcare-associated infections among mothers and newborns.

MARK HAMILTON MD FRCOG is a graduate of the University of Glasgow. His subspecialty interest in infertility started in the early 1980s and he trained in Glasgow and Singapore. He was appointed consultant in Obstetrics and Gynaecology in NHS Grampian in 1990 and became Honorary Senior Lecturer to the University of Aberdeen where he directed reproductive medicine clinical services for 25 years until his retirement in 2015. He served on the British Fertility Society Committee for many years and led the Society as Chair 2006–8. He now chairs the Board of Trustees of the British Fertility Society Ltd and is a member of the Executive Board of the International Federation of Fertility Societies. He has published over 90 papers in reproductive medicine, contributed several chapters in major textbooks and co-edits a popular RCOG textbook in infertility.

ALISON T MCCALL LLB, BA (Hons) MLitt PhD is a gender historian, with particular interests in women and education in Victorian Scotland. She is a former Convener of Women's History Scotland and is involved in the Mapping Memorials to Women project. She has enjoyed studying the Maternity Hospital from an academic viewpoint, having previously experienced it as a 'satisfied customer'.

MIKE MUNRO is a Neonatal Consultant currently based in Aberdeen Maternity Hospital. Born in Edinburgh, Mike graduated from the University of Aberdeen in 1989. After beginning his postgraduate training in Aberdeen, Mike moved with his family to Melbourne, Australia. There he worked in neonatology at the Monash Medical Centre, where he became the first ever Ritchie Institute fellow. In 2000, he returned to Aberdeen to become one of four consultant neonatologists. Over the years he has been the clinical lead for neonatal services for NHS Grampian. He is currently the lead for northern neonatal transport services and the clinical lead for the new Baird Family Hospital.

DONALD WM PEARSON BSC (Hons) FRCPE FRCPG is a retired honorary Professor of Medicine with interest in diabetes. After undergraduate study in biochemistry and medicine in Glasgow, Donald completed his post graduate training in Glasgow, Inverness and Aberdeen. He was appointed consultant physician and diabetologist at Aberdeen Royal Infirmary in 1984 and retired in 2014. Throughout his clinical practice in Aberdeen, he was involved with the combined obstetric diabetes service at AMH. During his consultant career he spent some time as head of the diabetes specialist services and lead clinician for the Grampian diabetes managed clinical network. He chaired the Diabetes in Pregnancy subgroup for the SIGN guideline 55 in 2001. From 2006 until 2010 he was lead clinician for diabetes in Scotland and chair of the Scottish diabetes group. His research interests and publications cover a range of topics including pregnancy (the previous chair of the Diabetic Pregnancy Study Group of the EASD), diabetes in adolescence, therapeutic interventions, and the epidemiology of diabetes. He was awarded an Honorary Professorship by the University of Aberdeen.

FIONA RENNIE is a proud Aberdonian and interested in the history of the city. In 2013, she joined Aberdeen Women's Alliance and became one of the history detectives who researched the history of the women of Aberdeen and their pioneering accolades. By 2014, the Aberdeen Women's Alliance started a city centre heritage walk and Fiona became a volunteer walk tour guide to tell the stories of these remarkable women and, with the opportunity through Aberdeen Women's Alliance, she has been able to find more inspiring women through other projects. She was the coordinator of the group that got memories of the heritage walk on the Silver City Vault, Aberdeen City Libraries' online resource.

PATRICIA SMITH MB ChB DRCOG MD PGCME oversaw the Ultrasound Department at Aberdeen Maternity Hospital 1986–2013. She is an Aberdeen medical graduate and trained in Obstetric Ultrasound at the Queen Mothers Hospital, Glasgow where ultrasound was first developed for use in pregnancy. She gained an MD thesis in 1993 from her alma mater on 'The Ultrasound Assessment of Multiple Pregnancy'. She has written books on obstetric ultrasound as well as numerous papers on the subject. She ran numerous courses on obstetric ultrasound both in the UK and overseas.

NORMAN C SMITH MB ChB FRCOG MD was a Consultant Obstetrician at Aberdeen Maternity Hospital 1986–2000 and developed the subspecialty of foetal and maternal medicine in the department. He is a University of Aberdeen graduate and received postgraduate training at Aberdeen Maternity Hospital, the Queen Mothers Hospital, Glasgow and Groote Schuur, Cape Town. He gained an MD thesis from his alma mater on 'Fetal scalp blood lactate as an indicator of intrapartum asphyxia'.

HAMISH W SUTHERLAND MB CHB FRCOG graduated in medicine from the University of St Andrews in 1957. After initial specialty training during his national service, he completed his post graduate training in obstetrics and gynaecology in Dundee, Glasgow and Falkirk. He was appointed lecturer at the University of Aberdeen in 1965, senior lecturer and consultant in Obstetrics and Gynaecology in 1971, elected FRCOG in 1976 and was awarded a personal Readership in 1977. He became Acting Head of the University Department of Obstetrics and Gynaecology in October 1984. He retired from clinical practice in the mid-1990s. He has published more than 90 works on a range of topics in his specialty. During the 1970s and 1980s he convened four international colloquia on diabetes in pregnancy in Aberdeen and chaired the European diabetes in pregnancy study group in 1984. He was visiting Professor at the University of Cape Town in 1991 and was the appointed obstetrician on the UK Central Councils for Nursing, Midwifery and Health Visiting (1983–88, 1988–93).

GEORGE G YOUNGSON CBE MB ChB PhD FRCPE FRCSEd is Emeritus Professor of Paediatric Surgery at the University of Aberdeen and Royal Aberdeen Children's Hospital. He graduated from the University of Aberdeen Medical School in 1973, undertook his surgical training in Scotland and Canada and was appointed as a Consultant General Surgeon to Aberdeen Royal Infirmary in 1984 and as a Consultant Paediatric and Neonatal Surgeon to the Royal Aberdeen Children's Hospital in 1988. He was a council member of the Aberdeen Medico-Chirurgical Society and is part of their heritage group.

Acknowledgements

The editors would like to recognise the advice and assistance provided by the following:

Nicole Bauwens, Lead Neonatal Nurse, Neonatal Unit

Fiona Donald SANDS, Stillbirth and Neonatal Death Society

Hannah Falconer Medical Student, University of Aberdeen

Andy Gaffron Design and Graphics Officer, Aberdeen City Council, External Communications

Hilary Hinton Honorary Librarian, Aberdeen Medico-Chirurgical Society

Local Studies Aberdeen Central Library

Dr David Lloyd Formerly Consultant in Neonatal and Perinatal Medicine

Fiona Musk Archivist, NHS Grampian

Kat Masterson Grampian Maternity Voices Partnership

Ann Oakley Professor of Sociology and Social Policy, UCL Institute of Education, University of London

Gill Skene Birth Trauma Association

Else Smaaskjaer Aberdeen Women's Alliance History Group

Janette Douglas Aberdeen Women's Alliance History Group

Gail Thompson Deputy Project Director, Baird Family Hospital, NHS Grampian

Marilene Walker Administrator, Aberdeen Medico-Chirurgical Society

We would like to thank all the women who shared their stories and experiences with us.

Index of Persons and Places

Luath Press Limited

committed to publishing well written books worth reading

LUATH PRESS takes its name from Robert Burns, whose little collie Luath (*Gael.*, swift or nimble) tripped up Jean Armour at a wedding and gave him the chance to speak to the woman who was to be his wife and the abiding love of his life. Burns called one of the 'Twa Dogs' Luath after Cuchullin's hunting dog in Ossian's *Fingal*. Luath Press was established in 1981 in the heart of Burns country, and is now based a few steps up the road from Burns' first lodgings on Edinburgh's Royal Mile. Luath offers you distinctive writing with a hint of unexpected pleasures.

Most bookshops in the UK, the US, Canada, Australia, New Zealand and parts of Europe, either carry our books in stock or can order them for you. To order direct from us, please send a £sterling cheque, postal order, international money order or your credit card details (number, address of cardholder and expiry date) to us at the address below. Please add post and packing as follows: UK – £1.00 per delivery address; overseas surface mail – £2.50 per delivery address; overseas airmail – £3.50 for the first book to each delivery address, plus £1.00 for each additional book by airmail to the same address. If your order is a gift, we will happily enclose your card or message at no extra charge.

Luath Press Limited
543/2 Castlehill
The Royal Mile
Edinburgh EH1 2ND
Scotland
Telephone: 0131 225 4326 (24 hours)
Fax: 0131 225 4324
email: sales@luath.co.uk
Website: www.luath.co.uk